BULBS

BULBS

John E. Bryan, Editor

Photography by

Andrew Lawson

HEARST BOOKS
New York

Library of Congress Cataloging-in-Publication Data

Bulbs / compiled from the Good housekeeping illustrated encyclopedia of gardening; completely revised by John E. Bryan; photography by Andrew Lawson. — 1st U.S. ed.
    p.   cm. — (The Hearst garden guides)
    Includes index.
    ISBN 0-688-10040-6 (alk. paper)
    1. Bulbs. 2. Bulbs—United States.   I. Bryan, John E., 1931–
  II. Good housekeeping illustrated encyclopedia of gardening.
  III. Series.
  SB425.B87 1992
  635.9′447—dc20   92-6148
                                                  CIP

Printed in Singapore
First U.S. Edition

1 2 3 4 5 6 7 8 9 10

Editors: Charles A. de Kay and Ruth Lively
Designer: Michelle Wiener
Illustrators: Laura B. Goodwin and Lisa Zador
Managing Editor: Robin Haywood

Produced by Smallwood and Stewart, Inc.
New York City

HEARST
GARDEN
GUIDES

CONTENTS

1

I N T R O D U C T I O N

This volume of the *Hearst Garden Guides* presents a selection of the bulbs best suited for home landscape and garden use. It combines the most commonly available species and cultivars, with other interesting and unusual plants, well worth the extra effort to find. The plants were selected for their beauty, their popularity, their availability and their capacity to grow in various climate zones. An encyclopedia at the heart of the book gives key facts and comments on each—an information capsule that outlines the planting, cultivation and care required for success in the garden for each variety.

There are some 250 genera that contain bulbous plants; many of these genera are rare, while others are not commercially available and can be seen only in the wild. But within the available genera there are thousands of species of bulbs and as many cultivars. It is estimated that there are several thousand cultivars of dahlias, irises and gladiolus alone.

For the purposes of this book all bulbous plants—true bulbs, corms, rhizomes and tubers—will be considered bulbs. For examples and complete descriptions of these "different types" of bulbs see the section entitled "The Botany of Bulbs" later in this chapter.

PLANT CLASSIFICATION

Over the ages, people have classified plants in various ways. The ancient Roman writer Pliny the Elder (A.D. 23–79) used size and form as his criteria, setting up three major groupings: trees, shrubs and herbs. In the Middle Ages, plants were classified according to whether they were medicinal, edible or poisonous. Later the great eighteenth-century Swedish botanist Carolus Linnaeus (1707–1778) used the number of stamens in plants as his basis for classification.

Such arbitrary systems are considered artificial today, and even though most gardeners continue to classify plants much as Pliny did, modern taxonomists have moved to a so-called natural system of classification in which plants are grouped according to their generic and evolutionary relationships. Under this system, related species of plants make up a genus. Related genera make up a family. Related families make up an order. Related orders make up a class. Related classes make up a subphylum. Related subphylla make up a phylum (or division). Related phylla make up a subkingdom. And the two subkingdoms make up the plant kingdom.

Starting at the top of the hierarchy, the living world is divided into two kingdoms, the plant kingdom and the animal kingdom. The plant kingdom is broken into two subkingdoms: the Thallophyta (plants not forming embryos), such as various algae, bacteria and slime molds, as well as the true fungi, and Embryophyta (plants forming embryos), which is the subkingdom of interest here.

The Embryophyta contains two phylla: one phyllum is the Bryophyta, which are plants lacking vascular tissues, such as mosses and liverworts, and the other, Tracheophyta, contains plants with vascular tissues. Subphyllum Pteropsida, within the Tracheophyta, contains seed plants and ferns. There are three classes in the subphyllum: Angiospermae, which contains the true flowering plants; Filicineae, which contains the ferns; and Gymnospermae, which includes the cone-bearing plants and relatives.

The Angiospermae are, in turn, broken down into the subclasses Dicotyledoneae and Monocotyledoneae, commonly called dicots and monocots. The monocot embryos bear one cotyledon (the first leaflike structure to appear after sprouting); the dicot embryos bear two. As the plants grow, the true leaves of monocots are alternate with parallel veins and show no secondary thickening; dicot leaves are net-veined, since their vascular strands contain cambium. These subclasses are divided into orders; each order contains one or more families. Each family contains one or more genera, and each genus contains one or more species.

Nomenclature

Because the common names are in English, they are easier to pronounce—which is probably why most gardeners prefer them. Unfortunately, using only common names leads to much confusion. First of all, many plants have not one but several common names. For example, *Schizostylis coccinea* is known as crimson-flag, kaffir lily and river lily. Frequently, two or more totally different plants have the same or similar common names: Who would imagine that the lily and the lily-of-the-Nile weren't related?

Because these problems made it difficult for people to communicate precisely about plants, 200 years ago botanists adopted a binomial system devised by Linnaeus, which identifies each plant more accurately by using two names—the genus followed by the species.

Both the generic and specific names are for the most part derived from Latin or Greek rendered into Latin. Both names are italicized or underlined when written, and the first (generic) name is always capitalized. Thus, the scientific name of the lily-of-the-Nile is *Agapanthus africanus* (which may be abbreviated *A. africanus* once the generic name has been spelled out in reasonably close context).

If a species of plant includes subspecies or varieties (defined below), that name is added directly after the specific name—in Latin for varieties or in modern language for cultivars. Thus, the naturally occurring variety of the trumpet narcissus is known as *Narcissus pseudonarcissus* ssp. *obvallaris*.

Genus

Structurally related plants make up a genus. (The plural of genus is genera.) While the lily and the tulip have the same arrangement of their flower parts, the same basic flower plan and are thus in the same family (*Liliaceae*), there is a great difference between them. The lily has a scaly bulb; the tulip has a truncated bulb. The lily has leaves on the flowering stem; the tulip does not. These plants are separated into two genera, *Lilium* and *Tulipa*.

Species

A species is the particular plant within a genus. Each species within a given genus will be different but will have common characteristics. In plant classification, a species (the word is both singular and plural) lies between a genus and a variety.

A genus may contain anywhere from one to over a thousand species. In turn, a species may encompass a number of varieties. Species, in contrast with most varieties, cultivars and hybrids, may reproduce themselves from seeds and may often be interbred; interbreeding among species of the same genus sometimes occurs naturally.

To the gardener, species are significant because they are individual types of plants. Having determined that a plant is a *Lilium*, one must identify it more exactly. The well-known Easter lily, for example, has the specific (or species) name *longiflorum*, which means that it flowers for a long time.

The specific name might denote a certain characteristic, its native habitat, the person who discovered it or any number of different attributes to separate it from the others. *Lilium canadense*, for example, grows wild in much of Canada.

Subspecies

While the genus and species cover the majority of plants, there are times when one plant is almost identical to a given species. If such a plant is consistently different in some aspect—perhaps the leaves are longer, but the flowers are identical—it merits a subspecies classification rather than its own species name. In botanical terminology the word "subspecies" is abbreviated as subsp. or ssp. For example, *Lilium canadense* subsp. *editorum*, which grows west of the Appalachian mountain range, produces smaller leaves than the species.

Variety

The lowest or final classification of plants found in nature is the variety. Not all species have natural varieties, but most species have several. Strictly speaking, the word "variety" is used to identify only *naturally* occurring variants of identified species. A variety retains the basic character of the species, but has one or more distinctive characteristics of its own. Varieties usually occur in populations, and exist whether or not people notice them. A common example of this is the red-flowering form of some flowers; the plant with this distinction could be called "var. *rubrum.*"

Cultivar

A cultivar (short for *culti*vated *vari*ety) or a hybrid (when the plant results from the crossing of two specific plants) is a new plant selected in cultivation, propagated and named. Cultivars are noted by the abbreviation cv. or by single quotation marks, are always capitalized and never appear in italics.

In the commercial world the name "variety" is frequently used to mean (albeit incorrectly) man-made cultivars. Strictly speaking, however, they are hybrids.

Hybrid

A hybrid is a plant resulting from the crossing of two specific plants. The process of hybridization is unusual in nature; most are developed as the result of human actions, either by accident or on purpose. An example is the commonly available foxtail, *Eremurus* × *shelfordii*, a hybrid of some importance to the garden.

Hybrids are noted with a multiplication sign "×." The symbol precedes the genus when the genus itself is a hybrid. It is written between the generic and specific names if the species is a hybrid. Cultivars are selected from hybrids.

Clones

Some plants are propagated asexually—without sex. For instance, one 'Enchantment' lily is exactly the same as another; they are all clones. Each 'Enchantment' is actually grown from a little piece of the original lily bulb. Rose 'Peace' and 'Golden Delicious' apple trees are other examples of clones.

Strains

Many nurseries produce flower strains. By crossing two named and known parents, the nurseries produce seeds which will grow to be very much like each other, varying little if at all. Golden Splendor and Pink Perfection are two such lily strains. Each Golden Splendor is almost but not quite identical to another; one might vary from another in height or in exact flowering time, but it would be immediately recognizable as a Golden Splendor lily.

THE BOTANY OF BULBS

In common parlance, we use bulbs to cover a wide range of plants that have some form of natural underground storage mechanism. In correct horticultural terminology, however, they are not all true bulbs.

True Bulbs

Perhaps the best known true bulb is the onion. When an onion is sliced in half, fleshy rings are revealed. These circles are, in fact, leaves modified to hold food for the bulb during a period of dormancy.

A true bulb consists of a stem, which is compressed into a flattened plate (the bottom of the onion from which the roots sprout), and the storage leaves. Small buds form inside the leaves attached to the basal plate, and the buds will in turn become stems and flowers.

Certain species of lilies will produce bulbils in the axis of the leaves. These are miniature plants and can be grown to become full-size bulbs. Under the ground, meanwhile, stem bulblets will form; these can be of considerable size, so that they will even flower the following year. They are generally white in color and will have their own root system. Certain Asiatic hybrids will produce so many stem bulblets that it is necessary to lift the bulbs to remove these bulblets, otherwise the plants will soon be overcrowded.

Corms

A corm is a stem modified for storage. The normal shape is rounded, flattened on top, concave below. Young buds, which will produce the stems and flowers, form on the top, while roots and cormels emerge from the bottom. Cormels are young growths that, when divided, become individual corms. *Crocus*, *Gladiolus* and *Watsonia* are all corms.

Rhizomes

A rhizome is an underground stem, sometimes breaking the surface of the soil. The growing ends (or apices) produce the leaf growth, while the roots emerge from the underside. The most commonly grown rhizome is the bearded iris. (Note, however, that some *Iris* are, in fact, true bulbs.)

Tubers

A tuber is an underground stem, but not the base of the stem as in a corm. Tubers are usually rounded and fleshy and covered with scaly leaves, which are often minute and concentrated towards the top of the tuber. One common example is the tuberous begonia; another is the dahlia, whose "eyes" or buds are found at the base of the older stem.

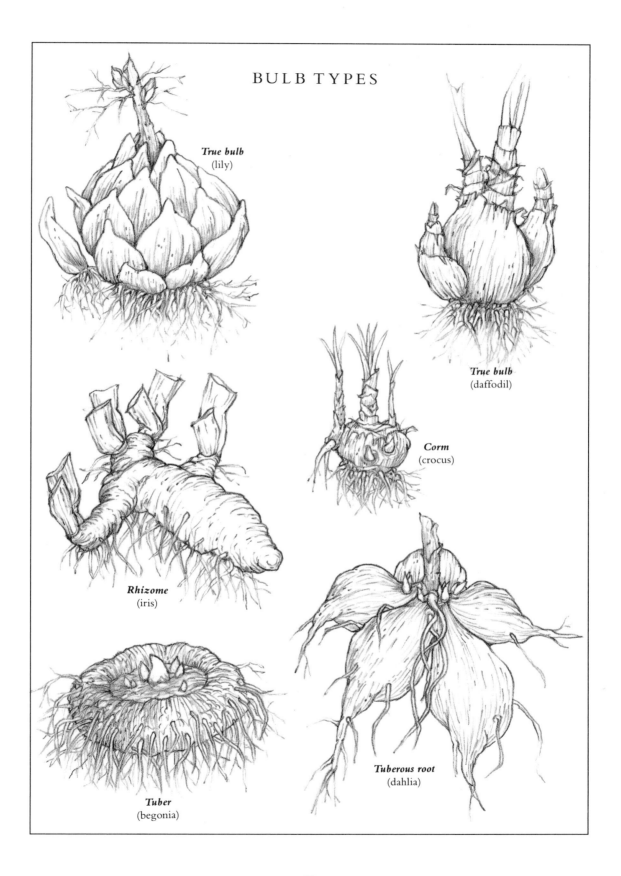

BULB TYPES

True bulb
(lily)

True bulb
(daffodil)

Rhizome
(iris)

Corm
(crocus)

Tuber
(begonia)

Tuberous root
(dahlia)

FLOWER FORMS

The word "flower" is the popular term for the combination of structures having to do with the reproduction of complex plants. The concept usually includes color and a definite organization. If these evolved plants did not have flowers, they could not produce seed with which to reproduce their kind.

The variety of colors, shapes and sizes of flowers is almost bewildering. In color, only a true black is missing. As to shape and form, while the majority of flowers are symmetrical, many, such as the bearded iris, are highly asymmetrical. In size they range from the microscopic to diameters of almost a foot. Some flowers are borne singly on the plant stems, others in clusters (see "Inflorescence" below).

The point at which the flower is connected to the stem is the receptacle. Next are the sepals, which collectively make up the calyx. These are the outermost, petal-like structures, which are usually green, that enclose and protect the flower bud before it opens.

Inside the sepals are the petals, which collectively form the corolla. (The petals and sepals together make up the perianth. In cases where the sepal and petals cannot be distinguished from one another, as for example in lilies, they are known as tepals.) Some flowers have only a few petals; others have hundreds. Usually the petals are separate, but they are often united into a single tube or cup.

The reproductive organs of the flower are surrounded by the petals. The male organs are the stamens, which are collectively called the Androecium, that produce pollen. The female organs are the seed-bearing carpels, collectively known as the pistil or Gynoecium, which collect pollen and protect the ovules.

Each stamen consists of a filament (usually a short, slender stalk) bearing at the apex a single, enlarged anther. The anthers form pollen.

Pistils may have three parts: the swollen ovary in which seeds are formed, above this the slender style, and at the end of the style the stigma—often rough or sticky—on which the pollen falls or is deposited to produce fertilization. The pollen germinates on the stigma, grows down the style and fertilizes the ovary, producing seed.

Flowers are also categorized as perfect and imperfect. Perfect flowers have both stamens and pistils and are thus capable of self-fertilization if pollen ripens and stigma becomes receptive to it at the same time. Daffodils, tulips and lilies are examples of perfect flowers. Imperfect flowers may have either stamens (these are called staminate flowers) or pistils (pistillate flowers). When the staminate (male) and pistillate (female) flowers (reproductive organs) are borne on separate plants the plants are said to be dioecious. The opposite of these are the monoecious plants (such as corn, walnuts and oaks) which have both staminate and pistillate flowers. All true bulbs produce perfect flowers.

In the case of iris flowers, a different arrangement of the parts calls for different terminology. The upright petals are called "standards," and those that grow below are called "falls." The upper part of the fall reaches an apex at the "crest," while in the center of the lower fall the "beard," which is often very decorative, appears. The stigma, style and anther are located between the two parts of the fall.

Inflorescence

Some plants will produce more than one flower in the flowerhead; the overall form, which these clusters take, varies with the type of plant. *Allium* flowers, for instance, form umbels, or flat or dome-shaped flower clusters. For an illustrative definition of each of the different types of inflorescences, see page 16.

PARTS OF A FLOWER

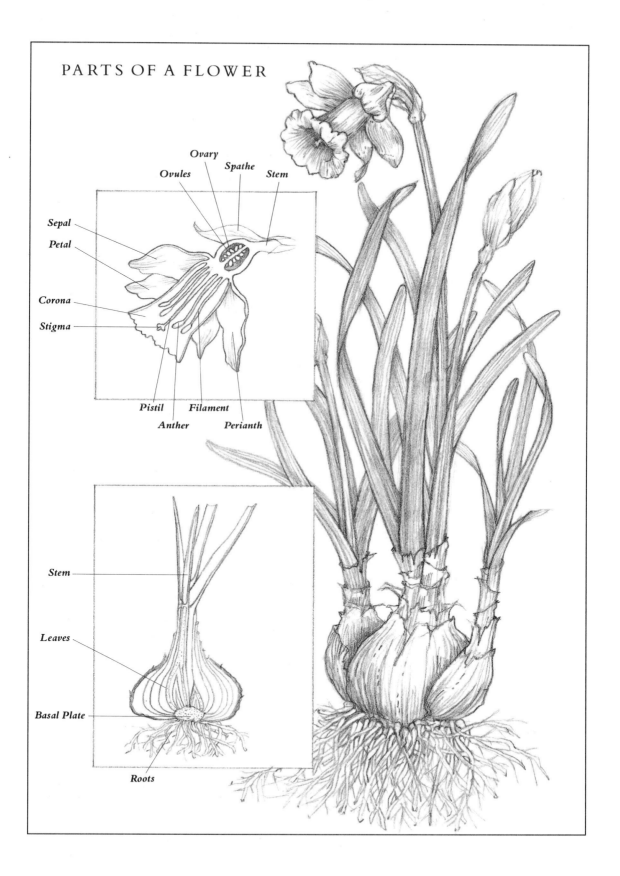

Ovary

Ovules   Spathe   Stem

Sepal

Petal

Corona

Stigma

Pistil   Filament

Anther   Perianth

Stem

Leaves

Basal Plate

Roots

FLOWER TYPES

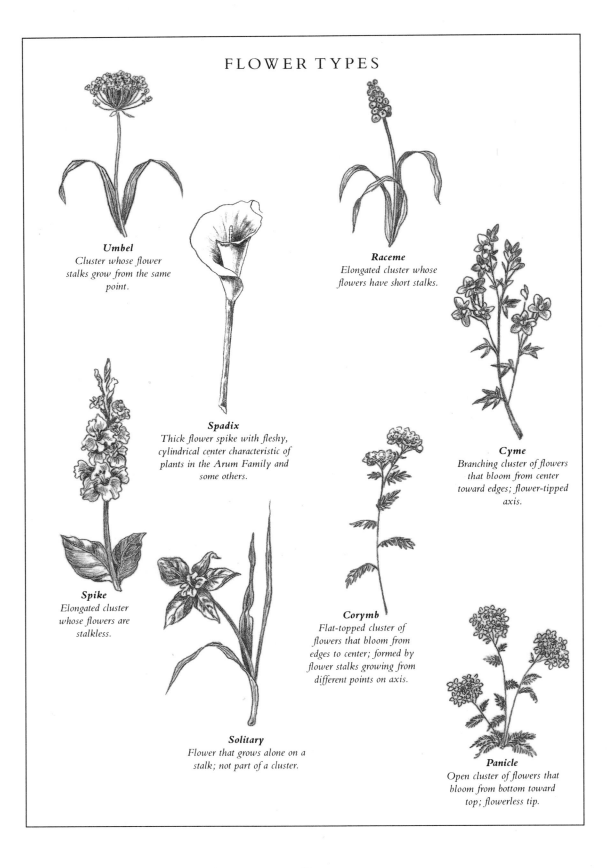

Umbel
Cluster whose flower stalks grow from the same point.

Spadix
Thick flower spike with fleshy, cylindrical center characteristic of plants in the Arum Family and some others.

Raceme
Elongated cluster whose flowers have short stalks.

Cyme
Branching cluster of flowers that bloom from center toward edges; flower-tipped axis.

Spike
Elongated cluster whose flowers are stalkless.

Solitary
Flower that grows alone on a stalk; not part of a cluster.

Corymb
Flat-topped cluster of flowers that bloom from edges to center; formed by flower stalks growing from different points on axis.

Panicle
Open cluster of flowers that bloom from bottom toward top; flowerless tip.

2

GARDEN FUNDAMENTALS

For the most part, the culture of bulbs is simple. What follows is intended to be a set of general guidelines to design considerations and cultural practices. Specific horticultural information peculiar to certain genera and species can be found with their entries in the encyclopedic portion of this book. There is also information about cultural requirements in Chapter 3.

DESIGNING WITH BULBS

When deciding just where to plant bulbs, keep several points in mind. The location must offer the sun or shade needed by the particular species and provide the good drainage or moisture needed. In any given area, plant the bulbs only if their cultural requirements can be met. Keep in mind that there are bulbs for almost every situation—there are those that thrive in the sun, others that require shade, some that need moisture, some that require superb drainage. With the great diversity of bulbs from which to choose, you can find suitable bulbs for almost any location.

Bulbs such as the English bluebell look superb in drifts in woodland settings, as well as adding complementary color to beds of azaleas and rhododendrons, but they would look out of place in a formal garden. Tulips look great in beds surrounded by annual color, such as is provided by primroses or pansies. They would not look as pretty in drifts under trees, where the bluebell is at its best. Lilies are marvelous for extending the seasons of interest of shrub borders, as well as for adding interest to the perennial border. Indeed, lilies are versatile. Certain varieties are striking in woodland settings, others are at home in more formal settings.

Bulbs that have a comparatively short flowering period should be planted where their great beauty and exciting colors can be appreciated. Choose a spot where they will be visible from as many angles from the house and comfortable niches in the property as possible. To site the beds, walk around the garden and make a note of the most visible areas—perfect spots for plantings of bright and exciting bulbs. Bulbs that become permanent residents of the garden, such as lilies, irises and muscari, must be planted where they can remain undisturbed for years. They will then naturalize and their numbers will increase. Selecting the site for various types of bulbs requires some knowledge of the bulbs under consideration, and this information can be found in this book.

Apart from cultural requirements, background and companion plants must be considered. Lilies seen against a dark background will stand out and be noticed. The same lilies planted among shrubs

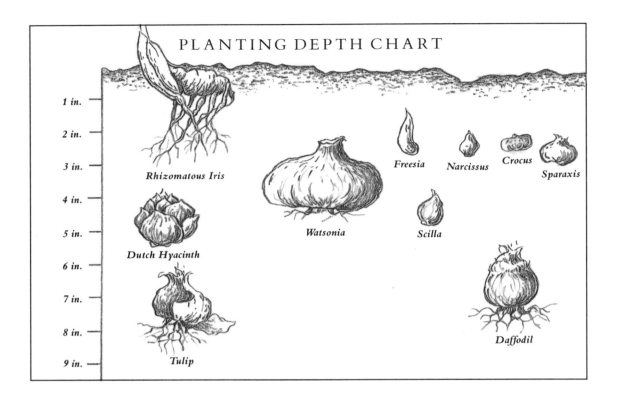

PLANTING DEPTH CHART

1 in.

2 in.

3 in.

Rhizomatous Iris

Freesia Narcissus Crocus Sparaxis

4 in.

5 in.

Dutch Hyacinth

Watsonia Scilla

6 in.

7 in.

8 in.

Daffodil

9 in.

Tulip

that are free-flowering and blooming at the same time as the lilies will detract from the brilliance of the lilies, unless they are of contrasting colors—white or yellow lilies paired with red-flowering shrubs, for example.

The topography of the site will always play a part in the design of a garden. Grading of any site is of great importance, as is drainage. These two factors combined can make or mar the beauty and the usefulness of a property. If the site is relatively flat, there will be few problems; increasing problems can be expected with the increasing steepness of any slope. Working with a professional is almost a must if your garden is on a steep slope. A few hours spent in consultation can save many hundreds of dollars in reducing the need for fill or excavation. Retaining walls are not inexpensive.

PLANTING BASICS

Planting time depends not only on the type of bulb in question but also in large part on the climate where it is to be planted. Consider the needs of the bulb.

First, before it flowers, a bulb must develop a strong root system, for physical support of the flowering spike and the ability to take in moisture and nutrients. Second, most hardy bulbs—daffodils, crocuses, hyacinths and tulips, for example—require a period of cold temperatures before they can start to grow and flower. Therefore, in cold-winter areas, hardy bulbs must be planted early enough to establish root systems before the soil gets cold enough to halt root growth—about 40°F. Tender bulbs, on the other hand, such as southern African natives like *Agapanthus*, are planted in spring, early enough to establish root systems before warm air and soil promote top growth.

Fall-flowering bulbs, such as colchicums and fall-blooming crocuses, should be planted as soon as they are available.

Spring-flowering bulbs should be planted in

PLANTING DEPTH CHART

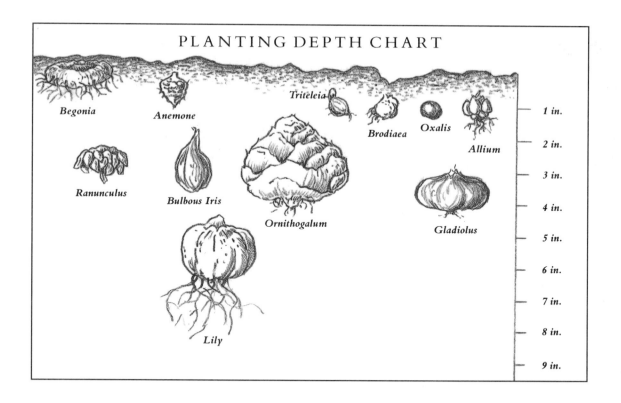

Begonia

Anemone

Triteleia

Brodiaea

Oxalis

Allium

Ranunculus

Bulbous Iris

Ornithogalum

Gladiolus

Lily

— 1 in.

— 2 in.

— 3 in.

— 4 in.

— 5 in.

— 6 in.

— 7 in.

— 8 in.

— 9 in.

fall, as early as Sept. or as late as Nov. or early Dec., depending on where you live. In Zones 6 and colder, plant hardy bulbs in Sept. or early Oct.; in Zone 7, plant in Oct.; in Zone 8, plant in late Oct. and Nov.; in Zones 9 and warmer, plant pre-chilled bulbs in late Nov. and Dec.

In Zones 9 to 11, you can buy hardy bulbs early and refrigerate them, simulating the cold requirement until proper planting time. It is possible to plant hardy bulbs too early, especially in warm climates. It is better to plant bulbs a week or ten days too late (no later) than too early. The warmer the climate, the more essential it is to satisfy the bulb's pre-cooling requirement.

Tender summer-flowering bulbs can be planted in fall or spring in warm-winter climates, Zones 9 to 11 (see USDA Hardiness Zone Map, pages 170–171). Elsewhere, plant them a week or ten days before your last frost date in spring. You do not want them to be up before the last frost is past.

Soil

Bulbs need a soil that is moisture-retentive and well-draining, but that is at no time without air; they do not like waterlogged soil. Plant bulbs in good garden loam that is moderately fertile. If your soil is sandy or heavy clay, add organic matter—leafmold or compost—and cultivate to a depth of 1 ft.

At several places in this book, reference is made to a basic potting mix. This is simply the kind of potting soil that you can buy in plastic bags at garden centers and nurseries, hardware stores and even supermarkets.

If you are making your own bulb soil, an ideal mixture is:

7 parts good loam,
3 parts peat or leafmold, and
2 parts sharp sand (not builder's sand, which is too fine).

TO STAKE, OR NOT TO STAKE?

Gardeners divide into two groups over this controversial subject—those who stake their plants, and those who do not. The first question is, is it necessary? The second, how to do it?

Many gardeners contend that most plants, grown well, do not need artificial support. Given good soil, adequate fertilizer, proper light, water and protection from wind, plants can stand up on their own. To avoid staking completely, learn the needs of the individual bulbs and cater to them well.

If soil is loose and friable, roots can work their way through it easily to form a good anchor. Adequate and appropriate fertilizer makes a strong plant, but too much can cause rank, lax growth, resulting in a weak plant. In fact, some gardeners grow plants on the lean side to prevent having to stake. Giving a plant less sun than it needs will cause it to stretch.

Finally, if a plant's stature is tall and thin, as is the case with lilies and gladioli, growing it in a windy spot without protection is asking for trouble. A tall plant, heavily laden with flowers, will have a hard time standing up to buffeting breezes. If the location is windy, plant in the shelter of a wall, hedge or shrub. Even if the site is not on a hilltop or near the sea or a lake, there will be wind occasionally. Breezes are more prevalent in some parts of a garden, such as at house corners. Pay attention to wind patterns and plant accordingly.

If the idea of staking is not offensive, do it properly. Put the stake in the soil as soon as the plants are up and it's still clear where the bulb ends and the soil begins. Be careful not to plunge the stake into the bulb or tuber. Place the stake on the back side of the plant so that it will be hidden. Likewise, when tying the plant, tie the knot against the stake, not the plant, so that the knot is on the back side of the stake. For aesthetic reasons, always use the same kind of stake and ties throughout your garden. Tie the plant's stalk every 6 to 8 in. And do not wait for a plant to lean before tying it to the stake, or it will wind up with a contorted stem.

When necessary, you can amend this ratio by increasing either the sand or the peat/leafmold. Where sharper drainage is indicated, increase the amount of sand to three or even four parts. Where more moisture-retentive soil is indicated, increase the peat or leafmold to four parts.

Planting depths vary depending on the bulb and to some extent on your soil. A good rule of thumb is to plant the base of the bulb at a depth three times the bulb's height. This holds true for soils that are normal to heavy. In light, sandy soil, plant deeper—cover the bulb with three to four times its height of soil. There are exceptions, which are described in the specific entries in Chapter 4, the Encyclopedia of Bulbs. For more information on planting depths, refer to the illustration above.

When planting only a few bulbs in one spot, use a trowel or a bulb planter, which removes a core of soil just big enough to allow a single bulb. If there a large number of bulbs to be planted, it is easiest to dig out the entire planting area with a spade, amend the soil if necessary, then set all the bulbs in at once and refill.

Watering

Immediately after planting, water the area well to settle the soil around the bulbs. Bulbs need moisture while in active growth. As soon as fall- and spring-flowering bulbs have finished flowering and the foliage has died down, however, they prefer to go on the dry side, with a very dry period in late summer, prior to being activated again at or around planting time.

The same general rule applies to tender bulbs: from the start of growth until they go dormant, they should never be dry or in water-laden soil. The exceptions are *Agapanthus*, *Clivia* and *Dietes*, which are evergreen. Although these bulbs retain their foliage year-round, they do have a resting period, during which they need much less moisture, but should not be allowed to go bone-dry.

Mulch

It is a good idea to mulch the planting area to retain moisture and to moderate the soil temperature. Match the type and depth of mulch to the bulbs you are planting; do not smother tiny flowers such as crocuses, *Eranthis* (winter aconite) or *Muscari* (grape hyacinth) in a deep or coarse mulch. The smaller the plant is overall, the finer-textured the mulch should be. Never use very large mulch, such as bark chips, to cover bulbs,

---

B U Y I N G   A N D   S T O R I N G
F E R T I L I Z E R S   A N D
P E S T I C I D E S

Fertilizer does not keep forever. If it gets damp or wet, its efficiency will decrease. Even so, it is still not a good idea to use more than the recommended rate. Instead, put the diminished fertilizer on the compost heap and buy a fresh product for your plants. If stored correctly—that is, completely dry—fertilizer should keep for two to possibly three seasons, but it is very hard to keep moisture out of an opened bag of fertilizer. The best bet is to buy only the amount you will use up in one season.

Pesticides have a longer shelf life than fertilizers, but it is still much better not to use old products. Buy the smallest quantities you need, and if you do not use them up after three years, dispose of them properly. Call your local EPA office or your county agricultural extension office for disposal instructions.

To keep track of how long you have had a product, write the purchase date on the label with an indelible marker. To keep the instructions on bottles of liquids legible, cover the entire label with clear packing tape. If spills occur, you will still be able to read how to apply the product. No matter what the product, never use more of it than the label recommends, and always follow directions.

---

because they take a long time to break down. Also, be sure to apply moist mulch to moist soil. A good gardening practice is to first rake the soil, put on an inch of mulch, work that together with the top layer of soil and then add the rest of the mulch.

Rules for Applying Fertilizer

A bulb contains everything it needs. Imagine a hyacinth flowering in a glass of water, or a narcissus in pebbles and water. But in order for a bulb to give sustained growth, fertilizing is important.

First, a few words of caution. Whenever using any garden chemical, whether fertilizer or pesticide, always follow package directions. Never use more than the label recommends, and never use a product on plants that are not indicated on the label. In areas with sandy soil and high rainfall, where nutrients leach quickly from the soil, it is better to use half the amount of fertilizer twice as frequently than it is to apply one heavy dose.

Commercial fertilizers are sold by the ratio of the chemicals they contain: nitrogen, phosphorus and potassium or N-P-K. Formulas mentioned below, such as 8-5-5, and on the actual packages represent this ratio of minerals in the order given.

For spring-flowering bulbs, at planting time add bone meal (or one of the commercial products called "bulb food") to the planting hole and mix it in well before setting the bulb. In spring, as soon as growth emerges from the ground, the bulbs should have a small amount of a fertilizer containing a little bit of nitrogen and a lesser amount of phosphate or potash, such as an 8-5-5 applied according to package directions, to get them stimulated into making growth. In fall, mix some 0-10-10 fertilizer into the soil.

For fall-flowering bulbs, apply 8-5-5 as soon as the foliage appears, after flowering.

For tender bulbs, in cold climates you can omit the bone meal when planting, because the bulbs probably will not benefit much from the slow-acting bone meal before it is time to lift and store them. Fertilize clivias in late summer with 8-5-5. After they flower, give them a feeding of 10-10-10 to carry them through the summer. Dahlias need to be fertilized as soon as they appear out of the ground. In good rich soil, there is no need for additional fertilizer after this initial boost. If soil fertility is average or worse, give dahlias weak liquid feedings until buds start to develop. Fertilize gladiolus with 8-5-5 when foliage appears.

Storing Bulbs

No matter where you live, there are probably some bulbs that need to be lifted and stored. Which ones depend on your climate. In cold-winter areas, tender bulbs are dug before winter and stored to protect them from frost; examples are *Gladiolus, Dahlia, Caladium* and Tuberous *Begonia*. In warm climates, dig hardy bulbs such as *Tulipa, Narcissus* (daffodils) and *Crocus* when they go dormant in early or midsummer. Later, prior to planting, put them in cold storage to meet their chilling requirement so they will bloom again. The important thing to remember is this: you want to maintain the status quo. If the bulb is fleshy or succulent, such as a *Caladium* or a *Dahlia*, store it without dehydration and without encouraging growth. If the bulb is dry, such as a *Gladiolus* corm or a tulip, store it dry.

Store tender bulbs in paper bags that have holes punched in them. Store one kind and color of bulb to a bag, and write this information on the bag. Keep the bags in a dry place where the temperature is about 45°F. Fleshy bulbs that need to be kept from shriveling can be stored in trays of damp pure peat, wood shavings or sawdust. Be sure the medium is not 100% dry; it should be barely moist, but not wet. If bulbs stored in peat or sawdust show shriveling, correct the condition

BULBS TO FORCE

The bulb is nature's well-wrapped marvel, a perfect holiday package. Late October or early November is the time to start the growth cycle that first sends roots down into moist soil or pebbles, then sends up fresh greening leaves, buds furling jewel colors and, finally, flowers as fragrant as spring. The best kinds to plant for flowering gifts and for decorating the house in December are the tender narcissus (paperwhite, golden 'Soleil d'Or' and Chinese sacred lily), amaryllis, hyacinths and precooled early tulips.

To grow narcissus, all you need is water, pebbles, the bulbs and a bowl or flowerpot at least 2 inches deep and large enough to hold three to twelve of them. Fill the container half full of pebbles. Set the bulbs on this surface, allowing about a half-inch of space between. Pour in more pebbles until a third of each bulb is in the gravel. Add water until it touches the bulbs and place the planting in a dark, cool place (60 to 70 deg. F.) for about two weeks to encourage root growth. After this time bring the planter to a sunny, warm place. Keep moist at all times, and avoid hot, dry drafts.

Hybrid amaryllis in white, pink, rose and red, or patterned reds and whites, send up splendid scapes of flowers two to eight weeks after planting. Plant in commercially prepared potting soil (or in a mixture of equal parts garden loam, peat moss and sand), allowing about an inch of space between bulb and pot, and leaving at least one-third of the bulb above the surface. Keep evenly moist at all times, but water more freely when growth becomes active. Am-

aryllis need a well-lighted, warm place until buds begin to open; then they may be moved to a cooler, shaded interior where the blooms will last longer.

Hyacinths

Fragrant hyacinths force into bloom easily in eight to ten weeks. Colors range from palest yellow to orange, from red to rose and pink, and through all the blues to delicate lavender. Plant the bulbs in the same kind of soil recommended for amaryllis, positioning them so that the tips are near the surface, even protruding slightly. Moisten well. Keep cool (less than 60 deg. F., if possible), moist and dark for two weeks, then move to a warmer place (about 70 deg. F.), but continue to keep in the dark until leaves are 4 or 5 inches tall. After this period, provide abundant light.

Precooled early tulips can also be forced to bloom by Christmas. Plant and care for as hyacinths, except keep tulips cool, moist and dark for three weeks, then move to a sunny, warm place to finish the growth cycle.

Other bulbs that may be planted and treated as tulips for flowers in late December and January include ixia, ornithogalum, sparaxis, freesia, ranunculus, *Iris reticulata* and *Iris danfordiae*. While lily-of-the-valley is not considered a bulb, its sweet-smelling flowers may be enjoyed any time after Thanksgiving by planting pips that have been specially prepared for forcing into bloom in 21 days.

by increasing the humidity in the medium. Moisten the tubers until they are plumped up before returning them to the damp medium. Check on the bulbs every month or so. Discard any that show signs of rot. To prevent rot from spreading to neighboring bulbs, shake the healthy bulbs in a plastic bag with a small amount of fungicide powder, then replace them in a new paper bag. Wear plastic gloves when doing this.

In warm-winter climates, dig hardy bulbs when the foliage has lightened and is obviously beginning to dry. Store in a light, airy place—but not in direct sun—until all clinging soil is dry. Remove the foliage and stem, then rub the bulb with your hands to clean off the dry soil. Store in a hole-punched paper bag in a cool, dry place. Refrigerate eight weeks prior to planting.

PROPAGATION TECHNIQUES

Bulbs lend themselves to many methods of propagation. Many of these techniques are easy and uncomplicated, but despite this few home gardeners propagate their bulbs.

Propagation is either sexual (by seed) or asexual (vegetative). Asexual propagation, such as division, gives rise to plants that are identical to the parent bulbs. Raising plants from seed opens up the chances of variation, which could be slight or considerable. It is from seed that new varieties are raised, which often takes thousands of seedlings before one worthwhile new variety is obtained.

Seed

If there is a disadvantage to propagating from seed, it is that with some genera it takes years for the seedlings to flower. In the case of *Dahlia*, *Ranunculus* and *Begonia*, flowers can be seen in the first year.

The size of the seeds varies. Lilies have large seeds which are easily handled. Begonias, on the other hand, have very fine seeds, there being millions in an ounce. The home gardener is well advised to purchase a seed mix or a soilless mix for the raising of seedlings, because such a mix will be free of weed seeds and of soil-borne diseases. There are many such mixes on the market, and it may take some experimentation to determine the best type.

The seed of most bulbs is sown in the spring, with temperatures at night in the 55° to 65°F range. If it is not possible to manage these conditions, simply wait until the weather warms and sow the seed outdoors in a sheltered location or in a cold frame. Although each genus has some special requirement, most will germinate in a comparatively short space of time. Some seed must have a cold period before germinating. Bulbs in this category are *Allium*, *Anemone*, *Arum*, *Camassia*, *Chionodoxa*, *Crocus*, *Cyclamen*, *Erythronium*, *Fritillaria*, *Gladiolus*, *Hyacinthus*, *Iris*, *Muscari*, *Narcissus*, *Nerine*, *Scilla* and *Tulipa*. Such seed should be sown as soon as ripe; barely cover the seed and then place the pots in a cold area where they will experience and enjoy the cold of winter. Come the following spring they will germinate. Some seed will take more than one season to germinate; among these genera are *Colchicum*, *Galanthus* and *Sternbergia*. If the temperatures in the garden do not fall below freezing, it may be necessary to mix the seed of such species with sand and place them in the freezer for a month or so.

Most seed purchased from commercial sources will have received the needed cold treatment and be ready for sowing.

After sowing seed in the warmth of spring, keep them evenly moist, maintain constant temperatures and give them good light, especially as soon as germination has occurred. Keep growing the seedlings on, hardening them off slowly. As soon as they are large enough to handle, place

Separating Bulbs

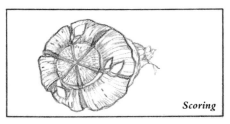

Bulblets and Bulbils

To separate a clump of bulbs, dig them up after the leaves have died. Replant immediately.

Separate and plant bulblets in fall and bulbils when they are ripe, 1 to 2 inches deep.

BULB PROPAGATION

Scaling

Scoring

Break scales, dust, store until bulblets form, refrigerate two months, then plant.

In early summer, make three cuts through the basal plate, then store in a dry place until the cuts spread (a few days).

Cormels

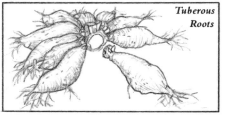

Tuberous Roots

Tiny corms are formed around edges of the bulb; the shallower the corm is planted, the more cormels are formed.

When, in spring, the eyes become clearly swollen, divide the root into segments, each with at least one eye.

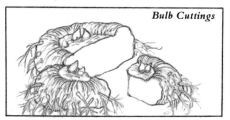

Bulb Cuttings

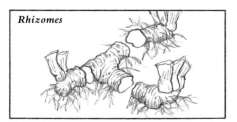

Rhizomes

Cut between scales and cut the basal plate so there are four scale segments per section of basal plate, then plant these cuttings. Treat like stem cuttings.

Pull up rhizomes after plant has flowered, then discard those without leaves before cutting the rest into sections, each with one fan of leaves.

them into their own individual containers, using a regular potting mix, which again is best purchased from a nursery. After a season of growth, the bulbs may be of a size to plant out. If they are large, plant them in permanent locations in the garden. If they are not, plant them in nursery rows to grow on until they can be planted out. Never let seedlings dry out while growing, but do respect the genus' normal resting periods.

Though many gardeners may be discouraged from sowing seed that will not produce any flowers for a number of years, it is worthwhile remembering that after a few years a constant delight of seedlings will be coming into flower.

When sowing seed, make sure that all containers are clean. Keep accurate records for easy reference during subsequent sowings. Many tips regarding the finer points of raising plants from seed can be obtained by corresponding with other growers of a particular genus. Membership in one of the specialized societies is highly recommended.

Stem Cuttings

Dahlias and begonias can be raised from cuttings. Given a temperature of about 55°F at night, dahlia tubers set in peat moss early in the year will start to produce shoots. When these are 4 to 5 in. in length, they can be removed with a sharp knife and placed in a sandy soil mix. It is preferable to keep the cuttings in a humid atmosphere such as is provided by putting them in a plastic frame. This will reduce the loss of moisture from the cuttings and allow them to root more easily. After five to ten days the cuttings will have rooted and can be potted individually into small containers.

Begonias can be propagated by two types of cuttings. The simplest method is to start the tubers into growth, then when the shoots are 3 to 4 in. long, remove them and root them, in much

the same way as described for dahlias. The other way is to start the tubers into growth, and as soon as the little buds are clearly visible, cut the tubers into sections, each with an eye that can develop into a full-grown plant.

Division

This is by far the easiest way to increase the stock of bulbs. The time to do this is when the bulbs have just gone into their dormant period. Lift the bulbs, separate the clumps and plant back the larger-sized bulbs; plant the smaller ones in nursery rows if maximum production is required. If there are many larger bulbs derived from this division, save the largest and soundest bulbs and discard the remainder.

Evergreen bulbs that do not go into an obvious dormant period should be divided in the springtime before the plants break into active growth. Species of *Clivia* and *Agapanthus* require such treatment. After division of evergreen species, it is recommended that you remove, at least in part, some of the foliage so that the roots do not have to sustain too much leaf area. This will bring the ratio of roots to foliage into balance and the bulbs will have a better chance of growing well.

For the rhizomes of *Iris*, such as bearded irises, the best time to lift and divide is in June or July. Lift the entire root, discard the older roots (which are darker in color), and with a knife cut sections of the root, each having at one end a young bud with growth buds and leaves. The leaves can be reduced in size, and planting should be carried out as soon as possible. If the roots are not to be planted for a while, cover them with sand or moist peat moss so that they do not dehydrate. Planting should not be delayed too long, however, or few if any flowers will be produced the following year. All such roots should be in the ground again in their final location by late August. If planted later, the plants will be fine, but flowering will be delayed by a season.

Lilies can be propagated by several different methods. One way is to remove the outer scales from the bulbs and sow them barely covered in a sandy soil. They will soon produce small bulbs at their base. These can be lifted after a season and grown on in nursery rows until they reach flowering size, which is about 2 to 4 in. in diameter, sometimes less, depending on variety.

Other methods of lily propagation involve bulblets and bulbils. Some lily species produce stem bulblets underground. These are treated in the same way as the young bulbs produced on the bases of the scales and grown on as described above. Bulbils produced on the stems above ground are also treated in the same way, but being small they should hardly be covered when planted. Some varieties will produce more stem bulbils if the stems are buried, but this method of propagation is best left to commercial growers, as often the parent bulb is lost.

Corms of various genera, including *Gladiolus*, are often prolific in the production of little corms, called cormels. It is not unusual for a corm to produce up to a hundred cormels. These can be treated much the same as the bulbils and bulblets of lilies. Lined out in nursery rows, planted 1 to 1½ in. deep, they will grow on to flowering size within a couple of seasons.

The following are some other ways of propagating specific kinds of bulbs.

Canna

In the spring, prior to planting the parent roots out, separate younger sections (each with a growing point) from the parent root either by cutting with a knife or by just pulling them apart.

Cyclamen

Treat the large tubers in the same way as tuberous begonias. Cut them into sections, each section having a bud.

Eremurus

The unusual-looking roots are fleshy and are easily broken, thus requiring extreme care in handling. After flowering, lift and separate the roots, making sure that each portion to be planted back has a prominent bud. Roots without such buds should be discarded.

Hippeastrum

When handling large bulbs such as *Hippeastrum*, take care not to harm the fleshy roots when separating the young bulbs from the parent bulb.

Polianthes

Tuberoses are propagated after they have finished flowering. Lift the tubers and remove or separate young ones with a growing point from the parent tuber. Store in sand and plant the following spring.

Zantedeschia

In late summer or early fall, lift the roots and divide, cutting the roots as necessary. The separated portions must have an eye or bud. Plant back as soon as possible; if this is not possible, store in sand and plant in the spring. If portions must be stored over winter, dust the cut surfaces with a fungicide to prevent rotting. Sections planted immediately do not require this treatment.

All bulbs can be propagated in one way or another. Narcissus, tulips and many others will produce smaller bulbs alongside the bulbs that have flowered that spring. Many times the offspring will not be of sufficient size to produce flowers the following spring and will have to be grown on for yet another season before the bulbs reach flowering size. When growing such bulbs on, be sure to remove any flowers that are produced as soon as possible so that the bulbs can focus their energy on producing larger bulbs.

Remember that the production of a flower demands a great effort on the part of the young bulb. Only when bulbs are of good size can they be expected to produce flowers of good size.

The propagation of bulbs is a fascinating subject. To fully understand the many facets of bulb production takes time, experience and patience. Yet the satisfaction obtained by such work is great, and home gardeners are encouraged to try their hand at propagating their bulbs. Some disappointments must be expected, but some techniques, such as stem cuttings from dahlias or the division of iris rhizomes, should provide good results with the minimum of effort.

PESTS & DISEASES

Bulbs purchased from reputable firms will be free of pests and diseases. If good hygiene is practiced, the gardener should have few problems with bulbs. When well cultivated, fertilized as needed, given the correct amount of moisture and grown in an area with good air circulation, most bulbs will flower and give pleasure without the gardener having to confront a myriad of problems.

If a plant does not look well, most people at once suspect an attack by some pest or disease. It is far more likely, however, that the plant's failing health is due to a lack of attention to correct cultural procedures. Before rushing off to purchase some chemical or mechanical "fix," first examine the possibility of other causes of the problem. Once you have ruled out incorrect cultural practices, then you can proceed with other solutions to the problem.

Plants will, from time to time, become infested by some insect or infected with some disease. Your first response should be the least-toxic approach—a jet of water to dislodge insects or perhaps an insecticidal soap, which has no harmful effect on the environment. Sometimes a more powerful product might have to be used. If and when any product is purchased for use in the garden, pay attention to the instructions on the package label. Use only as directed and only on those plants for which the product has received approval from authorities. If at any time you have any doubt about the use of a product, ask for advice from a fully qualified person, such as your county agricultural commissioner, extension agent, licensed pest-control operator or a member of the staff at your local nursery.

To determine the best plan of attack to control or eliminate pests or diseases in the garden, it is first necessary to identify the culprits. The following are the pests and diseases most likely to be encountered by a gardener growing a wide selection of bulbous plants.

Pests

Ants

These do not cause much damage to bulbous plants. They are generally found on plants that have colonies of aphids or other insects that exude honeydew, on which the ants feed. If you see ants, check for another pest. To control the ants, trace them to their nest and pour boiling water over it. If this fails, seek professional help.

Aphids

Probably the most common plant pest, aphids are sucking insects that weaken plants and can transmit viruses from one plant to another. They are small and generally dark green or brown. Multiplying rapidly, they congregate on bud tips and petals, and can cause distortion of plant tissue and yellowing of foliage. Sometimes a jet of water will dislodge them; if there are only a few they can be squashed by hand. Insecticidal soap can be used and repeat sprayings made, following the directions on the label. If after such methods of control the pests persist, obtain a suitable product from your nursery. Natural controls include lady-bugs, which will control but not eradicate the problem.

European Corn Borer

If a great number of cornstalks are left around at the end of summer, they could provide a home for this pest. In late summer or early spring the caterpillar emerges and will attack plants similar to corn, such as dahlias and gladioli. The larva is pink, ¾ in. long; the egg-laying moth is yellow-brown and nocturnal and thus difficult to spot. Cleanliness is one of the best controls. If you do find this borer on or in plants, remove the plants and dispose of them at once.

Stalk Borer

Dahlias, lilies (late-flowering types) and irises are the most susceptible to the pest, which is found mainly east of the Rocky Mountains. The cater-pillar is about l in. long and is pale yellow with a purplish band, the colors becoming fainter with age. Spray with a product approved for use on the crop under attack.

Japanese Beetle

These insects are a problem mainly east of the Mississippi. The grub, ½ in. long, overwinters in the soil. In spring it moves toward the surface and feeds on roots of grasses. In early summer the adult beetle, which is bronze in color, emerges and continues to feed until late summer or early fall, devouring buds, flowers and leaves and the soft stems of bulbs such as cannas, dahlias and lilies as well. If the attack is limited, remove the beetles by hand; traps are also a valid control. If an infestation is severe, spray with a suitable insec-ticide, following directions.

Wireworms

These pests are beetle larvae and are seldom visi-ble. They spend their lives in the soil and eat into the roots of dahlias, gladioli and other bulbs, causing the plant to collapse. One of the best controls is good cultivation, which exposes the pests to their natural enemies and also discour-ages the laying of eggs.

Nematodes

These are microscopic roundworms, not visible to the naked eye, of which there are many species. They are one of the main causes of root decay, which in turn causes deformed foliage, the split-ting of leaves and the browning of bulb tissue. If you have such a problem, it is best to consult a local authority, as the only sound control is soil fumigation, which must be done by pro-fessionals.

Narcissus Fly

This pest is found not only on narcissus but also at times on *Amaryllis, Galanthus* and *Leucojum*. The adult fly lays eggs in the neck of the bulb as the foliage dies; the larvae eat the bulb underground, destroying it. If any foliage is produced the fol-lowing year, it will be weak and yellow. Practical control consists of keeping the soil cultivated as the foliage dies, covering any holes leading into the bulb. Any attacked bulbs should be destroyed.

Whitefly

Plant damage caused by this common pest is not due to the adult flies but to the nymphs, which hatch from light-yellow eggs and suck the juices from the plants. Several generations are produced in a year, but overwintering is in the nymphal or pupal stage. Control using a product approved for use on the plants attacked. The adult flies can often be seen in the summer months as clouds of tiny white flies that suddenly appear when the foliage of the plants is disturbed. Spraying plants with a fine spray of cold water discourages these pests but is not an effective control.

Mealybugs

These insects are found mostly on bulbs with persistant foliage. They surround themselves with a white waxlike substance that looks like white wool. Generally, many are found together, and they are usually more of a problem with bulbs grown indoors than with bulbs in the garden. Denatured alcohol applied with a cotton swab will clear away small infestations.

Cutworms

The larvae of various moths make up a group of pests known as cutworms. One, the variegated cutworm, the larva of *Peridroma saucia*, is found worldwide. The larvae cut off stems at ground level but can also climb the stems and attack leaves and buds. The cutworm spends the winter as a naked brown pupa in the soil. Adult moths emerge in early spring, laying eggs which in a week become plump smooth caterpillars; these feed for several weeks, become more than 1 in. long, then burrow into the soil to pupate. Three or more generations can be expected in one year. Hand-picking is the most effective control, but chemicals can be used.

Thrips

There are several species of this insect. The two most common are the gladiolus thrips and the onion thrips; the latter also attacks dahlias and gloxinias as well as other garden flowers. These pests rasp the surface of the leaves, causing strips of yellow-to-brown foliage and giving a silvery appearance to gladiolus leaves. Clean cultural practices help prevent infestations. Dusting of the corms or bulbs during storage and prior to plant-ing is a good control method, and plantings should not be made without such dustings if attacks of these pests have been noted in the area. Spraying can be done during the season. Use appropriate products approved for use on the plants attacked.

Mites

These are tiny pests that suck juices from plants and leave the plants weakened. Their presence can be detected by a dry, yellowish appearance in the leaves. Close inspection will sometimes reveal webs, and if a clean piece of white paper is held below the foliage and the foliage tapped, specks, which soon start to move, can be seen on the paper. Hosing the foliage offers some control, but spraying with a miticide is often necessary. If severely attacked, the plants are best discarded.

Slugs and Snails

These common garden pests are not insects but mollusks. They often will attack the tender young shoots of bulbous plants. There are many controls, including various baits and traps.

Rodents

Many rodents eat bulbs; gophers are particularly bad. Keeping or encouraging predators, such as cats and snakes, can help deter rodents, but trap-ping is the only really effective way to eradicate them. Another option is to protect the plants. Some gardeners in gopher country line planting holes or entire beds with chicken wire or aviary cloth, leaving the wire protruding 2 in. above the ground. Single bulbs can be planted in deep clay pots, which are then sunk in the ground and covered with wire mesh. These pots can simply be left in place until it is time to dig the bulb to divide it.

Diseases

The majority of plant diseases flourish where there is poor air circulation and high humidity. Poor gardening practices such as using dirty containers and pots and allowing weeds to flourish also contribute to the likelihood of diseases.

Botrytis

A fungus, this causes several plant blights. During the summer months, small yellow or orange-brown spots may appear on the foliage. In a short time the entire leaf is covered with a gray mold. The ability of the plant to produce food to be stored in the bulb for the following season is adversely affected, the bulb is weakened and poor growth will result the following year. Bulbs that prefer shade, such as tuberous begonias, lilies and other woodland bulbs, are frequently susceptible to the disease, but even tulips and other sun-loving bulbs can be attacked. To control botrytis, spray with Benlate, Ferbam or other fungicides approved for use on the crop attacked. Generally, several sprayings are required for control.

Mildew

Both downy and powdery mildews will attack certain bulbs, but powdery mildew is the more common fungal disease. Spores are spread by the wind. First seen on the undersides of the leaves as white spots, the mildew soon takes on a weblike appearance that spreads to cover the entire underside. When severe, the leaf yellows, then browns, and is thus useless to the plant. Benlate will control this problem, but more than one application is required. Again, always follow directions on the package label.

Onion Smut

Dark blisters appear on the stalks of ornamental onions and can be severe; dark blisters appear on shoots and the plant is destroyed. If this fungal disease is common on edible onions in your area, think twice before planting any ornamental species.

Verticillium Wilt

This is a soil-borne disease that attacks a wide range of plant material. It enters the plant through the roots and the plant slowly dwindles away. It can also affect plants under stress in hot weather; even though these plants will recover in the cool of the evening, they will gradually weaken and die. Fumigation of the soil and rotation are the only means to control the problem.

Damping-off Disease

Another soil-borne disease, this attacks young seedlings, causing them to keel over right at soil level, the stems looking as if they had been pinched. Good air circulation will help control damping-off, as will the use of sterilized soil for seed sowing.

Viruses

All plants are susceptible. In tulips, viruses can cause "breaking" or mottling of the colors in the flowers. In lilies, the plants are weak, the flowers can be distorted and the foliage is mottled. There is little that can be done to save infected plants, but as such problems are spread by aphids, control of these pests is essential. All plants attacked should be destroyed.

With the great number of pests and diseases that can afflict bulbous plants, it seems that raising healthy crops in the garden would be difficult. Such is not the case, and many years may well pass before the home gardener is confronted with the pests or diseases listed above. Keeping weeds away from plants, keeping borders cultivated and following good cultural practices will result in many enjoyable displays of your favorite bulbs. Maintaining a constant eye toward potential problems and taking immediate action to correct any that do occur should enable home gardeners to enjoy spring-, summer- and fall-flowering bulbs.

CONSERVATION OF ENDANGERED SPECIES

Only in comparatively recent times has the appreciation for the need to conserve wild species of plants in their native habitats received the attention and publicity it deserves. For years those concerned were doing their best to alert the general public to the great harm that was being done to the environment by the practice of collecting bulbs from the wild. Steps have been taken to curtail this damaging practice. But collections from the wild are still undertaken, and although the number of species that are so collected and the actual numbers collected have diminished, your attention to just where bulbs are obtained is of great importance.

How can you know if the bulbs you purchase were propagated in a nursery or collected in the wild? There are two ways. First, you can purchase your bulbs from dealers who have publicly pledged to sell only propagated bulbs. Second, you can purchase only those packages of bulbs that are labeled "Bulbs grown from cultivated stock;" a similar statement should also appear in the catalogs. If in doubt, ask the mail-order nursery or the sales staff in locations where bulbs are sold.

Look for the label or catalog description when buying the following bulbs: *Anemone blanda*; *Cardiocrinum giganteum*; *Cyclamen* species, except the florist's cyclamen, *C. persicum*; *Eranthis cilicica* and *E. hyemalis*; *Galanthus* species, except *G. nivalis*; *Leucojum aestivum* and *L. vernum*; *Narcissus asturiensis*, *N. bulbocodium*, and *N. triandrus*; *Sternbergia* species; and *Trillium* species (pay particular attention to this genus—while a limited number are propagated in nurseries, many are still gathered in the wild).

There are many organizations working together to protect species of plants. Among them are the National Resources Defense Council (NRDC), the World Wildlife Fund (WWF), the Garden Club of America (GCA) and the Flora and Fauna Preservation Society (FFPS). These groups are working with the flower-bulb industry to educate gardeners about the probable wild origin of certain plants. At this time there is a lack of scientific knowledge of and research on the life cycles of many plants in the wild. Such information is essential if the ecological needs that would determine sustainable harvest requirements are to be exactly established. Concerned gardeners are encouraged to support all organizations that are undertaking this good work.

Responding to ecological concerns, the Dutch bulb industry is gradually putting in place a labeling program. Since 1990, bulbs harvested in the wild bear the label "Bulbs from wild sources." Bulbs of the same species propagated in nurseries may or may not bear the label "Bulbs grown from cultivated stock." These statements are appearing in catalogs issued by Dutch companies as well. Beginning in 1995, all bulbs exported by Dutch firms, including hybrid tulips, daffodils and hyacinths, will be labeled either "Bulbs grown from cultivated stock" or "Bulbs from wild sources." Unfortunately, American dealers are not obliged to comply with the labeling program, and while some have pledged not to sell wild-collected bulbs, others continue to do so. Ask your dealer if you are in doubt as to the origin of any bulbs you are considering purchasing.

3

BULBS:
FLOWERS FOR
ALL SEASONS

Bulbs are, or at least should be, the gardener's best friends. Spring would not be spring without them. But gardeners who think of bulbs as blooming only in spring miss a great deal, for some of the most beautiful ones belong to summer and fall. There is a wide choice of bulbs for all seasons, and every year long-sought treasures and new introductions turn up in the catalogs. In cold as well as warmer climates, such as Calif. and Fla., correct selection of suitable species will enable a gardener to have bulbs in flower for almost every, if not every, month of the year.

The majority of bulbs are easy to grow, have few troubles and require little care. Order your bulbs early. Apply bone meal, special bulb fertilizer or superphosphate at planting time. As a rule of thumb, place the top of the bulb twice its height beneath the surface of the ground. Bulbs

permanently in the garden seem to seek their own level. If possible, always allow the foliage to die away completely before removing it, as this enriches the bulb for the following season.

SPRING BULBS
Earliest

The first flowers of spring come to my North Carolina garden with the new year. A few years ago, for example, *Crocus sieberi* was in bloom on New Year's Day, Crocus 'Snow Bunting' on the 12th, *C. fleischeri* on the 21st. On the 28th, *Leucojum* 'Summer Snowflake' bloomed, and on the 30th, *Crocus* 'Vanguard', *Ipheion* 'Spring Starflower', *Narcissus* 'February Gold', *Anemone blanda*, *Scilla tubergeniana*, *Eranthis hyemalis*, *Crocus flavus* and *Crocus tomasinianus* 'Whitewells Purple' all came to flower. This does not happen every year, but it is indeed a cold Jan. when no bulbs are in bloom.

The late Elizabeth Lawrence (1910–1985), author of the following essay, gardened in Raleigh and then in Charlotte, N.C. and was a weekly garden columnist for the *Charlotte Observer*. She wrote several gardening books during her lifetime, including *The Little Bulbs* and *A Southern Garden: A Handbook for the Middle South*, which remain in print to this day; many of her columns were collected by Allan Lacey and published posthumously under the title *Gardening for Love* in the late 1980s. While she lived and gardened in the South, her garden writings are based on broad experience. She was trained as a landscape architect in the North and she kept up a running correspondence with numerous gardeners around the country. This piece has been updated to reflect changes in taxonomy and advances in new cultivars.

Perhaps so much bloom is not surprising in N.C., but even in colder climates the little bulbs are early risers. Winter aconites (*Eranthis*) bloom at the end of Jan. in Ohio and W. Va., the first flowers of *Crocus tomasinianus* appear in the Brooklyn Botanic Garden sometime in Feb., and *Narcissus bulbocodium* subsp. *romieuxii* has been reported to open in Jan. against a south wall in a garden on Long Island, N.Y.

Most crocuses will establish themselves anywhere in cooler climates, and flourish and multiply. They will bloom in the open, or under deciduous trees, or even under pines if the branches are high. *C. sieberi* and *C. tomasinianus* flower in tones of translucent violet, *C. tomasinianus* 'Whitewell Purple' in a dark but glowing violet, and 'Vanguard' in violet within, pearl-gray without. Two of the best forms of *C. chrysanthus* are 'Snow Bunting', white with a yellow throat, and 'E. A. Bowles', a clear soft yellow. All of these crocuses are easily grown.

Anemone blanda is just as easy and just as enduring as the crocuses. Like winter aconite (*Eranthis*), glory-of-the-snow (*Chionodoxa*), snowdrops (*Galanthus*), snowflakes (*Leucojum*), and some of the squills (*Scilla*), *A. blanda* becomes naturalized if it is in the right spot. It will bloom under trees if there is enough spring sunlight to open the wide flowers that look like *A. hepatica*, to which it is related. The various forms flower in tints of lavender and lilac, but most beautiful of all is the intense gentian-blue of the cultivar 'Atrocaerulea'. If you are in doubt as to the top and bottom of the anemone tubers, put them in the ground horizontally.

You may have some difficulty in getting winter aconite started, but once established, it blooms indefinitely. Success depends upon getting fresh tubers and planting them at once. Unlike crocuses, they are insignificant when they are planted in small groups. Plant them in quantity to make a carpet of gold. They do appreciate cooler winters and thus are not entirely suitable for warmer areas.

The pale flowers of *Scilla tubergeniana* are very good performers. The best of the early squills are *S. siberica* 'Spring Beauty' and *S. bifolia*. 'Spring Beauty' is such a brilliant blue that the little flowers are striking even as they emerge from the ground already open, sometimes at the end of Jan. in N.C., early Feb. in colder places and early May in Mass. They bloom profusely, often for two months, and the stems lengthen as they bloom until they are 4 in. long. *S. bifolia* blooms a little later. Its flowers are a softer blue, but equally beautiful.

Even in N.Y., snowdrops bloom in sheltered places early in Feb., sometimes before that. *Galanthus elwesii*, which is larger, handsomer and earlier than *G. nivalis*, the common snowdrop, is almost always in bloom before the end of Jan. Both grow in shade and in soil that has enough humus to keep it from drying out in summer, but *G. elwesii* blooms better in full sun.

The true spring snowflake (*Leucojum vernum*) flowers in Feb. or March. It is very rare in America. Although the plants may bloom the first year, they soon disappear. The solitary flowers are green-tipped bells on short stems, opening just as the foliage emerges from the ground.

In N.C., it is unusual for the spring starflower (*Ipheion uniflorum*, better known as *Triteleia*) to bloom in Jan. It usually comes in Feb. or early March, a little later in northern gardens and not until early May in Mass., where it usually needs protection. This bulb from Argentina grows north of Philadelphia, and it is definitely hardy in New York City. The six-pointed stars are typically white with violet stripes, and there is a form with pale bluish-violet flowers.

Narcissus bulbocodium is not the only small early daffodil, though it is one of the most dependable.

N. pseudonarcissus subsp. *obvallaris* produces drooping, bright yellow flowers in Feb. Even smaller, *N. asturiensis* is the tiniest of all, and it blooms in Jan. or Feb. in mild, almost frost-free climates, late Feb. or March in the North.

The brilliant purple, violet-scented flowers of *Iris reticulata* open in my garden at the end of Feb. or early in March, and even as far north as Boston they bloom in March or April. The blue flowers of the cultivar 'Cantab' are earlier still, and in some gardens the cultivar is more permanent than the species. Both will bloom in part shade, but they are better off in full sun.

North or south, the glory-of-the-snow blooms in March. The large forms of *Chionodoxa luciliae* are the handsomest. The flowers of the cultivar 'Gigantea' are pale blue-violet; those of 'Alba' are pure white. 'Pink Giant' is pale amaranth-pink. *C. sardensis*, said to be earlier, has never proved so with me. It is smaller, but the color is an intense gentian-blue. Chionodoxas should be planted in full sun, though they will bloom in part shade, and they should be planted in quantity—hundreds, not dozens!

Grape Hyacinths (*Muscari armeniacum*) have so much unattractive foliage, early and late, that some gardeners think they are scarcely worthy of garden room. Much better is the bulb listed as *M. azureum* (correctly *Pseudomuscari azureum*). It puts up tiny conical spikes of sailor-blue in Feb., and these bloom on into April. The true hyacinth leaves, usually two to a bulb, remain neat.

Hyacinths are to the early garden what tulips are to mid-spring. After the first year, they produce more foliage than flowers, and if you want big flowers, it is best to plant new bulbs each fall. My favorite kinds are two early ones—the massive white 'L'Innocence' and the pale blue-violet 'Ostara'. Two fine late ones are rose-pink 'Lady Derby' and, most beautiful of all, 'Chestnut Flower', which is a delicate double pink.

A Host of Golden Daffodils

The early daffodils are most welcome. 'February Gold' lives up to its name in my garden and has even bloomed in Jan. In Ohio it sometimes blooms at the end of Feb., and even where there are no daffodils before St. Patrick's Day, its pale flowers, like a splash of early sunshine, are ahead of most of the garden varieties. As for trumpets, 'Golden Harvest', a larger flower of cool yellow with a heavily frilled crown, blooms here in Feb., often before the middle of the month. 'Charlton', 'Ice Follies', 'Sun Chariot' and 'Fortune' (a very early large-cupped variety) should never be allowed to disappear from the growers' lists.

Later in the season, 'Actea', a charming poet's narcissus (*N. poeticus*), blooms early in April in N.C. and a month later in Penn. *N. gracilis*, a dainty species worth growing if you can find it, sometimes listed in catalogs of firms that have unusual bulbs, is a pale yellow. It blooms here in N.C. in the middle of April, in Penn. the last of April and in Mass. so late in May that it often blooms on into June. 'Polar Ice', which is silvery-white except for the green eye of the small cup, bloomed in my garden on the 19th of April along with 'Thalia'. These were the last to bloom.

The following are among the most beautiful, durable and trouble-free daffodils in the various divisions (I omit the miniatures, for they are too difficult to sum up briefly). These are popular and garden-worthy in all parts of the country, except the warmer areas, where getting them to bloom well again presents some problems. In such areas it is essential to allow them a resting period after the foliage has died down, and they should not be given water, especially in mid- to late summer.

Trumpet Daffodils

'Golden Harvest' is clear yellow without being brassy, large without being coarse, and is early. 'King Alfred' is the general favorite among the very large ones. And the magnificent 'Kings-court' has now come down to a gardener's price. 'Music Hall' may be the best all-around bicolor trumpet. Of the really white trumpets, 'Beer-sheba' is the only one that is permanent in my garden, and I have had none that I like better. 'Mount Hood' is much larger, perhaps not so white. 'Broughshane' is larger still, and is a dependable garden variety.

Large-cupped Narcissus

'Carlton' is a fine, early, lemon-yellow, deliciously fragrant variety. 'Fortune' sometimes blooms here at the end of Feb.; in Penn. it flowers early in April. Though the crown is described as a vivid orange, I have found that it seldom has more than a slight orange flush. 'Quirinus' is really brilliant, with its wide yellow perianth and fiery cup. 'Scarlet O'Hara' is another with a striking contrast between the yellow perianth and the flame-scarlet cup. For contrast between a bright yellow-orange cup and a white perianth, 'Duke of Windsor' has qualities that make it outstanding among daffodils of all types. The large, frilly cup of 'Ice Follies' is such a pale yellow, and becomes white so quickly, that the effect is that of a pure-white trumpet. As for daffodils with red cups and white perianths, the best is 'Professor Einstein'. For pink cups, none is lovelier than 'Mrs. R. O. Backhouse', but this does not always prosper.

Small-cupped Narcissus

'Birma' is a reliable variety with clear yellow petals and an orange cup. The real beauties are those with white petals and orange-red cups, such as 'La Riante' and 'Barret Browning'. The all-white daffodils of this class bloom late. 'Polar Ice' has a green eye, which makes the whiteness of the petals even more sparkling in contrast.

Double-flowered Daffodils

There is great variety in double daffodils. 'Golden Ducat' is like a double golden-yellow; 'Texas', a combination of yellow and orange; 'Mary Copeland', white and orange. 'Cheerfulness' is a double white poetaz, and 'Yellow Cheerfulness' the same thing in pale citron-yellow.

Triandrus Hybrids

There are several very similar to the silvery-white 'Thalia' but none lovelier, and none that blooms and increases so prolifically. 'Hawera' has the same airy form, but it is a pale yellow. 'Silver Chimes', with its cluster of ivory and citron flowers, is somewhat tender, although it sometimes blooms in very cold gardens. (In the North it may need to be mulched each year.)

Cyclamineus Hybrids

These are the most graceful of all daffodils. This same grace is inherent in 'February Gold', which possesses the additional attribute of being a tidy daffodil for shallower containers. It nearly always blooms in Feb. for me and lives up to its name even in cold gardens. 'Beryl', which looks like a fragile poet's narcissus with tilted petals, is another graceful plant. To those who like bold flowers, 'Peeping Tom', with its long stem, exaggerated trumpet and brassy color, will be welcome.

Jonquilla Hybrids

'Trevithian' is the general favorite among the early, short-cupped jonquil hybrids. It blooms early in March for me and in warm areas, and early in April in the North. The later 'Golden Perfection' also has two or three flowers to a stem, but the flowers are larger. These have the characteristic delicate jonquil fragrance and clear yellow color.

Tazettas

'Cragford' and 'Geranium' are colorful, prolific and free-flowering, with white petals and orange cups. 'Cragford' is early, 'Geranium' later with larger flowers. The flowers of 'Martha Washington' are larger still but come only two to a stem. 'Scarlet Gem' is a distinct tazetta with a sharp contrast between the pale yellow petals and the scarlet cup.

Poet's Narcissus

'Actaea,' by far the largest poeticus variety, is very popular in Calif. and has an excellent flower. I like to keep a corner for pheasant's-eye, *N. poeticus* var. *recurvus*, because it blooms later.

Tulips for a Long Bloom Season

Every fall I buy as many tulips as I have time to plant and can afford, and in the spring I dig them up as soon as the flowers have faded and usually throw them away. Sometimes a friend who cannot bear such willful waste comes along and gathers up the outcasts. She keeps them in soil until the foliage has died down, then cures the bulbs and plants them in the fall. She says they bloom beautifully the next spring. Some of the old varieties such as 'Clara Butt' can be left in the ground, and they will bloom for years if they are planted deep (at least 10 in.) in poor soil, but the flowers will not be large.

Tulips are among the last bulbs to go into the ground. They should not be planted until Nov. in the North, and late Nov. or early Dec. in the warmer areas of the South. If they are to be taken up in the spring, they need not be planted with more than 5 in. of soil over the bulb. Put a handful of bone meal or special bulb fertilizer under each clump, and in early spring a sprinkling of a balanced commercial fertilizer should be worked among the plants as soon as they emerge from the soil.

The most effective tulips in the garden and containers are the multifloras. 'Georgette', a yellow narrowly edged with red, has four or five flowers to a stem and more than one stem to each bulb. This and two others, 'Toronto', a pink flower that darkens as it matures, and 'Wallflower', which is purple with a yellow base, are usually available.

Tulips bloom over a period of several weeks, beginning (in my garden) early in March and lasting into May. Even as far north as Boston the water-lily tulip (*Tulipa kaufmanniana*) is in bloom by the middle of March if the season is an early one. The single early tulips come soon afterward. Too little appreciated, these include some charming varieties, such as 'General de Wet', the snowy 'Diana', peachy 'Apricot Beauty' and 'Bellona', with globe-shaped flowers that look like cups of lemon sherbet. Unfortunately, such lovely plants do not do too well in warmer areas. In Calif. and Fla., for example, midseason and late-flowering tulips are the best types to grow.

Some of the Darwin cultivars bloom very early too—'Demeter' far ahead of the rest, and then 'Flying Dutchman' and 'Rose Copland'. The enormous flowers of 'Demeter' are a brilliant purple. 'Aristocrat', a classic Darwin in form and a soft rose in color, is another early one. These early Darwins are followed by 'Sunkist', a clear lemon-yellow, and the classic salmon-pink of 'Clara Butt'. And don't forget the "black" tulips! 'Black Diamond' is a jewel. 'Queen-of-Night' is the darkest of all; its maroon petals are almost black. It blooms early and lasts a long time.

'Advance' is a very early cottage tulip of brilliant coloring, a fiery red tinged with violet. The flowers of 'Rosy Wings' are the clearest pink of any tulip I know; when they open wide, the aptness of their name is apparent. 'Zomerschoon' has been blooming in gardens since 1620. The flowers are carmine with creamy-white feathering. Two good late yellows are 'Mrs. John T. Scheepers', a golden, and 'Asta Nielsen', a sulphur-yellow.

The parrot tulips, which bloom at the end of the season, are not effective in the garden, for their stems are not stiff enough to support the heavy-headed flowers. They are delightful for cutting, however, and show great variety in color and pattern. 'Black Parrot', 'White Parrot', 'Fantasy' (a soft rose with apple-green feathering), 'Orange Favorite' and 'Parrot Wonder' (an enormous cerise flower) are all beautiful. Then there are the fringed tulips. The petals of these are edged with fine fringe and lack the deep slashing of the parrots. 'Aleppo', which is apricot with pink hues, is a good example.

Four good doubles are 'Peach Blossom' and the lovely white 'Schoonoord' (early), the rose 'Eros' and the snowy 'Mount Tacoma' (late).

I have read that "broken" tulips should never be planted in a garden where lilies grow, as the virus that gives them their flames and flakes and feathers is the one that is fatal to lilies. Most gardeners would choose the lilies without hesitation, but I find the patterned tulips very hard to part with. The Rembrandt tulips consist of "broken" Darwins, which are white with markings of red and violet, the Bizarre types are yellow with featherings of scarlet, orange, brown, bronze and garnet, and the Bijbloemen types have flames of rose or violet on a white ground.

Tulip species may be planted to bloom all through the season. Some are difficult, some are easy. Some bloom in one garden and not in another. Here are a few that are generally satisfactory:

I have known *T. kaufmanniana* to be in full bloom the first week in March. Louise Beebe Wilder said that it sometimes bloomed for her by the end of the month, and I have read that it may bloom near Boston by the end of March. In all climates it varies greatly with the season. The wide, short-stemmed water-lily flowers are typically pink and white, but there are yellow forms and red ones, and hybrids in myriads of colors and patterns.

T. tarda (sometimes known as *T. dasystemon*) occasionally blooms too early in N.C., and the buds are nipped by cold. But it is generally a reliable species. It is a small multiflora type with several gold-centered white flowers to a stem. *T. turkestanica*, another little white-and-gold multiflora, persists and multiplies.

The peppermint-striped flowers of *T. clusiana*, with stems to 12 in. tall, usually bloom for me soon after the middle of March, although in N.Y. they may not open until early May. This is the best of all species for the South. I find it offered by a Mass. grower without any hint of winter tenderness, but some people consider it uncertain in N.Y. This species does well in warmer areas and can be left in the ground to reappear each year.

The *T. batalinii* that I've had for several years has never increased, but it produces regularly, the first week in April, bearing two perfect urn-shaped, pale yellow flowers. It is planted on a terrace wall in my garden, where it gets the spring sunshine, the summer baking and the sharp drainage that all tulip species need. As the wall has been raised several inches since the little bulb was put there, the bulb is now very deep, which may account for its not having increased. The yellow-flowered *T. chrysantha* and *T. linifolia*, which is vivid red even to the stems and the margins of the narrow leaves, come at the same time. In the North all these usually bloom in May.

T. sprengeri ends the season. This handsome and rather large plant comes at the end of April and blooms on into May. In the North it blooms at the end of May and lasts well into June.

Other Late Spring Bulbs

When the first flush of spring bloom is over, the Dutch irises are the bulbs that make a show. They are so small and the foliage is so scant that they can be tucked in among other plants without being in the way when they are out of bloom. I never take my bulbs up. Sometimes they bloom for several years, and occasionally a few become established. I plant new ones from time to time to replace those that gradually disappear. In the South and warmer climates the bulbs are planted late, at the end of Nov. or early in Dec. In the North and cooler areas they should be planted early in the fall and the ground mulched. There are a great many varieties, but the white ones are to me by far the most beautiful. By planting several kinds I manage to have them in bloom for several weeks. 'White Excelsior' is a good early one, opening here before the middle of April. 'Joan of Arc', also very early, has a large creamy flower with a wide yellow spot on each petal. 'Wedgwood', the best blue, is early. 'Golden Harvest', with its large, brassy-yellow flower, comes at the very end of the season. Many of the blues are perhaps not as showy, and the bronze and two-toned varieties are not really effective out-of-doors, but they are wonderful cut flowers, adding an air of distinction to any arrangement. In N.Y. the Dutch irises bloom late in May.

In cold gardens the summer snowflake (*Leucojum aestivum*) blooms in May. Where I live, it often blooms in Jan. and usually lasts until the second week in April, but the late form, 'Gravetye Giant', doesn't begin to bloom until the middle of March. The stout stems of the snowflakes are short when they begin to bloom, but they stretch until they reach 20 in. or more, with sprays of green-trimmed bells at the tips. The wide, dark, glossy leaves are about the same length as the stems. Snowflakes will grow in any part of the garden, even in deep shade, but will flower less in such areas. They increase abundantly, but it is not necessary to divide them unless you want to start additional colonies.

Scilla pratensis blooms early in April, a blue-violet mist of tiny flowers. Spanish bluebell (now listed as *Hyacinthoides hispanica*) blooms about the same time, some of the white ones—'White Triumphator' is large and handsome—coming in late March, and the variety 'Sky blue' in the middle of April. There are several other blue varieties, but they all look almost alike to me. These squills, like the early ones, do well in the open, but they endure shade and will even bloom under pine trees, provided they have light. When left to themselves, the spikes improve in both height and size. In northern gardens they bloom in late May.

The nodding star-of-Bethlehem (*Ornithogalum umbellatum*) is another bulb that thrives on neglect and is found in old, untended gardens. It blooms well in part shade but better in full sun. The fragrant bells, grape-green satin without, silvery-white within, are hung along one side of the 12-in. scape. They appear in late April in N.Y., in March here and in other warmer areas.

Camassias also bloom indefinitely if they are left undisturbed, and they will thrive in much wetter, heavier soil than most bulbs can put up with, but they will not tolerate much shade. The large flowers of *Camassia leichtlinii* have widely separated petals of hyssop-violet flushed with pink. The even lovelier white form blooms a little later. The flowers of *C. cusickii* are small, pale blue and close together on the scape. These two species are the best, and both grow to a height of 3 feet. They begin to bloom in March-April (May in the North) and sometimes last for a month.

Triteleias are western bulbs that are somewhat difficult to grow in eastern gardens. Some of the species are short-lived, but several are lifetime possessions. *Triteleia laxa* is hardy to Zone 8 and dependable. The large flowers open wide on 24-in. scapes. This is the Ithuriel's spear that blooms late, from mid-June to July, according to the geographic location. The bulbs must be planted in full sun and preferably in heavy soil. *Ipheion uniflora* comes ahead of the other, blooming here in April. Its flowers are white with a hint of lilac or lavender, according to the eye of the beholder.

The western fritillaries are lovely plants but have never prospered in my garden; however, *Fritillaria meleagris*, the checkered lily, will bloom for several seasons. It is so charming and costs so little that I am glad to renew it occasionally. The named cultivars are superior to the type, and the loveliest of these is 'Aphrodite', a tall, silvery-white flower that lacks the checks. The other forms are checkered in violet and purple on a gray background. I have read that fritillaries respond to lime, and perhaps this is the secret of keeping them. The bulbs should be planted in July and Aug., in soil that is very well drained and rich in humus.

SUMMER BULBS
Alliums

The earliest of these relatives of the onion, *Allium giganteum*, blooms for me in late spring, and I once found it just coming into bloom in the New York Botanical Garden on the last day of May. But July is the usual month for the bright lilac globes that tower above the lesser perennials and give character to the flower border even after their colors fade. I always cut the flower heads before the seeds ripen, and I save them for friends who like to make dried arrangements.

One of the nicest small bulbs for shady places is *A. triquetrum*, which spreads itself freely, though the seedlings never seem to be too numerous. In Calif., however, it grows so rapidly that it becomes a pest and must be confined. I plant the bulbs under trees where they can be left to themselves and forgotten until early April, when sprays of frosty white bells, trimmed with hairlines of bright green, hang from the tips of the triangular stems. Although this is a Medit. species, and masses can be seen in the hedgerows in England, it is hardy. *A. moly*, the golden garlic, blooms here early in May, though in the New York Botanical Garden I have found it in full bloom during the last part of April (it is even earlier in mild areas), and it is much finer there than in my garden. If I lived north of the Mason-Dixon line, I think it would be my first choice among the alliums. It is usually at its best in full sun, but in the South I have found that it demands a little shade. The spectacular *A. christophii* blooms in April for me and in June where the seasons are later. As many as eighty metallic-violet stars, on stiff, 4-in. pedicels, form a huge sphere at the tip of a 10-in. scape. If the flower heads are cut before they go to seed, they last forever. *Tulbaghia violacea*, called society garlic, looks, smells and tastes like an allium (I often use the leaves in salad), but the violet flowers have a pleasant, sweet fragrance, are prettier than those of any allium I know, and have a longer season, blooming from June into Oct. I always thought of this as a very tender bulb, but it is hardy against a south wall in New York City if heavily mulched in winter. Like the alliums, it blooms best in full sun and is not particular as to soil. It comes from S. Afr. and is becoming popular in Calif. and rightly so, as it is in flower from May though Dec., and even in Jan. and Feb. a few flowers are giving color. This plant *deserves* to become popular.

Lilies

In the North the lily season begins in June, but in the South it begins earlier with two species small enough to fit into the rock garden. The fragrant, pale-pink trumpets of *Lilium rubellum* come first, and a few days later the shining scarlet flowers of the miniature Turk's-cap (*L. pumilum*). The bulbs are planted 6 in. deep, the former in part shade and the latter in full sun.

Provided I plant new bulbs every season, the Madonna lily (*L. candidum*) usually blooms in my garden in May. I have never been able to keep it, though established clumps bloom for years in country gardens. Bulbs of this and the lovely apricot-flowered Nankeen lily (*L. × testaceum*) must be planted very early and covered with only 2 to 3 in. of soil. Both are sun lovers and, unlike most lilies, do not like an acid soil.

The meadow lily (*L. canadense*) makes itself at home in gardens more readily than do other American species and is quite as lovely as any of the hybrids, though the maroon-spotted yellow flowers are not large. It blooms in June in my region. This species grows naturally in wet meadows, but while it needs more moisture than do most lilies, good drainage is still essential. Plant it 6 in. deep in partial shade. The European Turk's-cap (*L. martagon*) blooms about the same time, and its lovely white variety, *album*, a little earlier. The typical purple-flowered form grows in sun or shade, the white one in shade only. Plant the bulbs 4 in. deep. Another species for shade, *L. hansonii*, blooms in my garden early in June. The flowers are a soft orange-yellow, sprinkled toward the center with mahogany dots. Plant these bulbs deeper.

The wonderful strains that the hybridizers have developed in recent years have brought lilies into many more gardens than ever before, making summer an entirely new affair. The Bellingham hybrids, based on American lilies, are the result of a history of years of experimentation. They vary in the shape of the flowers, some being funnel-form, some recurved and some bell-like, in color from palest yellow to deepest red, and

in both height and season. Their garden value is increased by the lasting quality of the flowers; the first to open is still fresh when the last one comes out. Two of the Griffith cultivars, 'Shuksan' and 'Kulshan', have bloomed in the test garden of the Garden Club of Virginia during the first half of June. Plant bulbs 6 in. deep in well-drained soil, in partial shade such as is found in woodlands.

The Olympic hybrids and other trumpet lilies, such as 'Pink Perfection', 'Golden Splendor' and 'Black Dragon', come into bloom in July. The stems are tall, up to 5 ft. or more, and the flowers are fragrant. In color they are white, pink, or golden-yellow with a wash of green, brown or wine on the outside. Plant the bulbs 6 in. deep where their heads will be in sun, feet in shade. In warm climates with strong sun, light shade during the heat of the day helps to prolong the period of flowering and the lovely colors.

The Mid-Century and Asiatic hybrids follow one another through the early and middle summer. The colors range from yellow to red, and there are many bicolors and even tricolors; the flowers are upright, outfacing or pendant; the plants are from 2 to 4 ft. in height. 'Enchantment', with flowers the color of red nasturtiums, is outstanding; another is 'Polyana', a superb golden-yellow. All of these are superb container plants.

L. henryi is a handsome, healthy and easygoing lily, but the stems will not stand up unless they are staked. This fault has been overcome in its offspring, the Aurelian hybrids, a strain that bears cream or pale yellow flowers on strong, stiff stems, and in the Sunburst hybrid strain, which has Turk's-cap flowers in a series of pastels from almost white to orange.

Two late species are the most sumptuous lilies of all. When the great creamy flowers of *L. auratum*, the gold-banded lily of Japan, are open, the garden is filled, day and night, with fragrance.

The crimson-spotted flowers are up to 12 in. across. I have had as many as ten to a stalk in bloom from July into the second week of Aug. They seemed unmindful of the hottest summer sun, although they are supposed to need part shade. They were planted 8 in. deep. *L. speciosum* 'Rubrum', blooming here in late July and all through Aug., is just as striking in its own way. The graceful stalks bend just enough to show the rose-dotted flowers to advantage. I think the frosted white form is even more beautiful, but I find it practically impossible to grow. Some of the late forms bloom in Sept. Hybrids of these two species (*L. speciosum* × *L. auratum*) are even more outstanding. Named varieties of these Oriental hybrids can be found in the A-to-Z listing of *Lilium*.

Order lilies early and plant them as soon as you can. If they are shipped in sealed polyethylene bags, they can be kept for a while, but open the bags to prevent rot setting in. Late-flowering kinds that have been properly stored can be planted in the spring, if it is not possible to set them out in the fall.

Good drainage is an essential condition for successful lilies. Dig the soil to a depth of 18 in. and supply it with leafmold or peat moss. No manure should be used, but bone meal or super-phosphate can be mixed in when the bulbs are planted, and a sprinkling of bone meal, cotton-seed meal and wood ashes can be worked in over them in the spring. Do not allow your garden lilies to go to seed. If you cut the flowers, leave as much of the stem as possible. Mulches are helpful in hot weather, as are low-growing plants that shade the ground over the lily roots. When growing lilies in containers, feed the plants regularly with liquid fertilizer, stopping when you see the flower buds have formed.

Lycoris

The various species of *Lycoris* that are hardy in my garden bloom from the middle of July through the first week in Oct. The first one, *L. squamigera*, lasts for about three weeks; where more lavishly planted, for more than a month. The naked scapes spring from the ground and stretch up to 3 ft. almost overnight. Then a circle of six or seven rose-lilac trumpets bursts into bloom. Some days later, *L. radiata* follows with smaller, pink to deep red flowers. At the end of Aug. the golden-yellow flowers of *L. aurea*, the golden spider lily, appear. All bloom without foliage, which comes up about the middle of Jan. in my garden and two or three months later in the North. All bloom well in anything from shade to full sun.

The first species is hardy in Ohio, where a gardener I know grows these plants by the acre under the beeches and maples in his woods. They get no attention except that the woods are mowed before the scapes break through the ground. After about ten years the clumps are divided. As soon as the flowers have faded, the bulbs are dug and separated carefully, so that the roots are not cut, and planted again the same day. Dry, rootless bulbs will not bloom for several years. Growers are beginning to realize this and to ship them, like lilies, with live roots attached. The bulbs will often bloom better when they are planted with only an inch of soil on top of them. *L. squamigera* is said to be hardy in Mich. and Maine.

Scilla scilloides

Early in Aug. I begin to watch for the small spikes of *S. scilloides* to come up between the two or three narrow leaves that appear earlier in the summer. When they are about 6 in. tall, the blue-green buds begin to break open into fuzzy, pale pink flowers. This squill, unlike the spring-blooming kinds, does best in sun, though I have a planting that does very well at the foot of a tall pine tree. It is a charming bulb for the rock garden and is easily grown, although it does not increase very rapidly. Alas, this has become a rather rare bulb and is now seldom listed in catalogs.

Summer Bulbs for Spring Planting

Crinums

When I had a big garden, I grew more than forty kinds of crinums. Now that I have a small one, I grow only a few, for most of them take up a great deal of room. Two of the hardiest are two of the best: *Crinum × powellii* 'Album' and 'Cecil Houdyshel', both hybrids of *C. moorei* and *C. bulbispermum*. *C. × powellii* 'Album' blooms from late May into July. When the clumps are well established, up to thirty umbels of pure-white flowers (even the anthers are white) bloom in a rush. Scapes nearly 4 ft. tall hold the flowers well above the fountain of wide, tapering leaves. It is hardy in New York City with protection. The pink-flowered 'Cecil Houdyshel' blooms over a long period, from late May until the end of Aug., with sometimes as many as ten scapes in bloom at once. Mr. Houdyshel once told me that his namesake was hardy as far north as Independence, Mo., and that it had been wintered twice in Brooklyn. In northern Tex. it has survived −12°F, under shallow wooden boxes placed over the bulbs after the first hard freeze.

C. macowanii, one of the best, has large creamy flowers with a wine-colored stripe on each petal. It blooms at intervals all through the summer. This species is perfectly hardy in N.C., but I haven't any data on its performance farther north. *C. moorei* is a species with large pink flowers in Aug. The others are at their best in full sun, but this one must have shade.

In the South, crinums are planted with part of the bulb above the ground, but in the North, the bottom of the bulb should be 8 in. below the surface. Bulbs should be planted against a wall and heavily mulched. Once planted, they should be left alone, for they improve with age, and if they are given water and lots of well-rotted or dried cow manure, applied as a mulch, they will bloom better every year.

Dahlias

Dahlias need sun, perfect drainage, a rich soil and water. Plant tubers 4 to 6 in. deep, with a handful of bone meal to each tuber, putting the eye toward the stake, which should be set beforehand. Plant early for garden effect, later for exhibition. Mulch the roots heavily in the South and cut the tops back to the ground after the first hard frost. Lift the clumps in late spring; divide and replant. In the North, lift the tubers after the first frost and store them in sand or vermiculite in a cool place. The clumps can be most safely divided in the spring when the "eyes" are evident. Discard all tubers without eyes. Productive shoots develop only from roots with eyes.

See *Dahlia* in the encyclopedia listing for what I consider some of the best types and varieties for the average gardener.

Galtonia candicans

South of Philadelphia, where winter and spring are mild, the summer hyacinth is hardy. It is not really a good bulb where summers are likely to be wet but is an ideal plant for warmer, drier parts of the country. Bulbs planted in April may bloom in July or they may rot before they can bloom. Still, I plant more from time to time for the pleasure of seeing the spires of cool white bells in the midsummer heat. I like to plant them so that each spire stands alone; the beauty of form is lost when they are planted in clumps. In northern gardens, the summer hyacinth does well when the bulbs are planted 6 inches deep on a cushion of sand that is in rich, moist soil in full sun. Plant them in the spring and lift them in the fall, except in warmer areas, where they can remain undisturbed.

Gladiolus

In summer I depend on clumps of gladiolus to augment the bloom in the perennial border and to furnish spires to relieve the monotony of phlox and daylilies. I find it more effective to use only white varieties. In our part of the country and in warmer areas, the corms can be left in the ground. They bloom beautifully for several seasons; then, when the clumps become crowded, I lift them, replant the largest corms and throw away the rest. Since all corms left in the ground bloom during the early summer, I plant a few new ones each year in June and July to carry bloom on until frost. In northern areas the corms should be taken up after the leaves turn brown and before freezing weather arrives. Cut off the tops, remove the spent corms and store the new corms in shallow, screen-bottomed trays or old nylon stockings in a frost-proof place.

If gladiolus are grown in quantities, the only place for them is the cutting garden, where they can be planted in rows. For succession of bloom from early summer until frost, the corms can be planted at intervals of one to three weeks from early Feb. to early Aug. in the South, and from early March (or whenever the ground is workable) to early July in the North. Plant them 6 in. deep, preferably in full sun and in light soil. Good drainage is essential. Since too much nitrogen makes the stems and flowers weak, the fertilizer should be high in potassium. Use bone meal and superphosphate when planting, and a complete fertilizer when the leaves are a few inches high. A sprinkling of wood ashes makes sturdy stems and flowers of good substance. Water generously in dry weather. See *Gladiolus* in the encyclopedia section for suggested varieties.

Similar to the *Gladiolus* is *Acidanthera bicolor* var. *murielae*, which blooms in Aug. and Sept. The corms should be planted as early in the spring as possible because of the plant's long growing season, and they should be taken up in the fall even where they are hardy, since plants soon run to a clump of foliage without flowers if they are left in the ground. The flower is like a graceful, starry gladiolus (to 2 in. across), white with a dark wine center, and wonderfully fragrant.

Montbretias

Now classified under *Crocosmia*, these are more like gladiolus to me. They begin to bloom early in July and make a splash of bright orange in the border for at least a month. This is seldom offered by most dealers, but the handsome hybrids appear in the spring catalogs, and if planted early and in variety, these will bloom all summer and well into the fall. In the encyclopedia listing the question of selection of hybrids is discussed.

Montbretias may prove hardy around Philadelphia and even farther north with a heavy winter mulch. Unlike gladiolus, montbretia corms must not be allowed to dry out in storage but should be covered with soil that is barely moist. Therefore it is essential to buy them from a reliable dealer and plant them at once. They can be planted in April or May, 3 in. deep, in soil that is rich in humus. Full sun and plenty of water at all times are important.

In cold climates it is well worth while starting montbretias in a cold frame or greenhouse in early spring, being careful not to disturb their roots when they are set out in May. They are heavy feeders, and as soon as their leaves are a few inches above ground, they should be fertilized with liquid manure in a regular feeding program.

In the South, lift and divide the corms every

third spring. When the leaves die back and the plants go dormant, cut them back and use the leaves as a mulch. They also like a winter mulch of weathered ash. In the North, before storing, allow the corms to air-dry for two or three days.

Ismenes

Hymenocallis narcissiflora, the Peruvian daffodil, is commonly called by its old name, ismene. The fragrant, white crystalline flower has a flaring cup with bright green stripes and six narrow, slightly curled segments. There are six or seven flowers on a stout, 30 in. scape, blooming in June and July. The leaves are as exotic as the flowers, 2 in. wide and 2 ft. long and appearing dark and shining in two ranks.

In the North the bulbs should be planted in the latter half of May and taken up about the middle of October. The tops should be cut off, if this chore has not already been done by frost, and the bulbs dried and stored in a cool place in paper bags. The temperature must not fall below 55°F. The bulbs are surprisingly hardy, but the buds are killed by low temperatures. Some N.C. gardeners think that ismenes are better left in the garden all winter, but I find that they bloom better when they are taken up. They can be planted again as early as April, and I have on occasion kept them out of the ground safely as late as the middle of July. Those planted early bloom the first part of June; those planted later bloom almost at once and bloom just as well. I use no fertilizer, but well-rotted manure and bone meal can be recommended. Plenty of water is essential for ismenes, and full sun is preferred, though they will bloom well in part shade. While a light soil is supposedly best, mine thrive in stiff clay.

The variety 'Sulfur Queen' is almost more beautiful than the parent plant. The flowers are a pale, sparkling yellow. I have a single bulb that has bloomed faithfully for twenty years, but it has never increased. No wonder it is so rare. This one has always wintered outdoors in the garden.

'Festalis' is hardier than the Peruvian daffodil. Its delicate, pure white flowers have more slender crowns and narrower petals than those of the ismene. I leave the bulbs in the ground, and they bloom very well each year.

Other Summer Bulbs

St. James's lily (*Sprekelia formosissima*) is hardy in N.C. but not in northern Va. Even where hardy, it is uncertain as to bloom. One theory is that the bulbs bloom better if they are taken up and dried out each year; another is that they must not be disturbed because they do not bloom well until they become crowded. My theory is that it is a difficult bulb in any garden. But it takes up little space, and the red flowers, like delicately carved fleur-de-lis, are so beautiful that I keep a few bulbs and leave them to sulk or bloom as they choose. They bloom, when they bloom, in late May or early June. Full sun and poor soil are their preferences.

Tigridias are tropical bulbs originating on the high plateaus of Mex. They do not like hot nights and bloom better in northern gardens than in the South. Even where the bulbs are hardy, it is better to take them up in the fall and keep them dry during the winter. Dig them before frost, and do not divide the clusters until they are replanted—in April in the South, May in the North. Plant them 4 in. deep, and water well when they are coming into bloom. They need a rich, light soil. The flowers of *Tigridia pavonia* are brilliant. Their three broad outer petals form a heavily spotted cup with a flaring brim. There is a pure white form. Others are white with rose spots, rose with white spots, creamy-yellow with bright red spots, scarlet with white spots and so on. They bloom in late July and Aug.

Tuberoses (*Polianthes tuberosa*) bloom in my garden from late July until frost. When frost comes late, they bloom on into Nov. Here, the bulbs stay in the ground and are never disturbed except when I dig some to give away. The clumps bloom better every year. Where they will not winter out-of-doors—they are hardy to 20°F (Zone 9)—the bulbs can be taken up before heavy frost and stored in a dry place. In the spring they should be planted (preferably without division of the clumps) 3 in. deep, in April or May outdoors, or in Feb. in pots to be set in the border in June. Bulbs planted as late as the 1st of July have bloomed in Sept. Plant them in a sunny place. The single form called 'Mexican Everblooming' is the one that I have. Its slender, 3½-ft. wands are tipped with spikes of wax-white, perfumed flowers. I think it is hardier than the dwarf double form, 'The Pearl'.

Plants of the genus *Zephyranthes* bloom in the South from early spring until frost, popping up whenever showers invite a new crop of buds. *Z. atamasco*, a native of the southeasten U.S., is sometimes in bloom by the end of March. The fragrant white flowers are 3 in. long, and I have known them to have 12-in. stems. The raspberry-pink flowers of *Z. grandiflora* sometimes appear in May but more often in early June. They come at intervals all summer, and even in Sept., making this well worth planting if you can find the bulbs, which are not generally listed in catalogs. The white flowers of *Z. candida* are as small as crocuses, but on taller stems. From early June or July the clumps of shining, slender foliage are crowded with buds and flowers. They bloom on until hard frost, and when frost comes late, I have even found a few the first week in Nov. It is not necessary to worry about drainage with any of these three; they like wet ground. But they will grow in dry places, too. They need humus in the soil but not fertilizer. *Z. grandiflora* blooms better

in full sun, but the other two do just as well even in deep shade. *Z. robusta* is like the Atamasco lily except that the flowers are tinged with pink. It blooms off and on during the summer and is somewhat tender; after a hard winter it may not bloom at all. Plant all *Zephyranthes* species 2 to 3 in. deep. In the South these bulbs can be left in the ground indefinitely, dug only if you want to give some away or increase your planting. In gardens where they are not hardy, they can be lifted in the fall and stored in dry sand.

FALL BULBS
Amaryllids

Some members of the amaryllis family (*Amaryllidaceae*) have a pleasant habit of flowering after summer flowers are gone, bringing a sudden freshness to the autumn garden. The hardiest of these is *Sternbergia lutea*. Its flower of shining buttercup-yellow, which looks like a large, long-stemmed crocus, is most welcome in Sept. The leaves come up with the flowers and die down in the spring. The bulbs should be planted, or transplanted, during the summer dormant period, and not later than Aug. A depth of 3 in. is about right, as they need a summer baking. For the same reason, they are supposed to demand full sun, but I have seen great patches in bloom under a large oak tree, and the best clump in my garden is on the south side of a pine where the soil is poor and very dry.

Hippeastrum advenam, the oxblood lily, will stand a little frost. The bulbs must be planted deep enough for the long necks to be completely underground. They grow in any soil, in sun or part shade, and multiply rapidly. The flowers are cardinal-red bells, six or eight on a short, stout scape that appears before the masses of narrow leaves. I sometimes find them in bloom in the middle of Aug. and often there are still a few early in Oct. The rare pink form does not bloom as freely, and it increases very slowly, but to me it is one of the most beautiful fall bulbs.

Lycoris radiata, the red spider lily, is almost as hardy as the oxblood lily. Cover these bulbs with only an inch or so of soil, even in cold climates; otherwise they will not bloom until they have worked their way up by producing one bulb on top of another. The jasper-red flowers open in a circle at the tip of the tapered scape. They bloom as well in sun as in shade and require no special attention.

The white lycoris (*L. radiata* 'Alba'), which blooms about the same time, is less hardy than the red one, but I think it is dependable in the southern part of the country. The flowers are a little larger and the foliage a little broader, but the general effect is much the same. The flowers are pale coral as they open, gradually changing to creamy-white. If the bulbs are allowed to dry out, they will take several seasons to settle down and bloom. Where they are not hardy, they can be wintered in pots, but the roots must not be disturbed when plants are set out in the spring or when they are repotted in the fall.

Colchicums and Crocuses

Colchicums begin to bloom in early fall, often at the end of Aug. or even earlier. They are often called by the pretty name of meadow saffron and also, no more accurately, autumn crocus (they belong to the lily family, *Liliaceae*, and crocuses do not). The real autumn crocuses, which belong to the genus *Crocus* and the iris family (*Iridaceae*), come into bloom later, but the colchicum and crocus seasons overlap, so that they keep the garden in flowers of white or varying tones of violet from the end of summer to the beginning of spring.

Colchicum speciosum and its varieties start the season. The large, well-shaped, wide-petaled flowers are pure white in the extremely beautiful cultivar 'Album'; otherwise they are some shade or tint of violet with a white throat. The leaves are 3 to 4 in. wide and more than one foot long. When they first come up, in the spring, they look very pretty, but they are not so welcome when they grow large and turn yellow. This is to be remembered at planting time.

Of the other cultivars, 'Autumn Queen' is likely to bloom first, in a burst of purple. The flowers of 'The Giant' are like lilac tulips and the largest of all; spread out flat, they may measure 8 in. across. This and the pansy-violet 'Violet Queen' bloom early in Sept.

The flowers of *Colchicum autumnale* are smaller, but they make up for their size by profusion of bloom. *C. autumnale* is usually first to bloom in late Aug.; then the silvery-white 'Album' comes along in Sept. Early in Oct. the two exquisite double forms appear, one violet and one white. The leaves of this species are narrow, 2 in. wide or less, and therefore not so bothersome in spring.

Colchicums need some shade and will bloom even in deep shade. All they require in order to live, grow and bloom is a soil that is not too dry and is well supplied with leafmold. It is important to plant the bulbs as soon after midsummer as possible. They will bloom even if they are left out of the ground, but they bloom better if they are planted before the end of Aug. Although the bulbs are large, plant them only 3 to 4 in. deep.

The true autumn crocuses bloom in shade too, but they can also be planted in full sun. The earliest, *Crocus kotschyanus*, is easily established, and once it is settled, seedlings appear in all directions. This is delightful in Oct., when the pale lilac flowers come in crowds, but bear in mind the prospect of abundant spring foliage with untidy, narrow leaves up to one ft. long.

This species is followed by *C. speciosus*, the most popular fall-flowering crocus. It is extremely variable. Though it is called "blue," all of the kinds that I have had have been in tones of pure violet. The handsomest is 'Cassiope', a selected seedling with a very large flower of wisteria-violet delicately veined in a darker tone. The saffron crocus, so called because it is from the species *C. savitus*, from which saffron is harvested, flowers in Oct. It has an orange-red stigma (often protruding beyond the closed flower), which produces the saffron. The lilac-purple flowers with darker throats are 6 in. in height.

Hardy Cyclamen

I used to think that the hardy cyclamen would be too difficult for me to grow, and so for years I didn't have the pleasure of watching this most delightful of all little bulbs come into bloom at the very time that bloom is most wanted.

Cyclamen europaeum is really a summer bulb for me, and readily available. It blooms here in July, though in colder regions it comes along in late summer and fall. The round, dark, silver-marked leaves come first, and then little rose-colored flowers, about the size of a violet and as delicately scented. When the plant is satisfactorily grown, the leaves are evergreen, the old ones disappearing just before the new ones come along. *C. europaeum*, a native of the mountains of southern and central Europe, might be expected to be one of the hardiest cyclamens, but it is surprising to find that *C. neapolitanum* is another. These two survive severe weather, though when temperatures approach 0°F their foliage needs a light mulching.

Even in northern gardens the tubers must be planted very shallow, with only ½ in. of soil on top and a sprinkling of peat moss. A topdressing of bone meal and leafmold in late spring is the only supplement they need, but the soil should never be allowed to dry out. They must have part shade and will bloom in almost full shade. The tubers can be planted at any time if the leaves and roots are not allowed to dry.

C. neapolitanum is one of the most adaptable of garden bulbs; its one peculiarity is that its roots, along with the leaves and flowers, grow out of the top of the tuber, which must be planted with the smooth side down. Flowers of the faintest pink, marked at the base of the petals with a bright spot of magenta, begin to open in early fall, sometimes by the end of Aug. and once on the 4th of July (flowering at odd times seems to be characteristic of cyclamens). The flowers are unbelievably frost-proof, and they bloom on into Dec. Marbled leaves, each with a different silver pattern, begin to unfurl in Oct., making a green-and-silver carpet for winter and spring. In summer the ground is bare, and must be left so.

4

ENCYCLOPEDIA
OF BULBS

The following encyclopedia lists the bulbs best suited for garden and indoor use, including the most commonly available species and cultivars. It encapsulates essential information for making informed choices when selecting bulbs. Pointing out everyday gardening techniques for cultivating and propagating the plants, the encyclopedia serves as a basic reference to the best bulbs available.

In this chapter, bulbs are listed by genus under their botanical names (with a pronunciation key). Species of each genus appear for every entry, together with varieties and cultivars. For instance, the various kinds of daffodils are all listed under their genus, *Narcissus*. If only the common name is known, use the index to find its correct botanical name. Look up "daffodil" in the Common Name Index, for example, and it will point to the genus entry for *Narcissus*.

Plant Ratings

The encyclopedia singles out the most outstanding landscape plants for the garden. Virtually indispensible genera, such as *Tulipa* (tulips) and *Lilium* (lilies), are noted with two stars (✱✱). Outstanding species, varieties or cultivars, such as *Agapanthus africanus* (lily-of-the Nile), are indicated by a single star (✱).

The Encyclopedia Entries

General horticultural information, such as the type of soil and amount of light plants require, their susceptibility to disease, overall hardiness, planting times, depths and methods and appropriate methods of propagation, appears with each genus. General gardening information, such as the ornamental aspects of the plants that make the plants worthy of a place in the garden are outlined for an overview of the genus.

Each species entry contains a detailed botanical description of the plant, which includes: average mature height; flower shape, size, color and blooming period; and leaf structure, color, size and texture. Suggestions as to where plants might best be used in the garden or indoors highlight each species' aesthetic strong points. Recent and time-tested subspecies, nursery-introduced series, varieties, hybrids and clones worthy of their own place in the garden are included, and their variations from the species described.

Geographical information, such as the bulb's place of origin (which is a key to the conditions under which it thrives in nature) and hardiness zones alert gardeners to the ability of each species to grow well in their region. Wherever possible, a complete zone range, which features the southern boundaries (beyond which the summers or winters may be too warm for the plant to be healthy in the garden) as well as the more commonly known northern limits, has been supplied for the most complete hardiness treatment available. The U.S. Department of Agriculture Plant Hardiness Zone Map is reproduced on pages 170–171.

In addition, in-depth cultural and propagation information appears in features on such important plants as *Dahlia*, *Iris*, *Lilium*, *Narcissus* and *Tulipa*. Where there has been a great deal of work done to create new hybrids, detailed sections are designed for quick reference on the new varieties.

Snowdrops (*Galanthus nivalis* and *G. nivalis* 'Flore-Pleno') naturalize easily.

UNDERSTANDING
THE ENCYCLOPEDIA ENTRIES

Two stars indicating genus indispensable to the home garden. ———

Common name for the genus, *Dahlia*. ———

Common name of family to which this genus belongs. Cross-reference entry appears listed in the Index of Common Names.

Each entry gives a detailed description of the bulb, including average height; flower shape, size, color and blooming period; and leaf structure and size. In-depth cultivation information, including zone ranges where known, light and soil requirements and propagation techniques are covered. Design suggestions and reliable strains, varieties, cultivars, hybrids and clones complete the information.

✱✱Dahlia (*dal*-yuh). ———

DAHLIA.

Composite Family (*Compositae*). ———

Native to Mex. and C. Amer., these tuberous plants produce very colorful and attractive flowers from midsummer until frost, and are great additions to the summer garden. Each tuber will produce a number of stout stems, which are hollow and jointed; dark green, compound leaves arise from the joints. The height will vary from 1 ft. to over 12 ft., but the tallest species are seldom grown. Dahlias can be used as cut flowers, but make sure to seal the hollow stems by dipping the ends in hot water. Easy to grow and tolerant of a wide range of soils, the tubers should be set 3 to 4 in. deep about ten days before the last expected frost. Space plants 6 to 36 in. apart, depending on ultimate plant size at maturity. Where winter temperatures stay above freezing, the tubers can be left in the ground, but in other areas lift after the first frost and store over winter in a frost-free,

Genus. A plant group including many similar species.

Pronunciation key. Accent on italicized syllable.

Botanical name of the plant family.

Single star indicates species of outstanding merit.

Stands for *Hyacinthoides non-scripta*, a species belonging to the *Hyacinthoides* genus.

✱H. non-scripta (non-script-*tuh*).

ENGLISH BLUEBELL.

This plant has leaves up to 19 in. long and ½ in. wide. Flowers are tubular blue or white and sometimes a pinkish color. The plant reaches 18 in. in height, with the top of the spike bending over a little. Superb in woodlands. If planted with Spanish bluebell, some natural crossing will occur. Flowers in April. Zone 6. ———

Indicates this plant will survive cold weather generally prevailing in Zone 6. Zone map showing which areas of the continent this zone covers is reprinted on pages 170–171.

Narcissus bulbocodium overtakes a meadow.

Achimenes (ah-*kim*-ee-neez).

JAPANESE PANSY.

HOT-WATER PLANT.

KIMONO PLANT.

Gesneria Family (*Gesneriaceae*).

Summer-flowering tender herbaceous perennials from C. Amer., newly rediscovered by twentieth-century gardeners. The plants were so popular with the Victorians that they gave them all manner of common names, and even formally named every new seedling whose flowers showed the slightest variation from existing varieties. Achimenes were probably as widely cultivated in the 1800s as the related African violets (*Saintpaulia*) are today.

The genus comprises erect or trailing perennials arising from catkinlike scaly, tuberous, underground rhizomes. Because the plants are not frost-hardy in most parts of this country, they are most often grown as pot plants. They are covered with flowers from early spring to fall. The tubular or trumpet-shaped flowers have a broad face and come in blue, crimson, lavender, pink, purple, scarlet, violet, white and yellow, some attractively marked with a contrasting hue. Flowers are borne singly, in pairs or in short cymes in the leaf axils.

Plant the rhizomes in late winter or early spring about 1 in. apart and 1 in. deep in equal parts garden loam, peat moss, sand and leafmold, or in a mixture of equal parts milled sphagnum moss, perlite and vermiculite. Achimenes need a minimum nighttime temperature of 60°F, but 70° to 80°F while seeds are being germinated or scaly rhizomes are being started. Provide semi-sun in spring, bright open shade in summer. Feed every ten days to two weeks through the growing season with a diluted liquid houseplant fertilizer such as fish emulsion. To encourage branching, pinch out the growing tips of young plants. Keep moist from planting time until about Oct., after flowering stops, withhold water to force dormancy in pot-grown plants. Set the containers in a dark place with a temperature range of 50° to 60°F and leave there nearly dry until time to start again. If the plants are grown in the border, dig up the rhizomes and allow them to die down and dry out. Store the rhizomes in dry perlite, peat or vermiculite or in their pots in a location with a temperature of 50°F over winter. For plants stored in their pots, replace the potting soil with fresh potting soil each spring.

Each scaly rhizome will multiply into several every year. Seeds planted in Nov. in warmth and high humidity on moist vermiculite and screened sphagnum moss will provide blooming plants the second season after germination. Stem cuttings taken in early summer root easily if provided with warmth, moisture, humidity and shade. *Achimenes*, when well grown and strong, will produce greenish or reddish rhizomes in the axils of the leaves. If these propagules are allowed to mature on the plants and are then removed and stored over winter in barely moist vermiculite, they will sprout in the spring and may be grown on in the same way as mature rhizomes.

✳**A. longiflora** (long-ji-*flor*-uh).

A native of C. Amer. from Mex. to Panama. Flowers vary in color from pale to dark blue, to lavender, to pink, with white throats. The type species has large blue flowers produced in profusion, and begins flowering in July. Today the most commonly grown achimenes are hybrids. 'Paul Arnold', with violet-blue flowers, has long been a favorite. Other blue-flowering cultivars are 'Blue Rose' and 'Valse Blue'. Among the pinks are 'Pink Rose' and 'Manuet'; 'Tarantella' is a very fine red-flowered introduction. Zones 9 to 11.

Acidanthera

Acidanthera (ass-i-*dan*-ther-uh).

FRAGRANT GLADIOLUS.

Iris Family (*Iridaceae*).

Tender, summer-blooming cormaceous perennials from tropical and S. Afr. The globose corms, flattened at the bottom, produce a fan of sword-shaped leaves. There are several species, but only one is commonly grown.

Acidanthera bicolor var. *murielae*
FRAGRANT GLADIOLUS

A. bicolor var. **murielae** (*bye*-cul-or; mew-ree-el-*lee*).

(Syn. *A. murielae; Gladiolus callianthus*.) Leaves are similar to those of a gladiolus but narrower and more graceful. The creamy-white flowers are carried on stems that reach 36 in. in height and are tubular with a distinct purple coloration at the throat. While only six to eight flowers are produced per stem, they are often more than 3 in. in diameter and have a slight but pleasant fragrance, making them good cut flowers. Acidan-

theras grow in any good garden soil but prefer clay. The corms should be planted 4 to 6 in. deep and 6 to 10 in. apart in a sunny location. Plant in the spring, after the danger of frost has passed. In mild climates the corms can be left in the ground. In other areas lift them out in the fall when the foliage begins to turn yellow and store them in a cool, dry place over winter. Zones 7 to 11.

Agapanthus (ag-uh-*pan*-thus).

LILY-OF-THE-NILE.

HARRIET'S FLOWER.

Amaryllis Family (*Amaryllidaceae*).

Widely grown for their showy blue or white flowers, these tender evergreen or slightly hardier deciduous perennials are native to S. Afr. The roots are fleshy and produce clusters of thick, dark green leaves. The flowers are borne on stiff bare stalks in globe-shaped flower heads; the many individual flowers are funnel-shaped and are produced throughout the summer months. In areas where frost is common, the evergreen types are best grown in containers, in a good potting soil, so that they can be brought indoors for the winter. To keep their leaves inside they need partial sun and very light waterings—just enough moisture to keep the plants alive. In the spring they should be given more light, warmer temperatures and a feeding of a balanced fertilizer when new growth appears. After danger of frost has passed they can be placed outdoors. In the garden plant agapanthus in a sunny location in rich, well-drained soil. Leave the clumps undisturbed for years, lifting and dividing only when very crowded or if you wish to increase the number of plants.

★A. africanus (af-rik-*kan*-us).

(Often listed incorrectly as *A. umbellatus*.) The evergreen leaves are up to 36 in. long and 1½ in. wide. The flowers are borne on stems 24 in. or more in height. Flower heads are 4 to 8 in. in diameter, and the individual sky-blue flowers are long lasting. A white form is available. These plants need protection from frost. Zones 9 to 11.

Agapanthus africanus
LILY-OF-THE-NILE

A. campanulatus (cam-pan-yew-*lat*-us).
This deciduous species is hardier than the evergreens and will survive outdoors in as far north as Zone 5 provided it is heavily mulched during the winter. Pale to deep blue flowers are borne on stalks 18 to 24 in. high. Leaves are erect and strap shaped. Zones 9 to 11.

A. praecox (*pray*-cox).
Evergreen, this tender, tall species reaches 60 in. in height. Often as many as 100 pale to deep blue flowers in a very large head are produced through the summer months.

Recent introductions include 'Peter Pan', a dwarf some 24 in. in height with exceptional blue flowers, and 'Headbourne Hybrids', which has good blue flowers atop 36- to 48-in. stems with shorter foliage. White selections are also to be found that vary in height. Zones 9 to 11.

Allium (al-lee-um).
ONION.
Amaryllis Family (*Amaryllidaceae*).
Native to many parts of the N. Hemisphere, alliums are "onions," the edible onion being but one species of the 500 found in this genus. Almost all are hardy bulbous perennials. They have elongated leaves springing directly from the bulb, which in several American species grow close to the surface of the ground. The dark green foliage is practically pest-free, and gives off the typical onion odor when crushed. Leaves are straplike or hollow and round (terete). Easily grown, the ornamental species are good subjects for the herbaceous border, the rock garden, the wild garden and the cutting garden, especially since the flower heads are, in some species, sweet-scented. Globular clusters of white, yellow, pink, red, blue or purple flowers are carried on stalks that rise above the foliage. Alliums like a sandy, well-

Agapanthus praecox
'Headbourne Hybrids'

drained, ordinary soil; some prefer partial shade, but for most full sun is best. Propagate by seed, bulbils (which can often be found in the flower heads), and offsets from the parent bulbs. Or-

Allium

Allium aflatunense 'Purple Sensation'

Allium caeruleum

ganic gardeners often plant *Allium* species such as chives, garlic and onions with ornamentals to deter insects.

A. aflatunense (uh-flat-too-*nen*-see) 'Purple Sensation'.
A lovely species from central China. This selection from the species has attractive spherical umbels of violet-purple flowers, 30 to 36 in. in height. Leaves are 4 in. wide, 20 to 24 in. in length. Flowers in late spring to early summer. Zone 5.

A. albopilosum. See *A. christophii.*

A. azureum. See *A. caeruleum.*

A. caeruleum (seh-*rew*-lee-um).
(Syn. *A. azureum*) Very ornamental species, growing up to 24 in. in height with narrow, linear leaves to 18 in. long, which form a rushlike clump. Dense heads of bright blue flowers in midsummer. A variable species. Should enjoy full sun and perfect drainage, especially in winter. Zone 5.

A. christophii (kris-*tof*-ee-eye).
DOWNY ONION.
STAR-OF-PERSIA.
(Syn. *A. albopilosum.*) The 1-in.-wide, strap-shaped leaves have white hairs on their backs. The lilac flowers are in ball-shaped umbels 10 to 12 in. in diameter and made up of as many as 100 tiny flowers on 24-in. stems. Dramatic in early summer, the flowers are excellent in both fresh and dried arrangements. Plant in full sun in well-drained soil. The foliage dies as the flowers appear, and thus interplanting with plants of persistent foliage will mask the dying foliage. Zone 4.

A. giganteum (jye-*gan*-tee-um).
GIANT ONION.
This species produces immense heads of bright

Allium christophii
DOWNY ONION

blue flowers, reaching 48 in. in height. The bluish-green leaves are 2 in. wide, 30 in. long. Spectacular when used as a summer bedding plant. Zone 5.

A. karataviense (ka-ra-tah-vee-*en*-see).
TURKESTAN ONION.
Both foliage and flowers are ornamental. The flowers are silver-lilac on short 6- to 12-in. stems, produced in late spring. The foliage is blue and sometimes variegated, 4 to 6 in. wide, and lasts well into early summer. Ideal for the front of the border, in full sun with well-drained soil. Zone 4.

A. moly (*mah*-lee).
LILY LEEK.
GOLDEN GARLIC.
Produces two flat, lance-shaped leaves, 2 in. wide and 12 in. long, blue-green in color. Flowers appear in early summer and are bright cheery yellow in loose umbels on stems 12 in. in height.

Plant in full sun in a well-drained soil. These plants will form broad clumps and can become invasive. Zone 3.

A. neapolitanum (nee-uh-pol-i-*tay*-num).
NAPLES ONION.
The foliage is similar to that of daffodils. Loose umbels of white flowers appear in mid- to late spring and last for several weeks. One of the earliest ornamental onions to flower. The flowers are fragrant and are also good cut flowers. Plants need full sun and are tolerant of summer moisture. When well mulched or planted in a sunny spot, they will survive in quite cold climates. The cultivar 'Grandiflorum' is well worth growing for its large white flowers. Zone 7.

A. oreophilum (or-ee-oh-*fye*-lum).
(Syn. *A. ostrowskianum.*) Only 4 to 6 in. in height, this plant produces lovely carmine-pink flowers in midsummer. Zone 7.

A. ostrowskianum. See *A. oreophilum.*

A. rosenbachianum (rose-en-bak-ee-*ay*-num).
Dark violet flowers top 24-in. stems, each flower having prominent white stamens. Flowers in early summer with lance-shaped leaves 2 in. wide, 20 in. long. Zone 7.

A. siculum (*sick*-u-lum).
An unusual species, 30 in. in height, it flowers in early summer with greenish-white or maroon flowers with a green reverse to the petals. Needs full sun, well-drained soil and little summer moisture. Zone 8.

A. triquetrum (tri-*kwet*-trum).
This species has a unique three-sided stem. In late spring attractive white flowers with green-striped petals are produced on 18-in. stems. The leaves are dark green, basal and linear. Will grow

Allium

in light shade and can become invasive, and in milder climates should be planted only where it can be confined. Zone 6.

A. unifolium (u-ni-*fo*-lee-um).
Native to the West Coast, this species has attractive rose-colored flowers, produced in late spring or early summer above grasslike leaves, on 8- to 15-in. stems. Grows easily in moist soils, partial shade. Zone 8.

✱✱**Alstroemeria** (al-stro-*mare*-ee-uh).
PERUVIAN LILY.
Alstroemeria Family (*Alstroemeriaceae*).
Native to S. Amer. Superb cut flowers, they are lilylike, arise from rhizomes and are available in a multitude of colors. While individually only 1 to 2 in. in diameter, they bloom in profusion. The plants must have summer moisture and enjoy full sun to partial shade in the warmer climates. They are surprisingly hardy, and if well mulched will survive temperatures as low as 0°F for short periods. If in doubt, lift at the end of summer after the first frost, dry them, remove the foliage and store them in a cool, dry area, providing only sufficient moisture to prevent dehydration. The white fleshy roots (rhizomes) are brittle, a point to remember when handling them. Replant in the spring. Propagate by division; raising from seed is possible, but it is a slow process.

A. ligtu (*lig*-too).
Reaching 36 in. in height, this species produces trumpet-shaped flowers in midsummer, up to 2 in. long, variegated in color with hues of pink, pale lilac or off-white, with touches of yellow on the inner petals. Can become untidy in appearance. Zone 6.

A. 'Ligtu Hybrids'.
More vigorous than the species and slightly taller

growing, plants reach perhaps as much as 48 in. in height. Available in many colors, including attractive combinations of pink, flame, salmon, orange and yellow. Zone 6.

Alstroemeria 'Ligtu Hybrids'
PERUVIAN LILY

Amaryllis (am-ah-*rill*-iss).
NAKED-LADY LILY.
Amaryllis Family (*Amaryllidaceae*).
A genus containing only one species, a large, bulbous plant from S. Afr., closely related to and often confused with *Hippeastrum*. The pinkish lilylike flowers appear in late summer. It is grown indoors or out like hippeastrum. Zone 5.

A. belladonna (bell-uh-*don*-uh).
BELLADONNA LILY.
CAPE BELLADONNA.
This bulb is a hardy amaryllis similar to the pot or common amaryllis, which is actually in the genus *Hippeastrum*. The genus behaves differently and is more dramatic than most bulbs.

The attractive, straplike, 1½-ft.-long blue-green leaves appear in late fall in warm climates or early spring in cold climates and remain through the summer. By the end of the growing season the foliage matures and withers. In early fall the 2- to 2½-ft. flower stalk appears "naked," hence the common name. The delicate lilylike, funnel-shaped flowers of rose pink are 3 to 3½ in. long and are usually borne in a loose cluster of two to four, although sometimes more.

Plant in fall or spring. Although this bulb is considered frost-hardy and can survive in Zone 5, plant in a protected area, such as against a sunny wall. Plant in well-drained soil and cover with 3 to 6 in. of soil. Water only as required, cease watering during the summer, then start again when the plant is in flower. The foliage is a textural asset in the perennial border, but use care to mask the withering foliage when siting it so there will be no temptation to fill in the bare spot

Amaryllis belladonna
BELLADONNA LILY

that precedes the flower stalk. The bulbs can also be planted in pots; repot only when absolutely necessary, as they do not like to be disturbed and prefer to be overcrowded. Bring the pots inside for the winter to allow the foliage to mature, and treat as any other houseplant.

✶✶ Anemone (an-*nem*-oh-nee).
WINDFLOWER.
Buttercup Family (*Ranunculaceae*).
A large genus, native mostly to the N. Temp. Zone. Many species producing either rhizomes or tubers. Enormously varied in size, form and flowering characteristics, all have attractive fern-like foliage and are valuable in borders and rock, wild and cutting gardens. They like rich, sandy, well-drained soils and spring moisture. Bold plantings are the most effective. Propagate by seeds or by division of large established plants.

✶ A. blanda (*bland*-duh).
GREEK ANEMONE.
A delicate little tuberous plant from Greece and Asia Minor. It is 4 to 8 in. in height, with deeply divided leaves and bright blue flowers composed of many narrow petals. After flowering in early spring the foliage soon disappears. An excellent plant for the rock garden or the front of a sunny border, it will also perform well in light shade such as is found under deciduous trees. There are several cultivars, all great little plants. Among the best are 'White Splendor', 'Pink Star', 'Blue Star' and 'Radar', which is red with a white center. Zone 6.

A. coronaria (kor-oh-*nay*-ree-uh).
POPPY-FLOWERED ANEMONE.
Widely distributed in southern Eur., this lovely tuberous plant grows 18 in. high. It can be grown outdoors in Zones 9 to 11; in colder areas it can be grown for summer color by planting in the

Anemone

Anemone blanda
GREEK ANEMONE

Anemone coronaria
POPPY-FLOWERED ANEMONE

spring. It is a satisfactory greenhouse or conservatory plant. This species has been extensively hybridized, and today the St. Brigid double-flowered types and the de Caen single-flowered types are the most extensively grown. They are superb cut flowers and popular with florists, who particularly admire the bright, clean flower colors. The most popular St. Brigid cultivars are 'Lord Lieutenant', a bright blue; 'Mt. Everest', white; 'The Admiral', cyclamen-violet; and 'The Governor', vermillion-scarlet. Cultivars of the de Caen types include 'Blue Poppy', a lovely blue; 'The Bride', a dazzling white; and 'His Excellency', a bright scarlet.

Tubers should be planted 4 to 6 in. apart and 2 to 3 in. deep. They need moisture to grow successfully, but avoid overwatering. They can be grown indoors in a sunny but cool area with nighttime temperatures around 55°F. Plant the tubers in containers in Sept. or early Oct. using a regular potting-soil mix. Place them 1 in. deep and 2 to 3 in. apart. After planting, put the containers in a cool, dark place and keep moist but not wet until growth starts. Transfer to a sunny area and increase the water given as the plants grow, feeding every two weeks with a liquid houseplant fertilizer. Zones 9 to 11.

A. × fulgens (*full*-gens).
A naturally occurring hybrid between two species native to southern France, the most popular hybrids of this group are the St. Bavo Hybrids, which resulted from a cross between *A. × fulgens* and *A. coronaria*. Lovely plants, with a wide range of colors from white through pink, to salmon, brick and dark red, to violet-blue, they make excellent garden plants. These "peacock anemones" appreciate full sun—except in the warmest areas, where light shade should be given—and rich soil with good moisture. They grow 10 to 15 in. in height and should be planted 6 in. apart and 2 in. deep. The flowers are produced over a long

period from mid-spring to early summer. Zones 9 to 11.

A. nemorosa (nem-ur-*rose*-uh).
WOOD ANEMONE.

Found in the woods in Eur., these plants like moisture, shade and rich humus. Plant the creeping rhizomes 2 in. deep and 6 in. apart. The flowers are 1 in. in diameter, white with a tinge of pink, on stems that are 3 to 5 in. in height. The cultivar 'Alleni' has flowers of rose-lilac with a bluish interior. Flowers are produced in early spring. An ideal plant for naturalizing in wooded areas. Zone 5.

Arum (*ay*-rum).

Arum Family (*Araceae*).
Tuberous-rooted perennials, native to Eur. and Asia. Each tuber sends up a cluster of long-stalked, broad-bladed leaves shaped like arrowheads. The flowers are produced on single, leafless stalks about the same height as the leaves. The showy part of the flower is the spathe surrounding the spadix or flower spike, which is itself rather inconspicuous. The spathe may be white, green or purple and does not completely enclose the spadix. Mostly tender bulbs, arums are suitable for pot growing in a warm greenhouse or outdoors in warm regions. They require a moist, humusy soil. Plant 3 to 4 in. deep and 12 to 18 in. apart. Propagate by seeds or offsets.

A. italicum (i-*tal*-ick-um).
ITALIAN ARUM.

A tuberous perennial grown for its ornamental leaves, which appear in the fall and are followed by flowers enclosed in creamy-white to yellow spathes 18 in. in height. The leaves are arrow-shaped and a rich, glossy green with pale green to white veins. Red berries appear later in autumn. Plant in full sun in rich, moist soil. The variety

Anemone nemorosa 'Alleni'
WOOD ANEMONE

marmoratum (mar-moh-*ray*-tum), with white marbled foliage, is more ornamental. Zone 7.

Babiana (bay-be-*ain*-uh).

BABOON FLOWER.
BABOON ROOT.
Iris Family (*Iridaceae*).
Tender cormous plants from S. Afr. The corms produce a stalk made up of overlapping bases of slightly hairy, dark green leaves, pleated to give an effect of a flat spray of palmlike leaves. The flower shoot arises through the center of this stem, reaching a height of 15 to 18 in. Numerous flowers, 2 in. in diameter, are produced, and these are widely spaced and often fragrant. Flower colors are white, blue, red or purple. In warmer climates, where winter temperatures stay above 20°F., babianas can be grown outdoors in a sunny location; in colder areas they make excellent pot plants, growing well in a regular potting mix. Plant or pot the corms in early fall 4 to 6 in. deep

Babiana

and 6 in. apart. If at all possible allow them to remain undisturbed for years, so that they form large clumps. These can be lifted and divided, or seed can be sown in the summer, but as the corms produce many cormels, raising from seed is not necessary. The plants enjoy full sun with good moisture during their growing season but should be allowed to become dry after the foliage dies down.

B. stricta (*strick*-tuh).

The most commonly grown species, this produces flowers that can be cream, crimson or lilac to blue in mid-spring, 18 in. in height. One of the best cultivars is 'Tubergen's Blue', which displays lavender-violet flowers with a darker blotch in the center. Great garden plants for warmer areas. Zone 8 (with protection).

✱✱Begonia (bee-*go*-ni-uh).

Begonia Family (*Begoniaceae*).

A very large genus with well over 300 species, native to trop. and subtrop. areas of both hemispheres. Only a few of them produce tubers (only *B. socotrana*, which is rarely grown today, is a true bulb). The tuberous species and cultivars are superb garden plants with a wide range of forms and colors.

B. tuberhybrida (too-burr-*hye*-brid-uh).

The well-known tuberous begonias that are widely grown for summer bedding and in hanging baskets.

With the exception of the Multiflora begonias (see below), which appreciate more sun and less water, they like some shade and moisture-retentive soils.

Tuberous begonias will not tolerate frost. They need nighttime temperatures in the low 50°F range to grow well. As these tubers take twelve to fifteen weeks to come into flower, they should be started into growth indoors for planting in the garden when temperatures are suitable.

Place the tubers, concave side up, in a soil mix of equal parts peatmoss and sand, the convex side on the surface side, barely covering each tuber with the soil mix. Keep the soil moist, not wet, but never allow it to dry out. Buds, if not visible, will soon be formed, but growth will be slow. When growth is 2 in. long, plant in individual containers, one tuber per 4-in. pot being ideal, and use a regular potting soil with additional sand added. As soon as the tubers show signs of growth after potting, start feeding weekly with a complete liquid fertilizer. Keep all moisture off the crowns of the plants. Plant out in the garden when the plants are 6 to 8 in. in height. Select a planting area that has good sunlight except during the warmest parts of the day, and space the plants 12 to 18 in. apart, making sure the tubers are just at the surface of the soil. Better flower production will result if the first flower bud formed is removed and the plants are allowed to begin flowering only when well established. Many plants will need some support, but be careful not to damage the tubers when inserting the canes. Keep moist; on very hot days a light spray of water over the foliage will be appreciated. Toward the end of summer, when flower production decreases, stop feeding and the leaves will start to turn yellow. Cut the foliage back to 4 to 6 in. from the tuber and stop watering. Lift the tuber out of the soil, allow to dry, remove the remaining foliage and store in barely moist peat or perlite at a temperature of 50°F until it is time to start the tubers into growth again.

Propagation can be by seed sown in Feb. in sifted peat moss. Scatter the small fragile seeds over the surface and water carefully with a fine spray. Cover the container with glass and maintain a temperature of 65°F with full-spectrum light for a 14-hour photoperiod. Keep the glass dry. Germination will occur in seven to ten days. At this stage remove the glass during the day, replacing it at night. Seedlings will be of sufficient size to transplant into individual containers in several weeks, when the leaves start to touch each other.

Tubers can be cut into sections, provided each section has at least one bud, and planted in the same manner as whole tubers.

Cuttings can be taken from the stems but must be 4 to 5 in. long and inserted in a sandy soil mix. If the tubers produce a great number of shoots, these can be removed, along with a small portion of the tuber, when 4 to 5 in. long and grown on. Begonias can be grown in all zones for summer color; plant out only when temperatures are in the 50°F range at night.

Most cultivars are listed by color first, such as apricot shades or peach shades, and then by type. Recent introductions include 'Hanging Sensation Series' and 'Non-Stop'. A great variety of colors are available, with the exeception of blue shades. There are six types:

RUFFLED DOUBLE. Being those plants with double flowers, much like a camellia in shape, with fringed petals.

ROSE FORM. Having a formal shape with the central petal upstanding and longer than the outer.

PICOTEE. Very similar to the Rose Form types, but the outer petals have contrasting colors, in combinations such as cream with orange or white with pink.

HANGING BASKET. Producing pendulous stems and very large flowers.

Begonia 'Nelson'

Begonia 'Non-stop'

Begonia

HANGING BASKET PICOTEE. Producing pendulous stems with flowers that have combinations of colors.

MULTIFLORA. Compact bushy types, reaching a height of 12 to 18 in., produce flowers profusely throughout the summer.

Brimeura (bry-*mure*-uh).

Lily Family (*Liliaceae*).

Native to the Medit. region, the species in this genus were first included in *Hyacinthus* but in fact bear little resemblance to the hyacinth, looking more like a bluebell. The bulbs should be planted in the fall, 1 to 2 in. deep and 3 to 5 in. apart in full sun. They are quite hardy, withstanding temperatures down to 20°F, and are not bothered by heat or lack of moisture during the summer. They do appreciate moisture during their spring-growing season. If they enjoy their growing conditions, they will form large colonies and are ideal for the rock garden or sunny border. They also make good pot plants, requiring only ordinary potting soil. Propagation is by seed or by lifting and dividing large clumps.

B. amethystina (am-meth-thigh-*steen*-uh). Produces six to eight narrow leaves, bright green and up to 12 in. long. Five to fifteen flowers appear in April–May on each 8- to 10-in. stem. Flowers are bright blue, ½ in. long and bell-shaped. A white form, 'Alba', is often listed in catalogs and well worth growing. Zone 6.

Brodiaea laxa. See *Triteleia laxa*.

Brodiaea uniflora. See *Ipheion uniflorum*.

Bulbocodium (bulb-oh-*koh*-dee-um).

Lily Family (*Liliaceae*).

Native to Spain, the Alps and the Caucasus, the genus is closely related to *Colchicum*. While there are two species in this genus, only one is commonly grown.

B. vernum (*ver*-num).

SPRING-MEADOW SAFFRON.

The foliage, present when flowering, continues to grow when the flowers fade, and is just a little taller than the 4-in.-high flowers, which are in shades of purple and are produced in mid- to late spring. Plants need full sun and are ideal for the rock garden or the front of a sunny border. Plant in the fall, 4 to 5 in. deep and 5 to 6 in. apart. Leave undisturbed until the clumps become too large, which will be in about three to four years, then lift and divide in the fall. Plants need moisture when growing, then should enjoy dry conditions. They make excellent container plants; grow the corms in ordinary potting soil. Zone 4.

Caladium (kal-*lay*-dee-um).

FANCY-LEAVED CALADIUM.

Arum Family (*Araceae*).

Tuberous-rooted plants of trop. Amer., widely grown for their handsome, colorful foliage. The blade of the leaf is shaped like an arrowhead and is held horizontally. The flowers, usually hidden under the leaves, are in the calla-lily form that is typical of this family: a spathe surrounding the upright spike (spadix) that bears the tiny true flowers. Caladiums are stunning foliage plants for moist, shady spots in frost-free regions. In colder climates they should be grown in pots indoors or in a warm greenhouse. They are excellent plants for massing outdoors in the summer. To get the full effect of the colorful leaves, grow several plants of one variety together, either in individual pots or planted in the open round. If the bulbs are planted right side up, they will produce large leaves. If planted upside down, they will develop many more—but smaller—

Caladium hortulanum cultivar
FANCY-LEAVED CALADIUM

leaves. They need a rich loam and plenty of water during the growing season (summer) but are stored almost completely dry during the winter.

For pot plants use a basic potting mixture with doubled peat. All caladiums do best in partial shade; full sunlight tends to bleach or burn the leaves unless the plants have been carefully hardened off and are kept moist. Propagate by division prior to planting in the spring or by seed, which germinates quickly but produces highly variable offspring. Plant 2 in. deep, 12 to 18 in. apart, but do not place outside until the temperatures are consistently in the upper 50°F range at night. Start tubers indoors three to four weeks prior to planting, giving night temperatures in the upper 50°F range; keep moist, but increase the moisture as plants develop. Caladiums love high humidity when growing well.

✴C. hortulanum (hort-u-*lay*-num).

For decades hybridizers have introduced many wonderful foliage colors in cultivars of this species. Varying in height from 24 in. to as much as 36 to 48 in., these are found under such names as 'White Christmas', which is snow-white with green veining; 'Pink Symphony', pink with green veins; 'Frieda Hemple', crimson-red with green edges; and dwarf cultivars such as 'Little Miss Muffet', only 10 to 12 in. in height with lime-green leaves accented with wine-colored spots and blotches. The number of color variations is extensive, but remember to plant several of the same type for dramatic effects. Zones 10 to 11. Grown for annual color in other zones.

Calochortus (kal-oh-*kor*-tus).
MARIPOSA LILY.
GLOBE TULIP.
FAIRY-LANTERN.
Lily Family (*Liliaceae*).

These bulbs are native to the western U.S., particularly Calif., Colo., Oreg., Utah and Wash. While there are some sixty species, only a few are offered in catalogs. Flower color varies with the species and can be white, pink, lavender, purple or yellow, or shades in between these, usually with a streak of darker color in the center of the flowers. Flowers are produced on top of the stems or in the leaf axils. The bulbs grow best in a poor, light, well-drained, sandy soil with good moisture during the spring growing season, followed by a dry resting period in summer. They like sun but prefer light shade in the hotter times of the day. Plant 3 to 4 in. deep, 10 to 12 in. apart. Propagate by lifting and dividing established clumps after growth stops in early summer or by sowing seed as soon as it is ripe.

C. albus (*all*-bus).
Native to the coastal ranges of Calif. Up to 12 in. in height. Flowers pendulous, with fringed petals, inner petals 1 in. long, outer petals shorter;

Calochortus

mostly white, but pink selections are offered in some catalogs. April-May flowering. Will produce as many as four to eight flowers. The basal leaf is 12 to 24 in. in length, while the leaves on the flowering stem are 8 to 10 in. in length. Zones 8 to 10.

C. clavatus (cla-*vat*-tus).
A lovely species at home in the Sierra Nevada and Pacific coastal ranges. Deep yellow tulip-shaped flowers produced in early summer. Upright flowers atop 24-in. stems. The lower leaves are 4 to 8 in. long and linear, while the leaves on the stems are smaller. Zones 8 to 10.

C. venustus (ven-*nuss*-tuss).
WHITE MARIPOSA LILY.
WHITE MARIPOSA TULIP.
The upright flowers can measure 2 in. or more in diameter and range from white to yellow, purple to red, often with blotches of color on the petals and hairy inner segments. The height of the flowering stems can vary from 8 in. to as tall as 24 in. Selections of a specific color can be found listed in catalogs; all are lovely garden plants. Late spring to early summer flowering. Zones 8 to 10.

Camassia (ka-mass-si-uh).
CAMASS.
Lily Family (*Liliaceae*).
Except for one S. Amer. species, the species are found on the west coast of N.A. from Calif. to B. C. They are at home near streams or other areas where they have abundant summer moisture, and are ideal plants for bordering a pond when planted so that their roots can reach the moisture. Native Americans used to boil or roast the bulbs, but other parts of the plant are poisonous; eating any part is not recommended. The leaves are long and narrow. Flowers are produced in racemes, white to deep purplish-blue, depending on the species. Plant in the fall, 4 to 5 in. deep

and 12 to 18 in. apart, and leave undisturbed for years. Camassias grow well in full sun, provided summer moisture is given, and like a little shade during the warmest part of the day in hot climates. Seed is the best way to propagate these plants; sow them as soon as ripe in a soil mix that provides good moisture and good drainage. The bulbs do not produce many offsets. Plant *en masse* for good effect.

C. cusickii (koo-*sik*-ee-eye).
From Oreg. Produces a very large bulb. Foliage is blue-green, 16 in. long, 1½ in. wide. Flowers on strong stems reaching 36 in. in height; color is pale blue. When established, the flower heads are large and contain many individual flowers that open over a long period of time. Zone 5.

Camassia cusickii
CAMASS

Camassia quamash
CAMASS

C. esculenta. See *C. quamash*.

C. leichtlinii (lyekt-*lin*-ee-eye).
One of the tallest growing, reaching more than 36 in. in height. Leaves are 1 in. wide, 24 in. long. Flowers vary from white to deep purplish-blue. One of the best garden species, and several selections are sometimes offered, including semi-double flower forms. Zone 5.

C. quamash (*kwa*-mash).
Widespread habitat from B. C. to Calif. Great variation in flower color, from white to deep blue to purple. Hardy and of easy culture. Bulbs can become quite large and produce flower spikes that vary in height from 12 to 24 in. This was the species much used for food by Native Americans; hence the old name esculenta, meaning edible. The cultivar 'Orion' is deep blue; 'San Juan' is even deeper in color. Zones 5 to 8.

C. scilloides (sill-oi-*deez*).
WILD HYACINTH.
Reaches 24 in. in height. Grasslike leaves, 1 in. in width. Flowers vary from deep blue to white and number from eight to ten. Very easy to grow in average garden soil as long as moisture is present during the growing season. Zones 5 to 8.

Canna (*kan*-nah).
INDIAN-SHOT.
Canna Family (*Cannaceae*).
Native to trop. and subtrop. areas. The common name refers to plant's black, very hard seed, which resembles the shot or pellets in shotgun cartridges. Most of the plants grown in gardens today are hybrids and have stocky, often stubby rhizomes, used in some countries to make a sort of arrowroot, an edible starch. Most hybrids have been derived from *C. flaccida* (*flak*-sid-uh) a native of Fla. The flowers have three sepals, most commonly green, three long petals, which are colored, and up to five stamens, which look like petals and are broad and colored. One of these stamens forms the lower lip of the flower. The foliage can be green or bronzy, or a combination of these colors.

Cannas like full sun, ordinary garden soil, and moisture during the growing season. Cannas give great summer color in all areas, but they should be lifted at the end of the summer in cold areas and stored in a frost-free place, with the rhizomes kept just moist enough to prevent shriveling. Plant in the spring after danger of frost has passed; starting the plants indoors prior to planting out will speed flowering. Plant 4 to 6 in. deep. Spacing will depend on the height of the cultivar—set lower-growing plants 10 to 12 in. apart, taller ones up to 24 in. apart. If overwintered in the ground, lift and divide every three to four years, selecting pieces of roots that have buds. Plants like to be fertilized when in active

Canna

Canna 'King Midas'
INDIAN-SHOT

Cardiocrinum giganteum

growth, but not before. Plants from seed are very variable, and the seed must be soaked for twenty-four hours before sowing, or notched with a knife. Take care when transplanting, as the roots are quite brittle. With their bright flowers and varying foliage patterns, cannas are great for summer color, in the garden and in containers.

✷ Canna Cultivars.

The cultivars offered today are developed from *C. flaccida*, with the foliage variation being derived from *C. warscewiczii* (war-schew-*wick*-zee-eye). They are listed according to height, which can range from 18 in. to well over 6 ft. Among the cultivars are 'Ambassador', 42 in., red with bronze foliage; 'City of Portland', 48 in., salmon-pink with green foliage; 'Red King Humbert', 60 in., red with bronzy foliage; 'Rosamond Cole', 42 in., red with yellow backs and edges and dark green foliage; and 'The President', 36 in., bright red with deep green foliage.

Opera Series (all with green foliage): 'Aida', 60 in., salmon pink; 'La Traviata', 48 in., rose-pink; 'Madame Butterfly', 60 in., pink with deeper markings; 'La Boheme', 48 in., salmon-pink; and 'Rosenkavalier', 48 in., watermelon-pink. The lower-growing hybrids, raised by Wilhelm Pfitzer and frequently called 'Pfitzer Hybrids', include 'Crimson Beauty', 'Chinese Coral', 'Primrose Yellow' and 'Salmon Pink', all of which are between 24 and 36 in. in height with green foliage. Many other hybrids can be found in catalogs, ranging from 12 in. to more than 150 in. in height. Colors are very varied, and about the only color not found is blue. Many of these are reported to be hardier than the older types. While they will overwinter in the soil in warmer areas, they typically need the protection of a mulch in zones colder than Zone 7.

Cardiocrinum (kar-dee-oh-*cry*-num).

Lily Family (*Liliaceae*).

Native to Asia. For many years the plants in this genus were classified as lilies (*Lilium*). The flowers are like trumpet lilies, very fragrant, but the foliage is heart-shaped, the characteristic that separates these species from *Lilium*. Only one species is commonly grown.

C. giganteum (jye-*gan*-tee-um).

This Himalayan native is an ideal plant for the woodland garden, preferring light shade and good moisture. It is spectacular in flower, having as many as twenty pure white flowers with a hint of purple toward the base, 6 in. in diameter. Plant in the fall or early spring, with the top of the large bulb just at or below the surface of the soil. The bulbs send up nonflowering shoots each year, which then die back. After about four to five years the stems will produce flowers and then the plant will die, its place being taken by offsets that are produced at the base. As these can become quite crowded, it is best to lift and divide the plants when the principal plant in a clump dies. This will provide a good means of propagating these wonderful plants. Seed can be sown, but it may take seven to ten years before flowers are produced. The basal leaves form a rosette; other leaves are scattered up the strong stem and can be up to 18 in. long and almost as wide. While woodland settings are ideal, these plants can be grown in shrub borders, but they do not like to be grown in containers. They need protection in colder areas but with such a mulch as leaves will grow well in Zone 5.

Chionodoxa (kye-on-oh-*dock*-sa).

GLORY-OF-THE-SNOW.

Lily Family (*Liliaceae*).

One of the finest of the early flowering bulbs, native to the mountains of Crete and Turkey,

Chionodoxa luciliae
GLORY-OF-THE-SNOW

where they will peek above the melting snow in early spring. Foliage is basal, only two leaves per bulb, thick, stiff and dark green in color. Flowers are mostly blue, but white and pink forms are known. Plant 3 in. deep in fall, 2 to 3 in. apart. Mass plantings are best in well-drained soil with good moisture in winter and spring. Chionodoxas enjoy sun. Lift and divide only when crowded; seed sown when ripe germinates readily. These plants are ideal for the rock garden and for growing in containers to be brought into the house when in flower. Zone 5.

C. gigantea (jye-*gan*-tee-uh).

Light to medium blue flowers, up to 8 in. in height. A white form, *C. gigantea* 'Alba', is sometimes listed. Zone 5.

C. luciliae (lew-*sil*-ee-ay-ee).

This species can produce as many as ten flowers, each up to 1 in. in diameter, on each 6- to 8- in.-

Chionodoxa

high stem. The flowers are blue and have a white center, but selections have been made and are offered as 'Blue Giant', 'Alba' (white), 'Rosea' (rose) and 'Gigantea'. These are much like the species, only stronger-growing. Zone 5.

C. sardensis (czar-*den*-sis).
A good gentian blue with a white center, it reaches 6 in. in height, flowering a little later than the others. A rather rare plant but well worth growing. Zone 5.

C. siehei (*see*-hee-eye).
The largest-growing of the genus, 12 in. in height with as many as fifteen flowers per stem. The flowers are almost purple when they first open, turning to deep blue with a white center. This species deserves to be more commonly grown. Zone 5.

Clivia (*clive*-ee-uh).
Amaryllis Family (*Amaryllidaceae*).
A S. Afr. genus of evergreen bulbous plants that are among the finest for shady areas in warmer climates and for greenhouses in colder climes. They will not tolerate frost. The flowers are striking umbels of red, orange and yellow, tubular or funnel-shaped. They are produced in late fall and winter on strong stalks 24 in. or more in height, just above the deep green straplike leaves, which are up to 2 in. wide. Clivias love to grow in containers as well as in the open ground and should be left undisturbed for years. They should not be subjected to temperatures below 35°F, and they should be fertilized weekly after flowering until flower spikes are again produced. Plant in ordinary garden soil, with the base of the sheath that surrounds the base of the leaves just above soil level. Although clivias like shade, the light intensity should be fairly high.

Clivia miniata

✶**C. miniata** (minn-ee-*ah*-tah).
The most commonly grown species. There are a number of color variations offered, some bright orange, others redder, some a combination of these. A yellow variety, *C. miniata* var. *citrina* (sit-*treen*-uh), has recently been introduced and is highly prized and priced. Propagation is by division of established plants, or by seed sown in spring, when night temperatures remain above 55°F at night, in a soil with a good humus content. Keep moist, but do not allow to become too wet. Zone 9 in sheltered areas; Zones 10 to 11 otherwise.

Colchicum (*kol*-chi-cum).
AUTUMN CROCUS.
MEADOW SAFFRON.
Lily Family (*Liliaceae*).
Native to Eur., S. Afr. and Asia. These plants look like a crocus but have six stamens in place of the crocus's three. They have been grown for centuries for their colchicine content, which is made into a powder and used to treat gout. Flowers are produced in late summer or fall, after which the foliage grows, continuing throughout the summer and dying down before flowers reappear. Best planted in July or Aug., in full sun. Set the bulbs 4 in. deep and 4 to 6 in. apart. Though called autumn crocus, there are species that flower in the spring, but these are seldom grown.

Colchicum autumnale 'Waterlily'
AUTUMN CROCUS

Colchicums grow well in any sandy, well-drained soil and can be propagated by separating the young corms from the parents in late summer or by seed sown in July in sandy soil. They do not grow well in containers but are superb in shrub borders where fall color is scarce.

✳**C. autumnale** (au-tum-*nal*-ee).
Leaves are 8 to 12 in. long, 1 in. wide, turning yellow in late summer. One or more pale pink to white flowers are produced in late Aug. or early Sept., 4 to 6 in. in height. Nurseries offer several fine selections of this species, including 'Minor', a soft mauve; 'Plenum' (*plee*-num) or 'Alboplenum' (*al*-buh-plee-num), a double white form; 'The Giant'; 'Lilac Wonder'; 'Waterlily', a large double violet-pink; and 'Autumn Queen'. Zones 5 to 8.

C. byzantinum (by-zan-*tine*-um).
(Often listed as *C. autumnale* 'Major'.) This species has a very large corm, some 2 in. or more in length and as wide. It will produce as many as twenty flowers of lilac-purple, each 4 in. in diameter, from Sept. into Oct. It does not set seed. Zones 6 to 7.

C. cilicicum (sil-i-*sy*-cum).
Similar to *C. byzantinum*, but flowers are produced a little later in the season and foliage ap-

Colchicum speciosum
MEADOW SAFFRON

Colchicum speciosum var. *album*
WHITE MEADOW SAFFRON

pears almost with the last flowers; flowers are a deeper lilac and fragrant. *C. c.* var. *purpureum* (pur-pur-*ee*-um) flowers at the same time but has even deeper-hued flowers. Zones 3 to 7.

C. speciosum (spee-see-*oh*-sum).
Regarded as one of the finest for the garden, this species has deep reddish-violet, tulip-like flowers up to 12 in. in height. Left undisturbed, the corms become very large, often covering up to 1 sq. ft. in a couple of seasons, and then becoming even larger. Selections are offered, including *C. s.* var. *album* (*all*-bum). Zones 3 to 7.

Crinum x powellii

Crinum (*cry*-num).
Amaryllis Family (*Amaryllidaceae*).
More than 100 species of trop. bulbous plants, but few are in cultivation. They are not hardy. All species produce large bulbs and are evergreen. Leaves are straplike, often 24 to 36 in. in length and 2 to 4 in. wide, so that established plants

occupy a large area. The flowers are large and trumpet-shaped, on strong stalks often 24 in. in height. Up to twenty flowers are produced per head, but seldom more than five or six open at one time, hence crinums flower over a long period during the summer. Plant with the neck of the bulb just above ground, spacing 24 in. apart. Moisture is required during the growing season, but after flowering reduce the quantity given. Propagation is by separating the offsets from the parent bulbs or by seed; seeds are quite large and should be sown 1 in. deep in a soil rich in organic matter. Crinums like full sun but need protection from wind. Good container plants, they should be left undisturbed for years. In the open ground protect from frost by mulching heavily.

C. bulbispermum (bulb-be-*sper*-mum).
The flowers vary from pale pink to white with a rose-colored stripe through the center of each petal. The foliage curves back to the ground, throwing the flower spikes well above the foliage. It can often die back in the winter months, and water should be withheld. Often more than twenty flowers per stalk are produced in early summer. Zones 8 to 10.

C. macowanii (mack-ow-*ann*-ee-eye).
Easy to recognize, as the flowers have black anthers. A lovely species reaching 48 in. in height. Large trumpet flowers, white to pale pink with a crimson stripe in the center of each petal. Flowers in late summer. Zones 8 to 10.

C. moorei (*moor*-eye).
A favorite plant for cool greenhouses, flowering 48 in. in height on strong stalks, with white or pale pink flowers. The leaves are often 48 in. long and 4 in. wide. Needs a lot of summer moisture but little in the winter. Found in forests, it prefers a little shade. Zones 8 to 10.

C. × powellii (pow-*ell*-ee-eye).
A hybrid of *C. bulbispermum* and *C. moorei*, it is slightly hardier than other species and will withstand a little frost. Flowers vary from pure white to a good pink, on strong stalks 24 to 30 in. in height, and are fragrant; up to fifteen are produced per stalk. A good garden plant, this should be the first crinum you try in your garden. There are a number of cultivars offered, including 'J.C. Harvey', a coral pink with very long (60-in.) leaves; 'Ellen Bosanquet', a good red; 'Maureen Spinks', a red with a white stripe; and 'Mystery', a lovely pink. All flower over a long period of time. Zones 8 to 10.

Crocosmia (crow-*kos*-mee-uh).
Iris Family (*Iridaceae*)
(Syn. *Montbretia.*) Several cormous species native to S. Afr. They produce sword-shaped leaves and in late summer a slender branching flower spike. They like a light soil with good organic matter and should be planted 2 in. deep and 8 to 10 in. apart in an area where they can stay undis-

Crocosmia × *crocosmiiflora* 'Lucifer'

turbed and spread. They produce many offsets that can be removed and replanted; seed can be sown as soon as it is ripe, but it takes at least two seasons of growth to produce flowering-size corms. Flower color varies but is always in the red, orange, gold or yellow tones. Not very hardy, crocosmias should be treated like gladioli, to which they are closely related: plant in spring and lift in late summer in all but the warmer climates, where they will easily overwinter. A good cut flower, they will grow in full sun or light shade.

C. aurea (*aw*-ree-uh).
Up to 36 in. in height. Golden-yellow flowers on 24- to 36-in. spikes that branch, each carrying many flowers, often more than a total of thirty on one spike. Starts flowering in late summer and continues into fall. Individual flowers are often 2 in. in diameter. Leaves are narrow, arranged in a fan shape, 12 in. long. Zones 9 to 10.

C. × crocosmiiflora (crow-kos-mee-i-*flor*-uh).
A hybrid of *C. aurea* and *C. pottsii*. Foliage is sword-shaped, held in a fan shape. The flower

Crocosmia × *crocosmiiflora* cultivar

Crocosmia

Crocosmia x *crocosmiiflora* cultivar

spike zigzags to a height of 36 in. and carries many star-shaped orange-scarlet flowers that open over a long period starting in Aug.

There have been a number of hybrids introduced recently. In many cases the exact parentage is obscure. These plants are, however, listed under *Crocosmia* in the catalogs. Some outstanding hybrids are 'Jenny Bloom', a free-flowering plant with deep yellow trumpet-shaped flowers; 'Firebird', with rich flame-colored flowers; and 'Lucifer', with very long-lasting flowers of a good red color. The latter is reported to have flowers that last up to three weeks when used as a cut flower. The parentage of 'Lucifer' is given as a cross between *Crocosmia* and *Curtonus*. It is regarded as being hardier than many other plants of this type, wintering in Zurich, Switz. and Hartford, Conn. without any problems. Gardeners in colder areas may well wish to try this plant. Zones 5 to 8.

★★Crocus (*kroh*-kus).

Iris Family (*Iridaceae*).

Native to the Medit. region and Asia, these are the most popular of all spring-blooming bulbs, although several species flower in the fall and some in the winter. They are characterized by narrow, grasslike leaves (usually with the edges turned back and a white or silver streak along the midrib) growing directly from the round, slightly flattened corm. The low funnel-shaped flowers also grow directly from the corm and are white, pink, lavender, purple, yellow or orange, sometimes streaked or mottled. Although corms are often referred to as "bulbs," crocuses actually have roots correctly referred to as "corms," which are solid bulblike parts that grow below ground, being part of the stem modified for storage.

The hardy spring-flowering crocus is planted extensively in colder regions, where it is espe-

Crocus aureus
DUTCH CROCUS

cially appreciated for its early spring show of color. When the last snow is still white in the shaded areas, and grass and brush are brown and lifeless, crocuses bunched where the sun is hottest suddenly bloom in patches of gold, blue or white that the eye can't quite believe. They are charming clumped by stepping-stones and planted to carpet the earth beneath mature azaleas or rhododendrons, but they are perhaps most effective massed in naturalized settings backed by rock outcroppings or woodland. *C. tomasinianus* is an excellent species to plant in the lawn and its self-sown lavender and silver-gray seedlings spread with surprising speed.

The small winter-flowering crocuses are now better known and much more popular than they were, thanks to improved varieties. Where snow is deep and stays late, they are likely to bloom simultaneously with later-flowering species. But where snow is sparse in winter, they pop out well before spring.

Crocus

Crocus chrysanthus 'Cream Beauty'

Autumn-flowering crocuses last beyond the late asters. Plant them in areas that will not be mowed after the autumnal equinox (about Sept. 23 in the N. Hemisphere), around tree bases, in the flower border or in naturalized pockets. Ordered in spring or late summer, the bulbs should go into the ground as soon as they arrive and will bloom the first season. (*Colchicum*, which belongs to the lily family, is also called autumn crocus.)

Crocuses should be planted 3 to 4 in. deep and 2 to 3 in. apart in light, well-drained soil that is moist in the growing season and preferably dry the rest of the year. They do best in full sun, but some species will take partial shade. As with all bulbous plants, the foliage must be allowed to mature naturally if flowers are to be produced the following year. Propagate by removing bulb offsets or by sowing seeds. Left on their own, crocuses multiply rapidly. Although very hardy, species that bloom too early or too late may lose their flowers in severe frost. Crocuses may be grown in pots. Pot the corms in a basic potting mixture in fall, store in a cool, dark place till late winter and set on windowsills to bloom. Not always persistent in regions warmer than zone 7.

C. aureus (*aw*-ree-us).
DUTCH CROCUS OR DUTCH YELLOW.
Bright golden-yellow to orange flowers. An old

Crocus chrysanthus 'Blue Pearl'

and very popular species but now correctly called *C. flavus* (*flay*-vus). Flowers in very early spring, sometimes even in Jan. 3 to 4 in. in height. Zones 4 to 8.

C. chrysanthus (chris-*san*-thus).
The species has bright orange flowers feathered with bronze and orange anthers. Many of today's crocus hybrids were developed from this species and are grown and are thus listed under *C. chrysanthus*. The heights of these will vary, the majority being in the 3- to 4-in.-tall range. The leaves, which are produced with the flowers, reach up to 10 in. in length. 'Advance' is violet outside, yellow inside. 'Blue Pearl' is a soft blue with bronzy base and golden-yellow throat. 'Cream Beauty' is a soft creamy yellow, while 'E. A. Bowles' is a deep buttery yellow with bronze feathering. 'Fuscotinctus' (fuss-coh-*tinct*-tus) is a rich golden yellow, thought to be a selection from the species. 'Snow Bunting' has a white interior, the outer petals creamy with dark lilac feathering. 'White Triumphator' is a pure white with a yellow center. Zones 3 to 8.

C. fleischeri (*flesh*-her-eye).
White flowers striped with purple at the base. One of the first species to flower, often in late Jan. or early Feb., 2 to 3 in. in height with leaves up to 12 in. long. Zones 3 to 9.

C. goulimyi (ghoul-*lim*-ee-eye).
Flowers in Oct. or Nov. and has soft lilac flowers 3 to 4 in. in height. Zones 3 to 8.

C. kotschyanus (kot-she-*ay*-nus).
(Syn. *C. zonatus*.) One of the finest fall-flowering crocuses. The 12-in.-long leaves have a white band in the center and appear after the flowers, persisting through the winter. Large flowers of pale lilac with an orange band on the inside base

Crocus

Crocus sieberi

Crocus tomasinianus

Crocus speciosus

Crocus vernus

of the petals. It produces a lot of little corms (cormels) and increases rapidly. Well worth growing in any garden. Zones 3 to 8.

C. pulchellus (pull-*kel*-us).
Pale lilac flowers with darker veining, yellow throats and white anthers are produced in Sept. Foliage appears after flowering, maturing the following spring. One of the taller species, reaching 6 in. in height. Zone 6.

C. sativus (sat-*tye*-vus).
SAFFRON CROCUS.
Lilac purple with particularly deep throats. The unusual orange-red stigma, from which saffron is produced, is very large, often protruding beyond the closed flower and flopping to one side. The autumn flowers are quite large, up to 6 in. in height. The variety *C. sativus* var. *cashmerianus* (cash-mare-ee-*ay*-nus) has flowers that are slender with pointed segments. Zones 5 to 8.

C. sieberi (see-*bur*-eye).
A lovely species with fragrant white flowers stained purple on the exterior and having a yellow throat. It has a tapered, rounded perianth tube. Only 2 to 3 in. in height, it flowers in spring. Several selections are listed in catalogs, among them 'Firefly', a vivid lilac-pink with orange stamens; 'Violet Queen', violet with orange throat; and 'Bowles White', a pure white. Zones 3 to 9.

C. speciosus (spee-*see*-oh-sus).
Perhaps one of the easiest of the autumn-flowering crocuses to grow. The flowers are quite large, 5 to 6 in. in height, deep violet-blue but variable. Flowers are produced in Sept and Oct. Selections include 'Artabir' (*are*-tah-beer), a lavender-lilac-blue with a hint of white under the inner petals, a creamy white throat, a slight fragrance and reaching 5 to 6 in. in height, and

'Oxonian' (ox-*oh*-nee-an), with large blue flowers on blue stems. Zones 4 to 8.

C. susianus (su-see-*ay*-nus).
CLOTH-OF-GOLD.
A dwarf species only 2 in. in height. Deep golden yellow tinged with mahogany on the outside. Foliage reaches 10 in. in length. Early spring flowering, often in March. Zones 3 to 9.

C. tomasinianus (toe-mass-sin-ee-*ay*-nus)
With a long white throat and pale lavender petals that are often silvery-gray on the outside, this is a lovely March-flowering species which grows to 6 in. in height. The species seeds freely, and many forms and variations are known. Among them are 'Barr's Purple', rich purple-lilac, and 'Ruby Giant', a free-flowering deep violet-purple. Zones 3 to 9.

C. vernus (*ver*-nus).
COMMON CROCUS.
This is the wild crocus of the Alps and Pyrenees. Very variable in color, from pure white to purple, it has given birth to numerous selections. Flowers from Feb. to April. Height is around 3 in., and if happy with their situation they will increase in size rapidly. Among the selections offered are 'Grand Maître', a lavender-violet; 'Haarlem Gem', a lilac-blue; 'Joan of Arc', a pure white; 'Peter Pan', white with orange stamens; 'Pickwick', a white with lilac stripes; 'Remembrance', a silvery-purple and one of the earliest to flower; 'Snowstorm', ivory white with a purple base; 'Vanguard', a grayish blue; 'Yellow Mammoth', with large yellow flowers; and 'Purpurea Grandiflora', which has large flowers of purple-blue and is a good selection for growing in containers. Zones 3 to 9.

C. zonatus. See *C. kotschyanus*.

Cyclamen

Cyclamen coum

Cyclamen neapolitanum
IVY-LEAVED CYCLAMEN

Cyclamen (*sick*-lah-men).

Primrose Family (*Primulaceae*).

Native to the lands around the Medit., the "florist's cyclamen" is probably the best known species, but there are some 60 different species, all tuberous. A number of species are delightful garden plants and several are great woodland plants. All species thrive in rich, well-drained soil in partial shade. Tubers should be planted with the tops right at soil level, and spaced 3 to 5 in. apart. The popular indoor plants are easily raised from seed sown in Aug. for flowering about 15 months later. Seed should be sown in a regular potting mix with additional sand. Transplant the seedlings when they are large enough to handle, potting them into small individual pots. After about 120 days they should be moved to larger pots, in which they will flower. Temperature throughout their growing season must be cool, in the region of 55°F at night. Just before they flower, increase temperatures by about 10°F. Although plants that have flowered are often discarded, they can be grown outdoors in Zones 9 to 11. Plant them in a cool, shady place, making sure the tuber is at (and not below) soil level. They may lose their leaves but will soon recover and perform quite well. If the plants are kept in pots, allow them to dry out somewhat after the flowers have passed; the foliage will soon turn yellow and should then be removed. In late summer repot them and start to give moisture; leaves, followed by flowers, will be produced. Be careful not to expose the plants to direct sunlight, but keep them moist and cool and in the shade.

C. coum (koo-*um*).

This is a lovely spring-flowering, if very variable, species. Some authorities regard the different types as geographic variants, others give subspecies stature to each of the variants. It flowers between Dec. and March. Leaves are rounded, with few markings; the undersides are a dull crimson. Plant in light shade where the plants will receive good moisture during their growing season. Unlike many species, they should be placed about 1 in. deep. The flowers will often creep a short distance underground before emerging. The pure white 'Album' is an attractive cultivar. All plants of the species will survive temperatures down to 0°F provided there is snow cover. Zones 6 to 9.

C. hederifolium. See *C. neapolitanum.*

C. neapolitanum (nee-uh-pol-i-*tay*-num).
IVY-LEAVED CYCLAMEN.
NEAPOLITAN CYCLAMEN.
BABY CYCLAMEN.
(Syn. *C. hederifolium*) Native to Europe. The tubers are large, often more than 3 in. in diameter, and produce roots from the upper surface only. Free-flowering, the white to carmine flowers are 3 to 6 in. in height, produced in late summer, with the full complement of leaves appearing with the later flowers. Leaves are varied in shape, some round, others ivy- or lance-shaped. Plants soon become quite large and are ideal for bordering a path, as the flowers should be enjoyed close up. The cultivar 'Album' produces pretty white flowers. Zones 5 to 9.

C. pseudibericum (sue-di-*beer*-i-cum)
Possibly a variant of *C. coum*. The leaves have a serrated edge, often with yellowish-green mottling with crimson undersurface. Flowers in Feb. or March, 4 to 5 in. in height, large and fragrant blooms, dark purplish-crimson. Not very hardy; grow in protected areas even in Zone 8.

✶✶**Dahlia** (*dal*-yuh)
Composite Family (*Compositae*)
Native to Mex. and C. Amer., these tuberous plants produce very colorful and attractive flowers from midsummer until frost, and are great additions to the summer garden. Each tuber will produce a number of stout stems, which are hollow and jointed; dark green, compound leaves arise from the joints. The height will vary from 1 ft. to over 12 ft., but the tallest species are seldom grown. Dahlias can be used as cut flowers, but make sure to seal the hollow stems by dipping the ends in hot water. Easy to grow and tolerant of a wide range of soils, the tubers should be set 3 to 4 in. deep about ten days before the last expected frost. Space plants 6 to 36 in. apart, depending on ultimate plant size at maturity. Where winter temperatures stay above freezing, the tubers can be left in the ground, but in other areas lift after the first frost and store over winter in a frost-free, well-ventilated area.

During the growing season dahlias appreciate moisture, along with feeding at regular intervals until the flowers start to appear. Taller-growing types may need staking, but the lower-growing cultivars do not. All require full sun. The color range is extensive, with the exception of blue, the closest color being some of the lavenders. Propagation is by seed for the bedding types, sown in late March (or earlier in warmer areas); keep temperatures in the 50°F range at night, gradually hardening off the plants so they can be set outside after all frost has passed. Large tubers can be divided, but each portion must have its own "eye"—the growing bud that can be found on the stem. If no bud is present, there will be no growth. Cuttings, taken when the shoots are 3 to 4 in. long, are easy to root in a sandy soil mix.

When dahlias were first introduced into gardens, there were only three forms. Today there are many, and they are arranged in classes as listed below.

A great selection of many different types and colors of dahlias can be found in catalogs and

Dahlia

DAHLIAS

The dahlia was named in honor of Dr. Andreas Dahl, an eighteenth-century Swedish botanist and a pupil of Carolus Linnaeus. It was brought to Spain from its native Mex. in the late 1780s. While there are perhaps a dozen species of dahlia found in the wild in Mex., C. Amer. and Colombia, the great majority of plants grown today are variants of the true species and hybrids raised from variants that have arisen in cultivation. Aztec gardeners already had selected variants or hybrids long before the dahlia's introduction in Eur. The first cultivation was to exploit the plant's potential as a vegetable. The flower petals can be eaten and give color to a salad. (If they are to be used in this manner, it is essential that they have not been sprayed with any chemical.) The roots were used as food by the natives in Mex., but were not regarded with favor by Europeans. They do contain a valuable and healthful starchy substance called inulin, which is used today in the manufacture of certain chemicals. While used at one time in the preparation of a diabetic sugar, the contribution of the roots to medicine is in the testing of liver and kidney function.

The flowers are carried on long stalks. Although most species in the wild produce only single flowers, some, such as *D. variabilis*, have been found to produce many semidoubles. In singles, those known as perfect flowers have a yellow disk in the center, which is surrounded by ray florets. These are male flowers, where the pistils are petaloid. There is great variation in color. In doubles, the number of male flowers is greatly increased, and these are petaloid. Dahlias are not necessarily self-sterile, but the male pollen is ripe before the stigma is receptive, and the flowers are thus seldom self-pollinated.

The stem produced by a Dahlia tuber extends until a bud is produced at the top of the stem. Once the bud appears, extension growth of this main stem stops and the production of side shoots is stimulated. In some hybrids there is some side growth, but it is slow until the first bud is produced. For this reason this first bud is often known as the break bud. Many growers often pinch out the growing shoot after the plants have produced from four to six pairs of good, strong leaves, or when the plant has grown to a height of 10 to 12 in. This stimulates side growth and thus a bushier plant is produced.

A number of flower buds will be apparent at the top of the stems that carry the flowers. If all are allowed to develop, flower size will be reduced. If some buds are nipped out as soon as they appear, those that remain will produce larger flowers. Carried to the extreme, if only one bud is allowed to develop, the largest possible flower will be produced. (This is not the aim for most home gardeners, but it is of great interest for those producing flowers for exhibition or flower shows.) In general, it will take about six weeks from the time buds are removed until another series of buds is formed and about three weeks longer for the buds to open. The actual time span depends on the time of the year, temperature and light, as well as on the vigor of the plants. It should be noted, however, that pinching to form sturdier and bushier plants also delays the flowering.

Flowers to be enjoyed in home arrangements must be cut in the morning and must be fully open. After harvest, immerse the stems in warm (120°F) water. Then store the cut flowers in 39° to 41°F water, where they will last for several days. As with all flowers, no foliage should be allowed to remain on that part of the stem which is in the water, as the foliage will quickly rot. Also, if the cut stems are kept inside in low light, the leaves will quickly yellow, so it is best to place only a few stems in each vase and thus allow the light to reach the foliage.

When should Dahlia tubers be lifted? First, before the onset of any frost, make sure to label the plants; it is difficult to remember the flower color type when all you have is the tuber in hand. Next, allow the tubers to ripen as much as possible. A sign of ripening is that the plants seem to tire, blooms are poorly colored and become daisy-eyed, and bud production is slowed.

After a hot, dry summer, plants usually ripen quickly and lifting should be done in mid- to late Oct. But even in a late ripening season the tubers will be ready by early Nov. Cut the remaining foliage right down to soil level, if possible cutting the stem through a node where it will be solid. If you cut above or just below a node, the hollow stem will present a good spot for rain to collect, hastening spoiling. If the weather is dry, let the tubers stay in the ground for a week to ten days, the theory being that in

such a period the buds below ground will start to develop even if they do not break into growth. If, however, there is rain in the forecast, lift as soon as you can.

To lift, take a spade and cut into the soil about 8 to 10 in. away from the stem. Lift gently to pry the roots away from the soil. When all roots have been loosened, place the spade right under the tuber and firmly remove it with the ball of soil. Remove all loose soil, but leave some on the tuber to prevent loss of moisture. If the weather is dry, allow the tubers to remain outdoors for a day or two, as this will give them a chance to dry. In rainy weather or if there is danger of frost, take them indoors at once.

After a few days, more soil will have dried and can be removed. Once the tubers are more or less clean, keep them in a place where the temperature will remain in the 40° to 45° range and which is neither very dry nor very moist. They should never be exposed to frost. Shelves that are made up of slats a few inches apart are ideal, as they allow good air circulation. The tubers can be stored close together and covered with sand or peat, but be sure not to cover the stems, just the tubers.

Each month, check the tubers to make sure they are not shriveling, which will happen if they are kept too warm or too dry. Check also for any soft spots; remove them with a sharp knife and dust the cut surfaces with a fungicide to prevent rot. There is no need to worry if a small percentage of the tuber has to be removed. With just a little care, your dahlia tubers will overwinter easily.

Dahlia

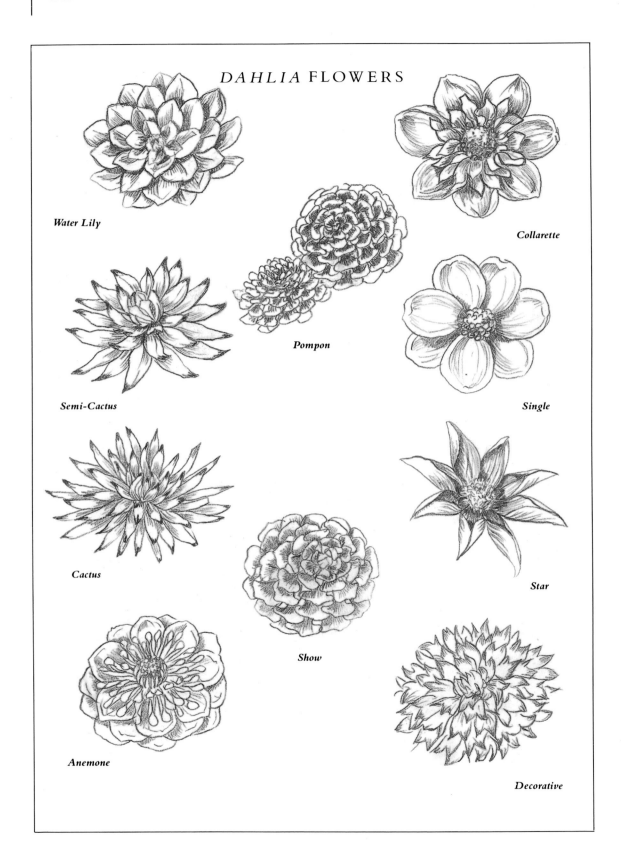

DAHLIA FLOWERS

Water Lily

Collarette

Pompon

Semi-Cactus

Single

Cactus

Star

Show

Anemone

Decorative

nurseries. Select tubers that are not shriveled but plump, preferably with an obvious "eye;" young plants should have good color and stout, sturdy stems. The following are particularly good cultivars.

Single Dahlias.

There are three subdivisions:
Show Singles–with heads not more than 3 in. across; Singles–petals not overlapping; Mignons–plants not more than 18 in. high.

'G.F. Hemerik', soft orange, 14 to 20 in. in height.

'Irene van der Zwet', soft yellow, 4 to 20 in. in height.

'Murillo', lilac-pink with a darker center, 14 to 20 in. in height.

'Nelly Geerlings', bright red, 10 to 12 in. in height.

'Sneezy', pure white, 16 to 20 in. in height.

Anemone-flowered Dahlias.

These have a dense group of tubular florets in the center of the flowers.

'Honey', apricot-pink, 10 to 18 in. in height.

'Sweden', rich yellow, 10 to 18 in. in height.

Collarette Dahlias.

There are three subdivisions:
Collarette Singles—having a single row of outer petals, a row of collarettes (usually of another color) and a yellow disk; Collarette Peony-flowered—two or three series of outer petals, then a collar and a yellow disk in the center; Collarette Decorative—fully double flowers.

'Awaikoe' (ah-*way*-koh), deep mahogany-red with white collar, 6 to 40 in. in height.

'Jack O'Lantern', Indian-orange with yellow collar, 48 in. in height.

Dahlia 'Claire de Lune'
COLLARETTE DAHLIA

Dahlia 'Christine'
FORMAL DECORATIVE DAHLIA

Dahlia

Peony-flowered Dahlias.
There are four subdivisions, based on size, all having two or three series of ray florets and a central disk: Large—more than 7 in. across; Medium—5 to 7 in. across; Small—less than 5 in. across; Dwarf—plants not more than 30 in. in height.

'Japanese Bishop', dark orange with almost black foliage, an older but lovely free-flowering cultivar, 36 in. in height.

Formal Decorative Dahlias.
These are fully double, all florets regularly arranged with margins slightly incurved, flattened tips.

'Daniel Edward', bright fuchsia-purple, 48 in. in height.

'Duet', red and white, 36 in. in height.

'Edinburgh', maroon and white, 36 in. in height.

Dahlia 'Viola'
COLLARETTE DAHLIA

Informal Decorative Dahlias.
Fully double, no disk, but rays not regularly arranged, more or less flat or slightly twisted.

'Envy', rich red, 36 to 48 in. in height.

'Playboy', pure yellow, 60 in. in height.

'Purple Taiheijo' (tie-*hee*-oh), purple, 48 in. in height.

Show Dahlias.
Flowers more than 3 in. across, almost globular; central florets similar to outer but smaller, margins incurved, tubular or cup-shaped, short and blunt at mouth.

Pompon Dahlias.
Similar to Show dahlias but not more than 2 in. across.

'Albino', pure white 36 to 48 in. in height.

'Lipoma', rose-pink, 36 in. in height.

'Nero', dark red with purple sheen, 36 to 48 in. in height.

Dahlia 'Hamari Gold'
INFORMAL DECORATIVE DAHLIA

'Yellow Gem', a clear yellow, 36 to 48 in. in height.

Cactus Dahlias.

Fully double flowers, margins revolute for not less than three-quarters of their length. Divided again by size:

Large are more than 4½ in. across; Small are under 4 in. across; and Dwarf are plants under 30 in. tall.

'Apple Blossom', rose with lighter center, 36 to 60 in. in height.

'Doris Day', cardinal-red, 42 in. in height.

'My Love', giant flowers of creamy white, 48 in. in height.

'Orchid Lace', white with purple tips, 60 in. in height.

Semi-cactus Dahlias.

Similar to previous class, but margins revolute

Dahlia 'Athalie'
CACTUS DAHLIA

Dahlia 'Abridge Ben'
SHOW DAHLIA

Dahlia 'Apple Blossom'
CACTUS DAHLIA

Dahlia

Dahlia 'Evening Mail'
SEMI-CACTUS DAHLIA

Dahlia 'Bishop of Llandaff'
SINGLE DAHLIA

Dahlia 'Flutterby'
WATER LILY DAHLIA

Dahlia 'Zorro'
POMPON DAHLIA

toward the tip, slightly twisted for about half their length. Again there are subclasses according to size.

Star Dahlias.

These have small flowers, with two or three series of slightly pointed rays barely overlapping, with more or less recurved margins.

These very popular plants have received a lot of attention from hybridizers, and each year new selections are listed in catalogs. There is good reason for dahlias' popularity, as they are colorful, easy to grow and not subject to many pests or diseases. Aphids and thrips may make an appearance but can be controlled with an application of insecticidal soap. (Check with your nursery for the correct product to use, and always follow the directions on the product label.) Ask your County Agent for advice if you run into any problem in your garden; he or she will know the problems that are to be expected in your area.

Dahlias from seed for bedding:

'Redskin', mixed colors, 12 to 14 in. in height.

'Rigoletto', mixed colors, doubles, 12 in. in height.

D. imperialis (im-peer-i-*ay*-lis).

Tall growing, this species can reach 10 to 15 ft. in height and has daisylike lavender to pale lavender, almost white, flowers produced late in summer. It is more of a novelty but is unusual. Often frost will kill the tops before the flowers appear, except in warmer areas. Zone 10.

Dierama (*dee*-ah-ram-ah).

ANGELS' FISHING ROD.

Iris Family (*Iridaceae*).

This S. Afr. cormous plant produces flower spikes that reach over 60 in. in height. These are thin, almost grasslike, and from the stalk hang

purple to carmine-red bell-shaped flowers from midsummer to late summer. The flowers are 2 in. in diameter and the spike waves in the slightest breeze. The corms should be planted in full sun, 3 to 5 in. deep and 12 to 18 in. apart. The plants like moisture and are ideal planted where the spikes reach out over water. Once planted leave them undisturbed except to propagate which can be accomplished by lifting and dividing the corms.

Dierama pulcherrimum
ANGELS' FISHING ROD

D. pulcherrimum (pull-*keer*-ri-mum).

Leaves are stiff and dark green, 36 in. in length and 2 to 3 in. wide. The tall, slender flowering spike emerges from the center of the clumped foliage. The species is variable in color in shades of red or pink to white. Several selections are to be found in catalogs, including 'Heron', a wine red; 'Kingfisher', pale purplish-red; and 'Windhover', a bright rose-pink. These all deserve a place in perennial borders in warmer areas of the country. Zone 8 in sheltered locations.

Dietes (*dye*-ee-teez).

Iris Family (*Iridaceae*).

There are several species native to trop. and S. Afr. but only one is commonly grown.

D. bicolor (*bye*-cul-or).

A native of S. Afr. and one of the S. Hemisphere's answers to its lack of a true Iris. The rootstock is a

Dietes

rhizome, and these should be planted just below the surface of the soil and spaced 18 in. apart. Flowers are produced throughout the summer months, but more heavily in early summer. They are cream, with brown blotches at the base of the broader petals, and are carried on branching stems to a height of 24 in. or more. Foliage is sword-shaped and broad, tapering to a fine point, and is evergreen. Hardy only in areas where the winters are mild, the plants can be grown in other areas in containers and protected during the winter months; they will not withstand any but the lightest of frosts. Lifting and dividing the rhizomes in late summer is the best way to propagate them. They can be used effectively in the garden in full sun but must have moisture and are thus ideal for planting alongside streams and pools, as well as in the border. Zone 9.

Eranthis (ee-*ran*-thiss).
WINTER ACONITE.
Buttercup Family (*Ranunculaceae*).
Hardy tuberous perennials from Eur. and Asia. In mid- to late winter each tuber produces a single flowering stem 3 to 6 in. high just above the rosette of leaves, which hug the ground. The little tubers hate to be dry, so plant as soon as you obtain them, in an area with good light such as in a shrub border or in open woodland areas where shade is not dense, especially during the winter months. Plant 1 in. deep, 3 in. apart, in masses, and allow them to naturalize. Lift only to divide, which should be done right after they have finished flowering.

E. cilicica (sill-*liss*-ih-cuh).
Foliage is bronzy-green. Flowers are deep yellow, a little earlier in flower than the species below, blooming in Jan. Zones 3 to 9.

Eranthis hyemalis
WINTER ACONITE

E. hyemalis (hi-em-*may*-liss).
Bright yellow cuplike flowers, 1½ in. in diameter, appear in Feb.–March. This species appreciates shade during the summer. Zones 3 to 9.

Eremurus (err-e-*mew*-rus).
FOXTAIL LILY.
DESERT-CANDLE.
Lily Family (*Liliaceae*).
Native to western and central Asia. The rootstock of this plant is shaped like a starfish and is brittle. Foliage is linear and straplike, its length varying by species. Tall, unbranched flower spikes are covered with many closely spaced small flowers of white, yellow or pink. The stalks often reach more than 6 ft. in height, making this one of the most spectacular tuberous-rooted plants to flower in early summer. Plant in Sept. in rich, well-drained soil in a sunny location, at least 6 in. deep and 36 in. apart. Eremurus must have

Eremurus x *shelford*
FOXTAIL LILY

good moisture during the growing season, less after they have finished flowering, but should never be allowed to completely dry out. Protect with straw if late frosts are expected, which would harm the developing spike; the plants are quite hardy, however, and in fact prefer to have some frost and do not flower well in warmer climates. The preferred method of propagation is to lift and divide the rootstocks of established plants as soon as the foliage has died down.

E. bungei. See *E. stenophyllus.*

E. himalaicus (him-uh-*lay*-eh-cuss).
Produces a flower spike 36 in. or more in height, crowded with pure white flowers. Foliage is about 12 to 18 in. long. Flowers in May. Zone 5.

E. robustus (roh-*buss*-tuss).
More than 72 in. in height with 4-in.-wide leaves, which are 48 in. long. Large, deep pink flowers

often cover more than 48 in. of the spike. June-flowering. Zone 5.

✷ **E. × shelford** (shell-*ford*).
The species has orange-buff flowers, but there are a number of cultivars offered in catalogs, including 'Cleopatra', with orange-pink flowers, and 'Moneymaker', with yellow-orange flowers. Flowering in early summer, these striking plants, 48 to 60 in. tall, are worthy of a place in any perennial border. Zone 5.

E. stenophyllus (sten-oh-*fye*-lus).
A shorter flower spike than most, only 24 to 36 in. in height. Leaves are long and narrow. Bright yellow flowers in early June. There are often selections such as 'Magnificus' or 'Sulphureus', listed in catalogs. Zone 5.

Erythronium (err-ih-*throw*-nee-um).
DOGTOOTH VIOLET.
ADDER'S-TONGUE.
TROUT LILY.
Lily Family (*Liliaceae*).
Hardy perennial corms, mostly native to N. Amer. The corms generally produce two leaves and a single slender flower stalk carrying a single flower, or as many as eight flowers, depending on the species. Flowers are lilylike, with narrow reflexed petals, and mostly around 12 in. in height. Most species flower in March or April. They grow in a wide range of soils, preferring those rich in organic matter with good moisture during their growing season and then enjoy a drier time in late summer and fall. Plant 3 to 4 in. deep, 8 to 10 in. apart, with some partial shade during the heat of the day. Grow in an area where they can remain undisturbed. Propagate by lifting and dividing when the foliage has almost disappeared, replanting at once. Sow seed as soon as it is ripe, but have patience as it takes six to eight weeks to

Erythronium

germinate. Never allow the seeds to dry out, and transplant when the seedlings are large enough to handle. It will take about three years to raise flowering-size plants. Erythronium make lovely plants in the woodland, rock or wild gardens.

E. americanum (ah-mare-i-*cay*-num).
COMMON FAWN-LILY.
The leaves are mottled purple and white. Height is 4 to 8 in. The corms produce stolons, which allow this species to spread, so give it room. The solitary flowers are yellow, April-flowering. Zones 3 to 9.

E. dens-canis (denz-*cay*-nis).
EUROPEAN FAWN-LILY.
Colors of the solitary flowers range from white through pink to dark purple. Loves to be in woodland settings, where it grows easily, reaching 12 in. in height and flowering from March to

Erythronium dens-canis
EUROPEAN FAWN-LILY

Erythronium revolutum

April. Leaves are heavily marbled, brown to bluish-green. Zones 2 to 7.

E. revolutum (rev-voh-*lute*-tum).
This species grows on the Pacific coast where summer moisture is provided by fog. Up to 12 in. in height. Flower color ranges from pure white to rose-pink, some with yellow or almost orange centers. Normally four to five flowers per stem appear in late April. Leaves are mottled. Cultivars are often listed, such as 'White Beauty', which is 4 to 5 in. in height, pure white with colored basal markings. Zones 5 to 9.

E. tuolumnense (tool-lume-*nen*-see).
The leaves are not mottled. Deep golden-yellow flowers open wide, so as to be almost flat, in March and early April, one to four per stem, 12 in. in height. Easy to grow, increases rapidly. The cultivar 'Pagoda' is a little taller and has larger sulfur-yellow flowers. Zones 3 to 9.

Erythronium toulumnense 'Pagoda'

✷✷ **Freesia** (*free*-zee-uh).

Iris Family (*Iridaceae*).

Tender, cormous plants from S. Afr. A number of named cultivars are offered by nurseries, and among these are both single- and double-flowered types. Thin, sword-shaped, light green leaves up to 1½ ft. high, with a slender flower stalk about the same height. As many as eight funnel-shaped flowers form a loose cluster at the top of each stalk and are sometimes fragrant. Where the flowers begin, the stem makes a sharp bend, so that the flowers face upward. Freesias may be grown outdoors only in warm climates, but even there they are so delicate and likely to be damaged by wind and rain that it is better to grow them in pots. In the North they are easily grown for winter flowering indoors. The corms should be planted rather close—six to a 5-in. pot—in a light, well-drained soil, with the top of each corm 1 in. below the surface of the soil. If they are planted in late summer or early fall, kept fairly cool until frosts are due and then brought inside, they may be kept on a windowsill or on a greenhouse bench to complete their growth cycle. They need full sun, a rather cool atmosphere (preferably 45° to 50°F at night) and plenty of water while leaves and flowers are developing. When the leaves begin to brown after the flowers have faded, the plants may be gradually dried off and the corms saved for the following year. Propagate by offsets and seeds. Zones 8 to 10.

Recommended Singles:
'Blue Wimple', a light blue;
'Matterhorn', a white;
'Royal Gold', a rich yellow;
'Washington', with orange flowers.

Recommended Doubles:
'Golden Crown', a deep gold;
'Princess Marijke', an orange;
'Royal Blue', blue;
'Snowdon', a white.

Freesia ✕ *hybrida*

Fritillaria

Fritillaria imperialis 'Lutea'
CROWN IMPERIAL

Fritillaria imperialis 'Rubra Maxima'
CROWN IMPERIAL

Fritillaria (frit-i-*lay*-ree-uh).

FRITILLARY.

Lily Family (*Liliaceae*).

Hardy bulbs native to western N. Amer., Eur., Asia, and N. Afr. Nodding flowers, some interestingly marked, blooming in spring. There is a wide variety of forms, sizes and colors. Plants require a deep, humus soil, well drained but never dry, and thrive in full sun or half shade. Most species have the peculiar habit of flowering in alternate years, sending up in the nonflowering year leaves that are somewhat different from those produced with flowers. Propagate by bulb offsets or seeds.

✱**F. imperialis** (im-peer-*ay*-lis).

CROWN IMPERIAL.

From Persia, suitable for grouping in the sunny flower border or in pockets of deep soil in the lower parts of a rock garden. It must have perfect drainage. The bulb is round and fleshy and has a

skunklike smell. It should be planted 6 to 8 in. deep, with at least 1 ft. of porous soil containing leafmold under it. In heavy soil, tip the bulb on its side. A cluster of wavy-edged, pointed leaves 6 to 8 in. long appears in early spring, and later in the season the flower spike pushes up through the center of this, to a height of from 2 to 4 ft., with a tight cluster of narrow leaves at the top. Under these leaves the flowers hang like a cluster of bells. Flowers are usually terra-cotta, but red, orange and yellow forms are available, including 'Aurora', with orange-red flowers; 'Lutea' (*lew*-tee-uh), golden yellow; and 'Rubra Maxima' (*rue*-bra *max*-i-ma), which has orange flowers with a hint of brown. Zone 5.

F. meleagris (mel-ee-*ay*-griss).

GUINEA-HEN FLOWER.

CHECKERED LILY.

Graceful woodland perennial. The stem grows to a height of 2 ft., with three narrow leaves and a

Fritillaria meleagris
CHECKERED LILY

Galanthus elwesii
GIANT SNOWDROP

single flower at the top. Flower color is dark red checkered with purple. Several cultivars are available, including 'Alba', a pure white. Zone 6.

F. michailovskyi (mick-ale-*ov*-skee-eye).
A lovely and comparatively recent introduction from Turkey. At 6 in. in height, the plant produces one to five pendant bells of dark reddish-purple with a gray bloom, the upper third of each segment bright yellow. Zone 8 with protection.

F. pallidiflora (pall-i-di-*floor*-uh).
Flowering in mid- to late spring, this species has up to twelve bell-shaped flowers arising from the leaf axils at the top of each 2-ft. stem. They are creamy-yellow to greenish-yellow with red or brown spots on the inside of the petals. Zone 5.

F. persica (*purr*-si-kuh).
One of the tallest, reaching 36 in. in height. Often as many as thirty small flowers per stem, dark

plum in color and long lasting. The cultivar 'Adiyaman' (ad-i-*yah*-man), named for the town near where it was found, is slightly taller. May-flowering; given light shade these flowers will last even longer. Zone 6.

Galanthus (ga-*lan*-thus).
SNOWDROP.
Amaryllis Family (*Amaryllidaceae*).
Hardy bulbs from Eur. and Asia Minor. Two or three straplike, dark green leaves grow from each bulb. The white flowers are usually borne singly, mostly in early spring but sometimes in mid- to late winter, which makes them the earliest of the flowering bulbs. These are very similar to snowflakes (*Leucojum*) but are smaller. The three inner petals have green tips and overlap the outer petals to form a tube. The bulbs should be planted 3 to 4 in. deep in early autumn, in fertile soil. They will thrive in full sun or partial shade. Excellent in rock gardens or as edging plants. May be left

Galanthus

Galanthus nivalis
COMMON SNOWDROP

undisturbed for many years. Propagate by bulb offsets or seeds. Best moved just as the flowers fade, rather than as dormant bulbs.

G. elwesii (el-*wee*-see-eye).
GIANT SNOWDROP.
Bluish-green leaves to 8 in. high and ¾ in. across, flowers borne on stalks to 1 ft., in winter or very early spring. Lower half of the inner segments, as well as the tips, flushed green. May flower even earlier than the following species. Zone 6.

G. nivalis (ni-*vay*-lis).
COMMON SNOWDROP.
Leaves about 8 in. high and ¼ in. across. Blooms from Jan. to early March. Flowers about 1 in. across, borne in early spring on 1-ft. stalks. Several varieties, differing chiefly in the placement and size of the green petal markings, are available, as well as the very large double-flowered form 'Flore Pleno' (*floh*-ree *plee*-noh). Among the best

are 'Simplex,' white with large, single blossoms, and *G. nivalis* ssp. *reginae-olgae* (ree-*ji*-nah ol-*gay*), which is unusual in that it flowers in the fall. Zones 3 to 9.

Galtonia (gol-*toh*-nee-uh).
SUMMER HYACINTH.
Lily Family (*Liliaceae*).
S. Afr. bulbs with straplike leaves and flower spikes vaguely like those of tall hyacinths in late summer. May be used in permanent outdoor plantings in warm climates, or with winter protection as far north as Wash., D.C. In the North, galtonias do well if handled like gladiolus. The bulbs should be dug and stored before frost for replanting in late spring. The white flower spikes appear in late summer, making a good accent for the taller part of a flower border. Propagate by planting bulb offsets in early spring. This is an excellent pot plant for the greenhouse or the plant room.

Galtonia candicans
SUMMER HYACINTH

G. candicans (*kan*-di-kanz).
Leaves up to 3 ft. long in a cluster from the bulb. Flower spikes up to 4 ft. high, with narrow-tubed, fragrant flowers like hanging bells on the upper half; white with a greenish tinge. Zones 8 to 9.

✶✶Gladiolus (glad-ee-*oh*-lus).

Iris Family (*Iridaceae*).

Among the most popular of flowers grown for cutting, these cormous plants are native to S. Africa and the Medit. area. An upright cluster of stiff leaves is sent up by each corm, with the flower spike appearing from the center late in the season. The flowers are borne one above another, all usually facing the same way, on the upper part of the stalk. Since the hybridization of gladiolus began in the early nineteenth century, a score or more of the wild species, including the relatively brief but representative list below, have been used

Gladiolus tristis

to produce the hundreds of garden varieties available today. These bear flowers in every color except "true" blue, and in a tremendous range of sizes, flower types, rufflings, fillings, blotchings and blooming times. Many of the varieties are hardy with winter protection as far north as Zone 7, but do best if dug, stored over winter in a cool, dry place and replanted annually.

Gladiolus are very useful as cut flowers. If you plant them in succession you can have cut flowers for most of the summer. Allow 100 to 120 days for the earliest plantings to flower, 90 days for those growing in the summer months, and time your plantings accordingly. Gladiolus make excellent container plants and can serve as accents in the perennial border or for adding interest to summer annual beds. They like to grow in almost any good garden soil and look best when planted in bold groupings.

As they grow in those areas of the world where the summers are warm, they appreciate a location in the garden where they can enjoy full sun, with plenty of moisture through the growing season. Flowering-size corms should be planted 6 to 8 in. apart and 6 to 8 in. deep—deeper in light soils—with the soil well loosened beneath them so that the roots can penetrate easily. If the corms are planted shallowly in light soil, the spikes will not stand upright. Work bone meal into the soil under the corms before planting, and use a side-dressing of commercial fertilizer when the flower spikes are forming. The best way to cut the blooms is to slide a knife blade between the leaves, cutting the stem well below the first flower but leaving most of the leaves to mature normally and so provide food for the bulb. The best time to cut is when the first flower is on the verge of opening.

Lift the corms before the first hard frost, cutting off the tops close to the corm immediately and then spreading the corms in a shady, slightly cool place to dry. The corms are ready to clean

Gladiolus

Gladiolus cultivar

Gladiolus cultivar

Gladiolus cultivar

Gladiolus cultivar

when the shriveled old corm, now useless, separates easily from the new one above it. The little cormels may be saved for planting out if more corms of any particular variety are wanted. After the corms have been cleaned, they should be allowed to dry for another few days, then stored in a dry, dark and cool location for the winter.

Pre-planting dips are available to prevent most of the diseases that attack gladiolus. If these are not used, or if plants become diseased anyway, they should be dug up and discarded. The worst gladiolus pests, however, are thrips, a tiny insect that makes its presence known by the appearance of fine white lines in the leaves and later by twisted, shriveled flowers that never open properly. Purchasing corms from reputable nurseries or catalogs of well-known firms will most often ensure pest-free stock. But if plants do become infested, ask your nursery for a product to control the pest and follow the directions on the package label. If you are growing gladiolus in containers, make sure that you plant only in deep containers, as these plants need at least 6 to 8 in. over and under the corms in order to grow well. While deep planting will ensure that the plants have the best chance to remain upright, in windy locations some support may need to be given, a small task when considering their beauty.

G. callianthus. See *Acidanthera bicolor* var. *murielae*.

G. nanus (*nay*-nus).
These are the winter-hardy gladiolus, and can be counted on to return each year. While often available in "mixed colors," certain selections such as 'Amanda Mahy' (coral in color), 'Charming Beauty' (a deep pink), 'Nymph' (snow white with rose markings) and 'Robinetta' (a fiery red) are available. These are all between 18 and 26 in. in height. Zones 5 to 10.

G. tristis (*tris*-tis).
The flowers are pale yellow, 3 in. in diameter and 24 to 36 in. in height, and fragrant. The plants are not fully hardy and should be lifted and stored over winter in areas where frost is expected. Zones 8 to 10.

Recommended Gladiolus cultivars:
'Black Swan', a deep red;
'Butterfly', yellow-rose;
'Dixieland', red with a white throat;
'Heather Hill', lavender;
'Pink Giant', pink;
'Polar Bear', a large-flowered white;
'Tiffany', orange;
'White Surf', white.

Gloriosa (glow-rew-*oh*-sa)
GLORY LILY.
Lily Family (*Liliaceae*).
The individual flowers of this Afr. and Asian genus are striking and popular with florists. They are not hardy and can be grown outdoors only in very warm areas. The tubers are fleshy and multiply quickly. Flowers are red and yellow, often crinkled along the edge, and frequently the tips of the six petals curl back, almost touching the flower stalk. Blooms are typically 4 to 6 in. in diameter. A sprawling plant, gloriosa climbs by means of tendrils at the ends of the leaves. They make excellent container plants in colder areas as long as they are protected from temperatures below 40°F. They like full sun and should be planted 1 to 2 in. deep, and 10 to 15 in. apart, in rich soil. They like to be well watered during the growing period and will flower from spring plantings from mid- to late summer.

G. superba (soo-*purr*-buh).
Regarded by many as the only species possessing the generic characteristics described above, it is a

Gloriosa

Gloriosa superba
GLORY LILY

Hippeastrum 'Appleblossom'

poisonous plant, but one that when seen in flower will delight you. Excellent cut flower. Zones 10 to 11.

Hippeastrum (hip-ee-*as*-trum).

AMARYLLIS.

Amaryllis Family (*Amaryllidaceae*).

Perennial, fleshy-rooted, bulbous plants mostly from S. Amer. These are handsome, bold plants with large, showy, lilylike flowers and long, strap-shaped leaves growing directly from the bulb. The leaves usually appear after the flowers. Easily grown outdoors in frost-free regions in good garden soil and partial sun, they also make elegant pot plants for home or greenhouse. The bulbs should be planted in a basic potting mixture with about half their tops showing. After the plants bloom in winter or spring keep the foliage growing until it yellows in late summer. (During the summer, the pots may be planted outdoors in a dry sunny location.) Then store the bulbs in

their pots until Nov.–Dec., when they can be repotted and started into growth again. There are many new hybrids and forms of the original species, offering a wide range of color, size and type of flower. Propagate by offsets, division or seeds (the latter is a lengthy process).

Amaryllis are among the easiest and most satisfactory houseplants. Being bulbous, they tolerate the amateur gardener's bumblings with water and exposure. Adaptable, they can live indoors year-round, or they can summer on a windy, air-polluted apartment terrace so long as ample water and fertilizer are provided. Ten dollars will purchase a bulb that contains bloom buds. Named cultivars cost more, and come in melting colors, and with soup-plate-size flowers. Generally three strains are recognized. The Dutch hybrids, entirely greenhouse grown, are probably the most perfect, with blue flowers, strong growth and temperamental habit due to their highly bred background. The S. Afr. strain is outdoor-bred;

the plants are more tolerant of varying cultural conditions; blossoms of moderate size are freely borne, and often a bulb makes several shapes. The Amer. hybrids, too, are of moderate size, tough and floriferous, often with narrower petals than the other two strains, a feature that is considered attractive by many.

Indoor gardeners can grow their own seeds and seedlings. When a blossom is wide open, transfer pollen daily with a cotton swab from the stamens to the tip of the stigma (the central greenish structure). After the seedpod matures and yellows, open it and sow the seed in a basic potting mixture, covering it to a depth of 1/16 in. Soak the pot from the bottom and hold at 70°F until germination is complete. When the seedlings are 2 in. high, water with a half-strength fish-emulsion solution. At six months, pot them up individually in 2-in. pots; continue to push with biweekly feeding and at least half-day sunlight. Move to larger pots as necessary. Seedlings bloom in about three years if not checked by moisture shortages.

The number of hybrids available is indicative of the increasing popularity of these bulbs. Available in a broad color range, among the most popular are 'African Sunset', a bright orange-red; 'Appleblossom', a salmon pink; 'Basuto', a deep, dark red; 'Desert Dawn', a lovely salmon; 'Springtime', a light rose marked with white; and 'Summertime', pink with a white stripe.

H. × papilio (pah-*pill*-ee-oh)

A new listing in some catalogs, known as the butterfly amaryllis, it has a white background to the petals, touched with green, with rich crimson markings and a broad band of red in the petals. Zones 9 to 10.

Hyacinthoides (hye-uh-sin-*thoi*-deez).

Lily Family (*Liliaceae*).

The plants in this genus, native to Eur., have been moved around by botanists, at one time classified as *Scilla, Agraphis* and *Endymion*. No matter how many times they are moved, they are lovely spring-flowering bulbs. The species in this genus like to grow in deciduous woodlands in leafy, humus-rich soil with light shade in the spring, when they flower, followed by deeper shade in the summer. They like plenty of moisture in the spring. Great for planting with azaleas and rhododendrons, the blue flowers add a distinctive color to such borders. Plant 4 in. deep, 4 to 6 in. apart, and make sure they are undisturbed so they can naturalize and multiply. They can be easily propagated by lifting and dividing established clumps after the foliage has died down.

H. hispanica (his-*pan*-i-cuh).

SPANISH BLUEBELL.

SPANISH SQUILL.

This species often has more than fifteen flowers per 20-in. stem. Leaves are strap-shaped, 1 in. wide, up to 24 in. in length. The flowers appear in April or May and vary in color from white to pink to violet. There are a number of named cultivars including 'Alba', with white flowers; 'Blue Bird', a deep, dark blue; and 'Rose Queen', a pure rose. Zone 5.

✶H. non-scripta (non-script-*tuh*).

ENGLISH BLUEBELL.

This plant has leaves up to 19 in. long and ½ in. wide. Flowers are tubular blue or white and sometimes a pinkish color. The plant reaches 18 in. in height, with the top of the spike bending over a little. Superb in woodlands. If planted with Spanish bluebell, some natural crossing will occur. Flowers in April. Zone 6.

Hyacinthus

Hyacinthoides hispanica
SPANISH BLUEBELL

Hyacinthoides non-scripta
ENGLISH BLUEBELL

Hyacinthus (hye-uh-*sin*-thus).

HYACINTH.

Lily Family (*Liliaceae*).

These spring-flowering plants, native to the eastern Medit., have tubular flowers that are delightfully fragrant. The foliage is linear. The bulbs should be planted in Oct. in colder areas, Nov. in warmer places. In cold climates plant 6 in. deep, in warmer areas 8 in., and space 6 to 9 in. apart. Although the bulbs are hardy, the flowers can be harmed by hard frosts, and where this is likely to happen (zones 3 and 4) they are best protected by a winter mulch of straw.

Hyacinths are ideal for container growing. After potting, the bulbs should be placed in a cold spot and allowed to form a good root system prior to being given warmer temperatures. These plants should be brought indoors when the shoots just emerge from the soil. Specially "prepared" bulbs can be obtained for such culture, and these can also be grown without soil—the bulbs are planted in special vases where each bulb is suspended just above the water in the lower part. If grown this way these bulbs need cool temperatures and darkness until the roots are well developed and top growth has started. Gradually increase the light and temperature. Hyacinths enjoy sun, and the broad selection in today's catalogs includes red, pink, yellow, white and blue cultivars.

Hyacinthus orientalis 'Delft Blue'
and 'L'Innocence'

Hyacinthus

H. orientalis (ore-ee-en-*tay*-lis).

COMMON HYACINTH.

FLORIST'S HYACINTH.

Among the cultivars often "prepared" for early forcing (growing out of season) are 'Anna Marie', a light pink; 'City of Haarlem', a pale yellow; 'L'Innocence', a white; and 'Pink Pearl', a deep pink. In addition to these, cultivars for the garden include 'Bismark', a large-flowered, clear blue;

Hyacinthus orientalis
COMMON HYACINTH

'Jan Bos', a carmine red; 'Lady Derby', a pink; 'Orange Boven', a lovely salmon, and 'Ostara', a bright blue with a band of deeper blue in the petals. Left in the ground the bulbs will return but are never quite as good as in their first season. If you are saving the bulbs, lift when the leaves have died and keep the bulbs in a dry frost-free area until planting time. Zones 4 to 8.

Hymenocallis (hye-me-noh-*kal*-is).

ISMENE.

SPIDER LILY.

Amaryllis Family (*Amaryllidaceae*).

Tender bulbs from warm N. and S. Amer. regions, including the U.S. and the Andes of Peru. Before the leaves appear, the bare flowering stem is produced bearing a cluster of white flowers, tubular at the base; the petals then flare outward from a cup formed by a membrane joining the lower parts of the stamens. In the warmest climates these plants will flower outdoors for a long period of time. In colder climes they can be grown in containers or used for summer bedding, then dug up and stored over winter in a frost-free area. They like a rich, moist soil and sunlight. Propagate by lifting and removing the offsets that the older bulbs produce.

H. calathina. See *H. narcissiflora*.

H. littoralis (lit-toh-*ray*-lis).

From Mex. and Guatemala, an evergreen with bright green foliage, 2 in. wide, narrowed at the base. It flowers on 20-in. stems, each with six to twelve sessile, fragrant flowers. The tube is often more than 5 in. long, and from the cup the petals splay outward forming a very large flower. Needs heat for good flower production throughout the year; flowers in midsummer. Should always have temperatures in the 50°F range at night. Zone 10.

H. narcissiflora (nar-siss-i-*floor*-uh).

(Syn. *H. calathina.*) This species can be grown outdoors in Zones 10 to 11 as long as some protection is given. Leaves are deciduous and form a false stem at their base that can be as much as 12 in. in length. Flowers are white and fragrant. The stem rises 18 to 20 in. above the false stalk; two to five flowers per stem are produced in the sum-

Hymenocallis narcissiflora
SPIDER LILY

mer. The tube is almost as long as the free segments, some 3 in. in length. Cultivars include 'Advance', 'Festalis', 'Pax' and 'Sulphur Queen', which has a light yellowish tinge to the petals. Zones 10 to 11.

Ipheion (if-*ee*-on).
Amaryllis Family (*Amaryllidaceae*).
A native of eastern S. Amer., this bulbous plant has narrow, grasslike leaves that when crushed have the smell of garlic. The flower stems are 6 in. high, each carrying a solitary star-shaped flower, but the bulbs will produce more than one stem. Colors vary from white to blue to deep purple. Plant in well-drained soil, 2 in. deep and 3 to 5 in. apart. Foliage appears in early spring, the flowers from March to early May. Once planted, leave the bulbs undisturbed for years, lifting only to divide in order to increase the stock. Moisture is needed in spring and early summer but not later. These plants look lovely in the open sunny border or among shrubs in light shade. They are quite hardy but need a mulch where the ground freezes.

I. uniflorum (u-nee-*floor*-um).
SPRING STARFLOWER.
(Syn. *Brodiaea uniflora*.) This species has foliage that is onion-scented when crushed. It produces solitary white flowers, sometimes with a hint of blue, on stems that are 6 in. in height. Flowers appear in spring. Propagation is by division of the older plants. Culture as for *Triteleia laxa*. Plant in the fall and leave undisturbed. Some cultivars are blue. The cultivar 'Wisley Blue', with large, deep blue flowers, is well worth growing, doing well in ordinary potting soil when grown in containers in colder climates. All appreciate a leaf mulch in the cooler regions of zone 7.

Ipheion uniflorum
SPRING STARFLOWER

Iris (*eye*-riss).
Iris Family (*Iridaceae*).
There are more than 200 species in the genus *Iris*, native mostly to the North Temperate Zone, and at least 100 of these and literally thousands of cultivars can be found in gardens today. They

Iris

range in size from plants small enough to fit under your cupped hands to regal plants 5 ft. in height and include the lovely wild flags. Irises are available in every imaginable color, except for a bright red, and make marvelous displays of color. The petals contain a high percentage of water and often are luminous. Some are frilly and ruffled, others chic and chiseled. These are highly prized for their contribution to planting compositions and as cut flowers.

Their rootstocks have different forms; some are bulbous, others are rhizomes that creep along the ground. Leaves are narrow, some sword-shaped, others grass-like. The flowers have six conspicuous parts. The three upright petals form "standards," while the three lower petals droop or are horizontal and are called "falls."

Irises are easy to grow, needing only lots of sun and good drainage. They thrive in most soils but are considered less susceptible to root rot when grown in soil of moderate fertility. Rich soil and subsequent lush growth contribute to disease, as do wet seasons and overdoses of fertilizers.

Bulbous irises go dormant in late summer and thus can be lifted and stored. Included in these types are *I. bucharica* (bew-*ker*-i-kuh), the best known of the Juno irises, which have thick fleshy roots; the Reticulata irises, having a netted covering to the bulbs; and the Xiphium irises, which have large standards and no fleshy roots when dormant. Included here are those called the Spanish, Dutch and English Irises.

When growing irises in containers, plant the bulbs in Oct., putting them 3 in. deep and about 1 in. apart. Set them in a cool place (a cool greenhouse is ideal) and out of the sunlight. When the leaves appear, bring them into bright light and give them some warmth, but not over 55°F at night.

I. danfordiae (dan-*ford*-ee-ay).
A lovely little plant, 4 in. high when in flower, and fragrant. Flowers are lemon-yellow with green markings, with bright yellowish-green to orange markings on the haft of the falls. Although hardy, it comes into flower in Jan.–Feb. and needs protection in areas where the weather is cold and wet to prevent damage to the flowers. The leaves are short at flowering time, elongating to 12 in. afterward. Plant 3 in. deep, 6 in. apart in a sunny location. Zone 5.

I. ensata. See *I. kaempferi.*

✳I. germanica (jer-*man*-i-cuh).
Nursery catalogs often list all of the "bearded" types of iris—by far the most commonly grown—as *I. germanica*, but as there were numerous species involved in the creation of the various members, this is not strictly correct. These are great garden plants, however, and deserving of a place in all gardens. They should be planted with the backs of the rhizomes just breaking the surface of the soil. Generally, they are listed in catalogs by color and by three classifications of height: Tall, 30 to 40 in.; Intermediate, 15 to 30 in.; and Dwarf, 5 to 15 in. in height. Among the blue cultivars are 'Babbling Brook', 'Blue Lustre', 'Mary Frances', 'Mystique' and 'Sapphire Hills', all of which are tall, over 30 in. in height. Yellow cultivars include 'Debby Rairdon', 'Joyce Terry' and 'West Coast'. Among the pinks are cultivars such as 'Beverly Sills', 'One Desire', 'Persian Berry' and 'Rancho Rose'. 'Superstition' has very dark flowers of ebony black and is possibly the darkest of them all. The list is almost endless, and practically any nursery catalog or the offering from one of the specialist iris growers will contain a palette of iris colors, even some two-tone combinations, to precisely fill the needs of any gardener.

Iris danfordiae

Iris germanica 'Florentina'

Iris 'Vice-Regal'
TALL-BEARDED IRIS

Iris kaempferi 'Hokkaido'
JAPANESE IRIS

Iris

I. kaempferi (*kam*-fer-eye).

JAPANESE IRIS.

One the largest flowered species, with flowers often 10 in. or more in diameter. Lovely near water, the stems reach 24 in. in height, generally branched, with each bearing one or two very showy flowers. Older plants flower over a long period but mainly in July. Colors are tones of red-purple, but there are many cultivars offered, including 'Nikko', a pale purple-blue marked with deeper purple, and 'Queen of the Blues', an orchid color with a blue cast veined white. The plants must have good moisture and sun. Zone 5.

Iris reticulata
RETICULATED IRIS

deep, 6 in. apart, in full sun. A variable species, several selections have been made, among them 'Cantab', a pale blue with an orange blotch on the blade of the falls, and 'Harmony', sky blue with a yellow central ridge on the blade of the falls. Zone 5.

Iris kaempferi 'Gei Sho-ui'
JAPANESE IRIS

I. reticulata (re-tik-you-*lay*-tuh).

RETICULATED IRIS.

A popular little iris, 4 to 6 in. tall, with small purple and golden-ridged flowers that open in late winter or early spring. Leaves are narrow and four-angled, and are short at flowering time, elongating to 12 to 18 in. afterward. Plant 3 in.

I. sibirica (sigh-*beer*-ih-cuh).

SIBERIAN IRIS.

Flowering in late spring and early summer, up to 36 in. in height. Drought resistant and very free flowering and trouble free. Set the rhizomes just below the surface in a sunny border, spacing them 12 in. apart. Colors are shades of blue-violet to white. A number of cultivars are offered, including 'Dreaming Spires', lavender with royal blue; 'Flight of the Butterfly', dark blue standards and white falls with a hint of blue and dark blue veining; and 'Little White', only 15 in. tall but a lovely plant. Zone 3.

Iris reticulata 'Cantab'
RETICULATED IRIS

I. xiphioides (zif-ee-oy-*deez*).
ENGLISH IRIS.
Foliage is linear, narrow, 18 in. long. In June–July flowers in a range of colors from white to blue to purple are produced, 5 in. in diameter, with each fall having a yellow blotch. This species needs moisture and full sun. Zone 7.

✱Dutch Iris.
A favorite of today's gardeners is the Dutch iris, a cross between *I. xiphium* (*zif*-i-um or *zye*-fi-um), and *I. tingitana* (tin-ji-*tay*-nuh). These will flower for years, giving glorious May–June displays in colder areas, March–April in warmer climes, and are superb cut flowers. Best when massed, they should be planted 3 in. deep (4 in. in sandy soils) and 6 in. apart, in a well-drained, sunny location. In colder climates, protect with a winter mulch.

   Among the best cultivars are 'Blue Ribbon', gentian blue with a gold blotch; 'Bronze Queen', a dark mahogany with a bronze blotch; and 'Im-

perator', which has dark blue standards and soft blue falls. 'Wedgwood', a tried and true favorite, has blue standards with a yellow blotch; it is very popular in the florist trade and is easy to grow in the garden and in containers. 'White Superior' is just that, one of the best pure whites.

Louisiana Iris.
These lovely hybrids are the result of crossing three different species. The results are a lovely race of garden irises that flower over a period of time. They do need abundant moisture, preferring to have their feet in or at least very near

Iris sibirica
SIBERIAN IRIS

water. The flowers are large, often 6 to 8 in. in diameter, on strong 36 in. stems that are often branched. Foliage is dark green, linear and up to 45 in. long. These plants form very large clumps. Generally offered as mixed colors, in shades of blue to white. Zones 4 to 9; a winter mulch is recommended north of zone 6.

Iris

IRISES

Iris, from the Greek for rainbow, is a name aptly given to the genus, whose flowers cover the entire spectrum of colors in the rainbow, with the exception of bright red. Lord Byron (1788–1824) wrote in his poem "Childe Harold:"

> The moon is up, and yet it is not night;
> Sunset divides the sky with her; a sea
> Of glory streams along the Alpine height
> Of blue Friuli's mountains; heaven is free
> From clouds, but of all colors seems to be—
> Melted to one vast Iris of the West
> Where the day joins the past Eternity.

Of the more than 200 species and many thousands of cultivars, two types of irises are responsible for making the genus so well known: the bearded irises, which are superb garden plants, and the Dutch irises, which are among the finest and most popular cut flowers. All members of the genus *Iris* are found in the N. Hemisphere. Although there are many genera found in the S. Hemisphere that belong to the same family (Iridaceae) and indeed at first glance look like an iris, these belong instead to such genera as *Dietes* and *Moraea*.

The most commonly grown irises in the garden are the bearded irises. They offer attractive sword-shaped leaves, strong stems that carry aloft large flowers, often three or four per stem, and rootstocks that like to be slightly exposed so they can bake in the sun—all of which contribute to the plant's popularity.

Walk the coasts of the U.S. from Maine to Tex. and you will see plants of *I. versicolor* at home among rocks and braving the sea air. Stroll the dry hills and coastal areas of Calif. and you will see the Douglas iris. Take a trip to La. and you will find the gentle hues of the Louisiana Irises, the happy result of crosses between two species, *I. brevicaulis* and *I. giganticaerulea*. Enter a plant lover's garden and you will find some of the species that are ideal for a rock garden, such as *I. histrioides* and *I. reticulata*. (These low-growing plants are not as widely grown as they deserve to be, but some nursery growers are finding these species to be a worthwhile commercial crop, planting six bulbs per small pot and getting them to the market when they come into flower.) If you visit Ireland in May, you will see fields of *I. pseudacorus* growing in damp areas, each strong stem crowned with the bright yellow flowers. Iris species are widely distributed throughout many parts of Eur.

Though adaptable to many different types of soil, irises will flower and grow best in moderately rich soil and in full sun. If given these conditions, they will not require any fertilizer or any special care. They do like to have a drier resting period after they have finished flowering. After a few years in one location, the roots will become a little crowded and it will be necessary to lift and divide the rhizomes. Bearded irises are one of the few plants that should be lifted and divided in the summer, preferably in June or July. If this work is done at a later time, the plants will not be harmed, but there will be a drop in flower production. In fact if the process of lifting, dividing and replanting is much delayed, there may be no flower production at all until the second year after division. In average soil, fertilizer may increase the amount of foliage produced but not necessarily the number of flowers. Feeding too heavily may increase vegetative growth but sharply reduce flower production.

Bearded irises are appealing for use in arrangements, but the blooms have a shorter vase life than Dutch irises. The cut flowers of bearded irises prefer to be in shallow water and the large blooms will last much longer if they receive a fine spray of water daily. Keeping these flowers as cool as possible will also extend their life.

The difference in the appearance of the Dutch and bearded irises dictates, to a certain degree, their best locations in the garden. The bearded types can hold their own and even stand alone in a large bed or in a mixed border of shrubs and perennials, as informal settings are more suitable to their appearance than are formal bedding schemes. Dutch irises are best combined with annuals or grown in bold groupings in more formal settings, since they do not have the form and mass to stand alone. Dutch irises, as well as other bulbous irises, do make great container plants, however. Bearded irises are not suitable for containers and will not give satisfaction if grown this way.

Each year many new and exciting hybrids are listed in various catalogs. For the gardener new to growing irises, it is advisable to purchase cultivars that are tried and true and generally available at a modest cost compared to the higher prices of the latest introductions. Once experience has been gained in growing these, then an investment in newer selections will be profitable.

The Dutch irises, which are the result of crossing several species belonging to the same group as *I. xiphium* (Spanish iris) and *I. xiphioides* (English iris), can be brought into flower at different times of the year if given specific cultural conditions, such as a period of cold storage followed by warmer greenhouse temperatures. This makes them very popular with florists, as they are a very reliable crop. They are easy to grow, and a selection such as 'Wedgwood' (a lovely blue), 'Yellow Queen' or 'White Excelsior' should find a place in every garden or in a container on every patio.

Dutch irises are superb cut flowers and will last many days in the home, particularly if they are to be held at cooler temperatures and brought into the warmer parts of the house only when they are to be enjoyed. The flowers should be harvested when the flower buds are well colored. If the plants are being grown out of season, such as in a greenhouse, wait for the first bud to open before harvesting. This is especially true if they are being grown during the winter months, when light intensity is low. The flowers should be placed in water as soon as possible. Cutting the ends off purchased stems prior to arranging them is a must. The use of a preservative in the water will prolong the blooms.

Iris

IRIS FLOWER FORMS

Tall Bearded

Crested

Juno

Siberian

Louisiana

Aril

Japanese

Reticulata

Spuria

DUTCH IRIS

Iris xiphium
SPANISH IRIS

Ixia (*ik*-see-uh).
CORN LILY.
Iris Family (*Iridaceae*).
These S. Afr. corms with sword-shaped leaves that are held erect look rugged, but they are not able to withstand temperatures below 20°F. They produce flowers that are bell-, saucer- or bowl-shaped in spring to midsummer. The flowers are red, violet, pink, yellow or white with the centers a darker color. Ixias will naturalize in warm areas and are excellent pot plants in cooler regions. They like a sandy soil and sun, except in the warmest areas, where a little shade is appreciated and will help preserve the lovely colors. In warm areas plant in the fall, in cooler areas in the spring, setting the corms 2 in. deep and 4 in. apart. The plants look best in groupings of fifteen or more. Moisture is needed during the growing season, after which water should be withheld so the bulbs can enter into a resting period.

✱**I. maculata** (mack-yew-*lay*-tuh).
Leaves are narrow and ribbed, 12 in. long. The flowers are yellow with a dark-toned area around the throat. Blooms in a dense spike up to 24 in. in height. Often listed by color in catalogs, ranging from white to orange, the plants may also be offered as "mixed" with the full range of colors in the selection. Zone 9.

Ixiolirion (iks-ee-oh-*leer*-ee-on).
Amaryllis Family (*Amaryllidaceae*).
The bulbs of this S. Afr. genus are very small, often less than ½ in. in diameter. Ixiolirions make excellent pot plants. The bulbs should be potted up in the spring and placed in a cool area so they can root well before they are exposed to stronger light and warmer temperatures. Propagate by lifting and dividing large established plantings, or sow the seed as soon as it is ripe. Seed does germinate easily, but it will take two to three seasons for the bulbs to reach flowering size.

Ixiolirion

Ixia maculata cultivar
CORN LILY

Ixiolirion tartaricum

I. tartaricum (tar-*ter*-ri-cum).
(Syn. *I. ledbourii* and *I. montanum.*) Flowers are a little over 1 inch in diameter, but as many as ten to fifteen can be found on each 12-in. spike, flowering in April–May. Despite their small size, the bulbs should be planted 4 in. deep in well-drained soil. They still need good moisture in winter but should be allowed to become dry in summer. They love the sun, and will perform even in poor soil, their only enemy being a late spring frost, from which they should be protected. Plant in the fall in warm areas (zones 7 to 9), in the spring in cooler regions (zones 3 to 6), lifting and storing the bulbs over winter in a frost-free area. Zones 8 to 9.

Lachenalia (lack-ee-*nay*-lee-uh).
Lily Family (*Liliaceae*).
Lovely plants from S. Afr., most producing two mottled leaves and tubular bell-shaped flowers. They were very popular pot plants at the turn of the century and have recently been rediscovered. Outdoor plants in only the warmest areas, they are great pot plants for the cool greenhouse as long as they are protected from frost and given light shade from direct sun. They like well-drained soil with a good percentage of humus and moisture while the leaves are growing, but as soon as the leaves start to wither water should be withheld. Plants should be started into growth in late summer; plant them 2 to 3 in. deep and 3 to 4 inches apart. The plants stay in flower for six to eight weeks, and after the foliage has died down older plants can be lifted and the offsets removed for growing on to flowering size. Sow seed as soon as it is ripe in a sandy soil mix and maintain temperatures of 65°F at night. Pot the seedlings into individual pots as soon as they can be handled with ease. These plants are superb in hanging baskets, as the foliage itself is attractive.

L. algoensis (al-goh-*en*-sis).
An interesting species, its seeds are rich in oil (elaiosome) and are spread by ants. It is not in cultivation and is indeed rare in the wild. Zone 10.

L. aloides (ah-*loi*-deez).
Grows 10 in. in height and produces, on 10-in. stems, green tubular flowers tipped with crimson, the outside of the petals a deep rose turning to yellow at the tips. Unusual and striking. The number of flowers varies from ten to twenty. *L. aloides* var. *aurea* has bright orange-yellow flowers. Spring-flowering. Zone 10.

L. bulbifera (bul-bif-*er*-uh).
Produces fifteen to twenty-five flowers on spikes 12 to 15 in. in height. Flowers are tubular, coral-red edged with green or purple. Blooms in Jan.–Feb. Leaves are erect, linear-lanceolate. Zone 10.

L. tricolor (*try*-cul-or).
This spring-flowering plant has flowers of red, yellow and green. Both the 10-in. stem and leaves are mottled with purple. Zone 10.

Leucojum (lew-*koh*-jum).
SNOWFLAKE.
Amaryllis Family (*Amaryllidaceae*).
Native to central Eur. and the western Medit. region, these hardy and half-hardy bulbs produce straplike leaves and nodding, bell-shaped white flowers with petal tips tinged with green. They should be planted 3 to 4 in. deep, 8 to 10 in. apart in the front of the border and left undisturbed. They require moisture throughout the year, especially in the growing season and up to flowering, which is in late spring or early summer. Winter protection is required in the colder regions, but the plants will stand temperatures down to 20°F without protection if in a sheltered area. In all but

Lachenalia tricolor

Leucojum aestivum
SUMMER SNOWFLAKE

the warmest areas give them full sun; light shade is needed in hot regions. Propagate by lifting and dividing established clumps. Seed can also be sown but should be barely covered. The seedling can remain in the seed containers for a season and then should be lifted out and placed into individual pots for planting out the following year.

✳ L. aestivum (ess-*tye*-vum).
SUMMER SNOWFLAKE.

Leaves are 12 in. long. Drooping flowers, two to eight per 12- to 14-in. stem, bloom in late spring or early summer. This plant grows quite quickly, forming large clumps. Hardier than other species. The cultivar 'Gravetye Giant' is more robust and more free-flowering. Zone 4.

Leucojum vernum
SPRING SNOWFLAKE

L. vernum (*vern*-um).
SPRING SNOWFLAKE.

Leaves are 9 in. long, ½ in. wide, 6 to 12 in. in height. Each stem carries only one flower, tubu-

lar and about ¾ in. long, but many stalks per plant are produced when established. Flowers appear in early spring. Zone 4, with protection in colder locations.

✳✳ Lilium (lih-*lee*-um).
LILY.
Lily Family (*Liliaceae*).

Words and phrases such as "highly prized," "stately," "flawless beauty," "rivaled only by the orchid" and "beauty of form and color" have been written about the lily. It is a rare gardener who does not respond in kind to these adjectives. The lily is indeed a lovely, regal flower, and the hybrids offered today span a dazzling array of colors, sizes, heights and profusion of blooms. The hybrids also offer new strains possessing a hardiness and resistance to disease not found in most of the species.

While it has been cultivated extensively in N. Amer. for only 60 years, the lily is among the oldest of cultivated plants. *L. candidum* was pictured on a Minoan vase dated to 1300 B.C. and many drawings of lilies have been found among the artifacts and monuments of the Assyrian and Egyptian civilizations. During the late nineteenth and early twentieth centuries here, gardeners would have liked to have grown lilies in their gardens. But the bulbs, which then were all grown in Eur. and Asia, did not survive the overseas trip well. The bulbs of most species are highly perishable and a typical shipment might include only one or two bulbs that would bloom.

Now most bulbs are sold and grown here, and shipments are often made in polyethylene bags to cut down on the possibility of drying out. And, as mentioned, the hybrids are stronger. Moreover, many varieties are grown from seed today, a means of producing very healthy plants (a method that many home gardeners are trying).

There are enough hybrids and varieties of lily

to spread a bloom of color in your garden from earliest June until frost bites in autumn (although most lilies bloom in the summer). Some lilies are very easy to grow; some offer a challenge. There are varieties low to the ground, and lilies that grow on stalks over 12 ft. tall. In short, there is probably a lily to suit every garden demand.

Including lilies in your garden plan calls for more than casual placement. For one thing, lilies are more attractive in groups of three or more. Singly, they appear a trifle gawky. Taller varieties appear best at the back of the border, perhaps outlined against evergreens. There are varieties to serve well in the front of the border, but you would do well to match the color, size and time of bloom with the other plants in the border. Another consideration: After blooms die, the stalks are not the most attractive element in the garden. Nor is it wise, as you'll see below, to cut down the stalks for the sake of appearance.

The lily is an erect plant, leafy-stemmed, with flowers borne at the tips of the stalks, one at a time or in clusters. There are generally three petals and three sepals, which together are called segments and make up the perianth. Ordinarily, the leaves are narrow—some almost grasslike—and scattered along the stalk or whorled around it. In certain species and hybrids derived from them, little bulbs will be produced in the axils of the leaves and can be grown on to flowering size which they will reach in 2 to 3 growing seasons.

Because in the past many foreign lily bulbs resisted travel, were prone to disease and bore blossoms weakly, the lily had earned a reputation for being temperamental and difficult to grow. With today's hybrids, this is no longer so. Nevertheless, there are several fundamentals of lily culture it is wise to follow.

Perhaps the most important is to provide a very well-drained soil. Water-holding soil is anathema to lily bulbs. Even the hardiest of hybrid bulbs

Lilium 'Star Gazer'
ORIENTAL LILY

Lilium auratum var. *platyphyllum*
GOLD-BAND LILY

Lilium

Lilium 'Golden Splendor'
TRUMPET HYBRID

Lilium 'Pink Perfection'
TRUMPET HYBRID

cannot survive in soggy soil. The soil should probably be slightly acid and mixed thoroughly with humus. Some gardeners use an all-purpose dry fertilizer, but this may make the soil too rich, so use with care. A few species, such as *L. canadense* and *L. martagon*, enjoy partial shade. Nearly all others blossom best in full sun where summer temperatures remain below 90°F. While some hybrid stalks are quite strong, it is still advisable to shield the lily plant from high winds. And despite protection, some of the taller species will need staking. Don't smother the plants, though. They require a good amount of air circulation, and the plants need water, but not an overdose. A summer mulch helps contain moisture in the soil and cuts down the need for watering. An herbaceous ground cover around the lily plants acts as a natural mulch. Otherwise, spread lawn clippings, well-rotted leafmold, peat—but not manure unless it is well rotted.

When the blossoms wither, cut them away. After the last blossom dies—and assuming you aren't going to save the seed—cut the stalk just below the lowermost blossom, but above the leaves. This gives the leaves a chance to continue their production of food for the bulb and root systems, thus producing a stronger and healthier bulb for next year. When the leaves die, cut down the stalk.

The best time to plant lily bulbs is in the fall, before frost. Prepare the soil well to a depth of 2 ft., especially if the soil leans to clay rather than sand. Work in plenty of humus and, around the area of the bulb, a handful of bone meal. Most lily bulbs are planted with from 4 to 6 in. of soil above the top of the bulb. Spread over the area a mulch of salt hay, straw or pine needles. Plant the bulbs as soon after you receive them as possible. If frost has already arrived, store the bulbs in dry sand at a very cool temperature (about 38 to 40°F.). Or pack each bulb in a polyethylene bag along with moist (not wet) sphagnum, and store in a home refrigerator or cool root cellar. But keep in mind that it is better to plant in autumn than to store the bulbs and plant in early spring; spring planting can be done, but during the first season the bulbs might be later flowering than normal. Lily bulbs do best when transplanted with roots attached. The roots ought to look healthy and soft, not dried up. Also check each bulb carefully for signs of rot or disease before planting. If you find any that are unhealthy, discard.

Propagation has become something of a hobby for many gardeners. There are two principal ways, and two further methods that apply to some species.

The first is by seed. When the lily seed pods turn from green to brown, and just before the pod splits, you can take the seeds. The seeds ought to flow freely. If they are sticking to one another, they are not quite ripe. One pod holds around 200 seeds.

As soon as the seeds ripen in the fall, sow them in a well-drained cold frame with a mixture of loam, leafmold and peat in about equal parts. Cover the seeds with about 1 in. of soil, and mulch with peat moss, salt hay or straw. Water gently through the mulch. During the second season, transplant the seedlings to a larger cold frame to allow them more space. Continue to mulch. In the spring of the third year, the bulbs should be ready to lift and plant in your garden where you want them. As a rule, the plants will bloom during the third summer.

The second and slightly faster method is by planting bulb scales, the outer curved covering on the bulb. Lift the bulb in early fall after the last bloom has faded, and be sure not to tear the basal roots. Strip away dried-up or rotted scales. Then carefully break off the healthy scales at the base, working around the bulb (the scales are overlapped). If the bulb core is unharmed, replant it,

and with modest good luck, blooms will begin again from the core next summer. Plant the scales right away in shallow drills mixed with sand or peat moss, base down and several inches apart. Good drainage—even slightly dry soil—is best to start scale propagation. Bulbs will begin forming on the scale edges in about 60 to 90 days, at which time the scales should be moved to a cold frame and planted so as to allow more space between them. Mulch with peat moss, salt hay or straw. By the following autumn, the bulbs ought to be ready for your garden.

Some species and cultivars produce bulbils— tiny bulbs that grow in the leaf axils. Typical are *L. bulbiferum* and *L. lancifolium*. Others, such as *L. regale*, bear bulblets, the same kind of tiny bulb, but they appear on the main stems on parts that are underground. Both bulbils and bulblets may be picked and propagated in the same way as seeds. Established plants will produce quite large-sized bulbs underground and these can be planted and will often flower the next year.

While it's true the new hybrids are more resistant to disease and insect pests than the species, there is still a chance for maladies to strike, and thus good reason to list the potential dangers. Two fungus diseases attack the bulbs; one strikes the leaves.

Botrytis rot shows up as spots on the leaves, stems and flower buds. The spots range from orange to brown, darker toward the center. The fungus spreads in cool, wet weather. Remove and discard all affected parts, and spray with fungicide, following directions on the package label. This problem occurs where air circulation is poor, so plant accordingly.

Bulb rot is due essentially to wet soil. A slightly darkened spot will appear on the bulb; then the bulb flesh will grow soft and eventually collapse. The above-ground sign of this rot is a dwarfed or disfigured blossom, or bent stalk. Lift

Lilium

Lilium 'Connecticut King'
ASIATIC HYBRID

the bulb, and if it is too far gone, discard it. Otherwise, you might try to cut away the affected portion and soak in a solution of a recommended fungicide or dust with powdered charcoal or fungicide powder; follow the directions on the label and after treatment replant the bulbs.

Leaf spot shows up on the leaves as a brown spot, turning later to a powdery, mildew-like covering. Again good air circulation helps; keep any irrigation water off the plants, and remove and discard infested leaves.

Mosaic or lily virus turns the leaves a mottled green, streaked with yellow. During the second season of this disease, the stem is attacked, and finally the bulb and roots. It is spread by the aphid so eliminating this pest will help cut down on the occurrence of the disease. Discard all diseased plants.

Pests include the aphids, already mentioned, and the stalk borer, a slim caterpillar about 1½ in. long that is a dusty gray when mature. It bores

into the stem causing the plant to wilt and break. Cut away and discard infested shoots.

Rodents consider the lily bulbs an epicurean delight. The most effective block is a layer of ¼ in. wire screen lining the sides, ends and bottom of the entire planting bed. Laying out poison is not recommended, since there is too much chance for birds, cats and dogs and even small children to eat the poison by mistake.

Below are the most important species and varieties and a few of the major hybrids, along with their principal characteristics.

While today's hybrid lilies are superb it must be remembered that they were derived from species and many of the species have unique qualities making them worthy of a place in any garden. The following hybrids and species are listed in many catalogs. Lilies are hardy in all zones, as long as they are protected by a good winter mulch in coldest areas.

Lilium lancifolium
TIGER LILY

Because there are so many different types of lilies, it became necessary to develop a classification system. This divided the lilies into 10 Divisions, with several sub-divisions in each to accommodate the shape of the flowers, such as flat-faced, bowl or trumpet-shaped, as well as how the flowers were held on the stem—upright, outward or pendant. As an aid this classification is most helpful and an abridged outline follows.

✳ Division I.

ASIATIC HYBRIDS.

Subdivisions: a. upright; b. outward-facing; c. pendant flowers.

Recommended hybrids:

'Chinook'. Lovely salmon, 12 or more flowers, 48 in. in height, July flowering.

'Connecticut King'. Unspotted bright yellow flowers. June flowering. 48 in. in height.

'Enchantment'. Nasturtium-red, tried and true hybrid, superb in every way, June–July flowering. 36 in. in height.

'Pixie Flame'. Brilliant orange-red, with golden blotch, 16 in. high. June flowering, a great plant for containers.

'Pollyanna'. Reaches 60 in. in height, large golden-yellow flowers 7 in. in diameter, with deeper golden colored blotch, July flowering.

'Rosefire'. A tricolor, tips are red, center of petals golden yellow, center of the flower bright orange-red. Free flowering, 48 in. in height, June flowering.

Division II.

MARTAGON HYBRIDS.

Hybrids in which one parent is *L. martagon*.

Division III.

CANDIDUM HYBRIDS.

Hybrids derived from *L. candidum*.

An outstanding strain is Cascade; it is an exceedingly vigorous and beautiful selection from the species. Zones 4 to 9.

Division IV.

AMERICAN HYBRIDS.

Hybrids derived from American species.

Division V.

LONGIFLORUM HYBRIDS.

Hybrids with "Easter Lily" blood.

✳ Division VI.

TRUMPET HYBRIDS.

Lilies with trumpet-shaped flowers derived from species from Asia but excluding the Oriental Types. Subdivisions are for Trumpet Type, Bowl-shaped flowers, Pendant flowers, and Sunburst Type, which are flowers that have a star-shaped, open flat face with petals separated from each other.

Recommended hybrids:

'Black Dragon'. Fragrant white flowers with maroon reverse, 6 ft. in height, up to 20 flowers 6 in. in diameter, July flowering.

'Golden Splendor'. Large golden-yellow fragrant flowers, same height and flowering time as 'Black Dragon'.

'Pink Perfection'. A non-fading pink, as many as 30 flowers on 6 ft. stems. Flowering in July–Aug.

Division VII.

ORIENTAL HYBRIDS.

Hybrids derived principally from *L. auratum* and *L. speciosum* and others, with subdivisions based on the shape of the flowers. They have bowl-shaped to flat-faced flowers that are often 9 in. or more in diameter, are fragrant and flower in late summer. Wonderful container plants, hardy and easy to grow, they appreciate liquid fertilizer feedings through mid-summer. Their height varies a little but generally they are 36 to 48 in. in height.

There are a number of "Elegance" lilies, all of which are superb, the name denoting the color of the flowers: 'Crimson Elegance', 'Gold Elegance', 'Rose Elegance' and 'Silver Elegance'. Another lovely lily is 'Jamboree', a crimson with silver edges to the recurved petals, but even recurved the flowers are 8 in. in diameter. An unusual cultivar is 'Star Gazer', with upright facing red flowers with white margins; this lily has

LILIES

The lily, especially *Lilium candidum*, is in the Christian tradition the symbol of purity, innocence, and chastity. In the Semitic world, it is the symbol of motherhood.

But this particular lily, known by the common name of Madonna lily, had found favor with mankind long before the Christian era. It was the flower of Aphrodite, the Greek goddess of love, and was later the flower of Diana and Venus, becoming part of the ceremonies and festivals of these Roman goddesses. The Romans in turn took it with them as they conquered their world.

In ancient times the bulbs of lilies were also used in medicine. The mucilaginous substance concocted when the bulbs were cooked was used in external compresses for tumors, ulcers and inflammations, as an anointment, and as an emollient.

The lily was also used in heraldry, becoming the heraldic symbol of the House of Bourbon, the Fleur des Lys. The English botanist John Parkinson (1596–1629) described *L. chalcedonicum* as the "Red Martagon" of Constantinople, indicating that the beauty of the lily was appreciated there. Lilies of the New World were soon introduced into Renaissance Eur., as evidenced by Parkinson's description of *L. canadense* in *Paradisus Terrestris* (1629). Lilies were also introduced from China and Japan.

The most significant lily cultivations were made by E.H. Wilson (1876–1931), the English director of the Arnold Arboretum in Boston. Soon after the turn of the century, he introduced *L. davidii*, *L regale* and *L. sargentiae*. *L. regale* in particular spurred greater interest in lilies, as it was a trumpet flower of beauty and fragrance that was of comparatively easy culture and propagation. Another lily, *L. auratum*, the gold-banded lily of Japan, was grown in the 1880s in both Amer. and Eng. Its fragrance and large flowers created a great demand for this species.

The Mid-century Hybrids, in particular the cultivar 'Enchantment', started to make inroads into the market. Today this widely grown cultivar is used as a container plant, a cut flower and in the garden. Colored trumpet lilies such as 'Black Dragon', 'Pink Perfection' and 'Golden Splendor' followed, enabling gardeners to grow top-quality stock. While lilies are cultivated all over the world, the majority of the hundreds of cultivars offered are the result of Amer. hybridizers.

The genus comprises some 80 species, and while there are many hybrids between the various species, the "blood lines" are comparatively clear. By carefully selecting the parentage of lily hybrids, we have today a selection of colors and forms that were undreamed of but a short time ago. It is possible to select hybrids that will perform well in almost every conceivable location—in shade and sun, in formal borders and informal woodland settings, in containers on decks and patios, in greenhouses and conservatories. With time has come an increased understanding of the needs of the bulbs, and lilies can now be stored for late flowering or treated to be forced into flower at earlier times than in the open ground. Today lilies can be found in flower throughout the year.

As cut flowers lilies are superb. With commercially grown lilies, a short amount of stem is cut off, the stems are placed in water, and in just an hour or two the flowers are opening; the foliage is turgid and one would never know that these stems had been as much as four to five days in transit. If you are cutting lilies from your garden for your home, try to leave as much of the stem as possible in the garden—cut off only the flower head. The leaves will continue to manufacture food for the bulb, ensuring a good flower production the following year.

Lilies should be left in the ground for many years. Indeed, some stands exist that have been in the same location for fifteen to twenty years. There will come a time when, due to their natural ability to produce bulblets underground, the clumps will become too crowded for good continued production of strong flowering stems. When this happens, it is time to intervene.

In the fall, after the foliage has died down, carefully lift the entire clump, taking care not to damage the bulbs. Then gently separate the bulbs. You will find that the bulbs will be of various sizes, some perhaps the size of an egg, others the size of a small turnip, while the smallest will be only the size of your thumbnail. Plant the largest bulbs where you want them to grow, making certain that they are deep enough, with 4 to 8 in. of soil over the tops. The heavier the clay, the shallower you plant, but in most garden soils you will need some 6 in. (8 in. in sandy soils).

The smaller bulbs should not be discarded, but planted quite close together in a row, spaced 1 to 2 in. apart and covered with about 2 in. of soil. These will increase in size, and after one or two seasons they can be lifted and planted into their flowering positions. Always discard any bulbs that are damaged, as rots can set in.

As soon as the shoots emerge from the soil in spring, give lilies a feeding of a balanced fertilizer. If the plants are growing in containers, feed them weekly with a weak solution of liquid fertilizer. Stop feeding as soon as flower buds appear.

Remember that the tender young growing shoot of a lily must be protected from physical damage. If the stem is broken, there will be no flowers produced. Mark the location of the bulbs to avoid any possible damage to the shoots when you are cultivating in the border prior to the shoots' emergence.

After the plants have been in one location for a few years, you will be pleasantly surprised at how vigorous they are and just how tall they can become. In many areas it might be necessary to give these older established plants some support. The flower heads can become quite heavy and cause the stems to bend over, and the flower heads then cannot be seen to advantage. This is more likely with Trumpet and Oriental types; the Asiatic Hybrids seldom need support.

To control aphids, squash them with your fingers or wash them off with a jet of water. If you need to spray, generally products that can be used on roses are fine on lilies. Always follow the directions given regarding strength of solution, frequency of application and precautions to take.

With the vigorous hybrids available today, and the exciting range of forms and colors offered in catalogs, there is no reason why you should not have a great and varied selection of lilies in your garden.

Lilium

become one of the most popular pot plants, being forced into flower early and being held back for late flowering so that at almost any month of the year you will find this in the florists' shops.

Division VIII.

Contains all hybrids not provided for in previous divisions.

Division IX.

Contains all true species and their forms. See listings below for recommended lilies.

Division X.

Contains species, varieties and forms of Cardiocrinum which was known for many years as *Lilium giganteum.*

Today's new hybrid lilies are superior to earlier introductions, the range of colors having dramatically increased; this is especially true of the earlier-flowering Asiatic hybrids, which are produced by the thousands for superb cut flowers and are great container plants.

L. auratum (or-*rate*-tum).
GOLD-BAND LILY.
GOLDEN RAYED LILY.
This lily has a wonderful fragrance, great form and texture and is a vigorous grower. When well established it can reach over 10 ft. in height and carry as many as 20 flowers, each 10 in. in diameter. Bowl-shaped, the tips of the petals recurving a little, pure white and spotted with crimson-brown spots and a gold band in the center of each petal, this can vary in intensity of color. Late summer flowering, a wonderful cut flower and good container plant. Zones 5 to 8.

L. bulbiferum (bulb-*bif*-err-um).
A native of Europe, it has upward-facing blooms of orange- or fire-red, 4 to 5 in. in diameter, 15 to 20 flowers on 36 in. stems. Bulbils are produced on the upper part of the stem. Flowers in June–July. Zones 5 to 8.

L. canadense (can-ah-*dense*-ee).
Native of the eastern part of N. Amer., it grows to a height of 60 in. and produces bell-shaped flowers of lemon-yellow, with their insides speckled with deep crimson to black spots. Leaves in whorls around the stem. Likes a little shade in warmer climates. The flowers are held away from the stem by long flower stalks, the lower being up to 6 in. in length, the upper ones shorter thus forming a flower-head of conal shape. The *L. canadense* var. *editorum* is found at the western limit of its habitat and has red flowers. Zones 4 to 8.

Lilium candidum
MADONNA LILY

L. candidum (can-did-*dum*).
MADONNA LILY.
The bulb should be planted close to the surface of the soil. It produces a rosette of basal leaves and then the flowering stem in June. The stem carries as many as 15 or more pure white fragrant flowers 5 in. in diameter, reaching a height of 48 in. or more. Zones 4 to 8.

L. hansonii (han-soh-*nee*-eye).
Reaches 48 in. in height. Orange flowers spotted with brown, flowering in June–July. This lily should be planted 8 in. deep as it produces many roots on the lower part of the stem. Leaves in whorls; this is a great plant for woodland areas in light shade. Zones 4 to 8.

L. lancifolium (lance-*see*-foal-ee-um).
TIGER LILY.
For years this species was known as *L. tigrinum* (tie-*grin*-um). Bright orange flowers with a pinkish tinge, carried on black stems on which bulbils are freely produced. Many flowers produced, pendant often with secondary flowers making a full head. 60 in. in height, July–Aug. flowering. One of the easiest lilies to grow and does well even in poor soil. Zones 4 to 8.

L. lankongense (lang-kon-*gen*-see).
The bulb produces stolons which may emerge as much as 12 in. away from the bulb, 36 to 48 in. in height, 15 to 20 pendant, scented flowers of soft pink which deepen in color with age. Loves the sun, and while appreciative of moisture will withstand drought well. Flowers in July. Zones 5 to 8.

Lilium 'Enchantment'
ASIATIC HYBRID

Lilium martagon

Lilium

Lilium regale

Lilium speciosum

L. longiflorum (lon-gee-*floor*-um).

EASTER LILY.

In the garden, where you should plant any Easter Lilies you purchase after they have finished flowering, this plant will reach 36 in. in height and carry up to 6–9 pure white flowers in late summer. Zone 8.

L. martagon (mar-tuh-*gone*).

Native to much of Europe, easy to grow and an outstanding woodland plant. Flowers are pendulous, purple with many spots and carried on stems reaching 6 ft. in height. Leaves in whorls, occasionally scattered along the stem. Early summer flowering, and on well-established plants as many as 50 flowers are produced. There are several varieties; *L. martagon* var. *dalmaticum* (dahl-*mat*-tea-cum) has deep mahogany flowers, while *L. martagon* var. *album* (*all*-bum) is white. Zones 4 to 8.

L. pumilum (pew-*mill*-lum).

This species has brilliant, nodding red flowers with 24 in. stems in June. Loves full sun. Leaves are grass-like and cover the stems. There are several forms, including 'Golden Gleam' and 'Yellow Bunting', which when planted with the species are great with contrasting colors complimenting each other. Zones 5 to 8.

L. regale (ree-*gall*-lee).

Perhaps the finest of the trumpet-shaped lilies. Fragrant, pure white flowers, 6 in. long, open to give flowers 6 in. or more in diameter on top of 48 to 72 in. stems. Fragrant, long lasting, easy to grow, great container plants. Flowers in July but the flowers do not fade even in strong sun, which this species enjoys along with good moisture. Zones 4 to 9.

L. speciosum (*spee*-see-oh-sum).

Commonly referred to as "Rubrum" Lily, a favorite of flower arrangers, who love the carmine-red flowers, often with petals edged with silver. Established plants can reach over 6 ft. in height, carrying more than thirty flowers which open in July and last for a long time. If possible plant 8 to 10 in. deep; support the stems if needed. Very fragrant, good in containers. Has been much used in the breeding of new hybrids. Zones 5 to 8.

L. superbum (sue-*perb*-um).
Unusual, as it is found growing in marshy ground on the east coast of the U.S. from Maine to Florida. Can reach 10 ft. but generally less, producing a pyramid of up to 40 orange flowers which become crimson at the tips, but flower color can vary a little. Leaves in whorls. Flowers in July–Aug. Zones 5 to 8.

L. × testaceum (test-*tase*-ee-um).
This old species is actually an old hybrid, being a cross between *L. candidum* and *L. chalcedonicum* (chal-*see*-don-ee-cum); now superseded by many new hybrids, it still has garden merit. Flowers are pale corn-yellow with red spots, 48 in. or more in height. June–July flowering. Zones 4 to 9.

Lycoris (lie-*core*-is).
SPIDER LILIES.

Amaryllis Family (*Amaryllidaceae*).

The bulbs of this genus are not unlike daffodil bulbs. Native to China and Japan, they are valuable garden plants flowering in late summer or early fall.

Flowers are funnel-shaped and irregular, petals often recurved. Foliage is strap-like. Bulbs should be planted in mid- to late summer, as soon as they become available, by setting them 4 in. deep, 8 to 10 in. apart in well-drained but moisture-retentive soil in a sunny border. The flower spikes will emerge first, and as soon as they appear more moisture should be given; the leaves follow the

Lilium superbum

Lilium × *testaceum*

flowers and as they appear a feeding of balanced fertilizer should be given. These plants grow well in containers; 3 bulbs to a 12 in. pot is about right. Plants are best left undisturbed, but can be lifted and divided when of good size in order to increase the stock. Seed can be sown as soon as ripe in a sandy soil mix, in light shade with temperatures in the 50° F range at night. Transplant to individual pots as soon as they can be handled; in two seasons these will be of a size suitable for planting out.

L. albiflora (all-*bee*-floor-ah).
Creamy flowers on 18 to 24 in. stems are produced in the fall. Flowers are 2 in. in length, about ½ of which is tubular, then petals recurve; three to five flowers per stem. Leaves 20 to 24 in. in length with a pale center line. Zone 7.

L. aurea (or-*ree*-ah).
GOLDEN SPIDER LILY.
Golden-yellow flowers, 24 in. in height and long lasting. Flowers in Aug.–Sept. Leaves are strap-shaped, slightly bluish with a paler stripe in the middle. Not as hardy as the other species and in colder regions should be grown in a greenhouse. Zone 9.

L. radiata (ray-*dee*-ah-tah).
Flowers vary in color from pink to deep red or scarlet, on stems 18 in. in height and flowering in Aug. or early Sept. The anthers are much exposed and for this reason the plants are known as Spider Lilies. Very free flowering. Foliage is narrow with lighter green stripe down the center. Zone 5.

L. squamigera (squah-mah-*jeer*-ah).
The hardiest of the species, it has rose-lilac flowers with a bluish hue. The flowers reach a height of 18 in. in Aug. Unstriped, straplike leaves are 12 in. long, 1 in. in width and may be produced long after the flowers have passed. Zone 3.

Moraea.
See *Dietes*.

Muscari (mus-*kay*-ree).
GRAPE HYACINTH.
Lily Family (*Liliaceae*).
Native to the Medit. region and southwest Asia. Few bulbs are as easy to grow or as quick to naturalize as these. Leaves will often appear in the fall, with the spikes of tightly held little flowers crowded together on the short stems arising in the spring. Foliage is grasslike. Muscari like the sun but tolerate some shade. Almost any soil suits them, but they must have moisture while growing. Plant 2 to 3 in. deep and 4 to 5 in. apart. After the foliage has died down, rake it off. To propagate, lift and divide established clumps after the foliage has died. Seed is freely produced and germinates well. Sow seeds in a flat, and after a season of growth, line out the seedlings in a row, grow on; in two seasons lift and plant in permanent locations. The plants grow well in containers, but allow several weeks for them to produce roots before bringing them indoors. Great for the rock garden and alongside paths.

✳M. armeniacum (ar-mee-nee-*ay*-kum).
Deep purple flowers, 6 to 8 in. in height, with a white rim at the mouth. Flowers in April–May. Several selections are offered, including 'Blue Spike', a very free-flowering blue, and 'Early Giant', cobalt-blue and lightly fragrant. Zones 3 to 8.

M. azureum (ah-zoo-*ree*-um).
(Syn. *Pseudomuscari azureum*.) Very hardy and

easy to grow. Flowers are bright blue, 4 to 6 in. in height. This species is earlier than others into flower, often in March. Zones 3 to 8.

M. botryoides (bot-ree-*oy*-deez).

The height can vary between 5 and 10 in. The flowers are sky-blue with a white rim at the mouth, produced in late spring or early summer. Several forms or selections offered by nurseries, including 'Album' (*all*-bum), a pure white. Zones 3 to 8.

M. comosum var. plumosum (coh-*moh*-sum) (plu-*moh*-sum).

FEATHER HYACINTH.

The flowers are mauve, on stems 8 to 12 in. in height, flowering in April. Foliage is broader than that of other species. The flowers are carried well above the leaves and are unusual in that they have a featherlike appearance. Zones 1 to 9.

Muscari armeniacum
GRAPE HYACINTH

M. latifolium (lat-i-*foh*-lee-um).

Unusual in that it generally produces only one broad leaf. It flowers on stems reaching almost 12 in. in height, with two different colors of flowers: violet on lower part of the stalk, deep blue on top. Quite striking in appearance. Flowers in April–May. Zones 3 to 8.

★★Narcissus (nar-*siss*-us).

DAFFODIL.

Amaryllis Family (*Amaryllidaceae*).

Spring-flowering bulbs, native to Eur., northern Afr. and western Amer., which are hardy outdoors and grown in cool, sunny windows and greenhouses for winter and spring bloom. Of all the spring-flowering bulbs, narcissus are among the most popular and most widely grown. They have been known and grown for hundreds of years. Shakespeare, in "The Winter's Tale," says that daffodils "take the winds of March with beauty." Many nurseries force narcissus for sale at Christmastime and through the winter months.

Narcissus come in a wide range of colors, heights and shapes. There are creamy-white and yellow, golden, glowing reddish-orange and "pink" cultivars. The kinds with trumpets are generally referred to as daffodils. Other types are called jonquils and narcissus. The paper-white narcissus, so often grown in pebbles indoors for winter bloom, and the poet's narcissus are the kinds usually referred to as narcissus.

Narcissus bulbs should be planted in fall for spring bloom. In almost all zones, plant in Oct.; in Zones 9 to 11, plant bulbs in mid to late Nov. This will give the bulbs time to develop the root systems needed to flower well. Plant the bulbs 6 to 8 in. deep and 6 in. apart, except for those species with small bulbs, which should be planted 3 to 4 in. deep. *Narcissus* are effective if planted in drifts or when naturalized in wooded

Narcissus

areas—they usually bloom before the new leaves form on trees. They like full sun, light shade in the warmest areas. They will continue to bloom for many seasons, and they will increase if left undisturbed and kept dry in late summer. Blooms will be larger but fewer if they are lifted, divided and replanted every two or three years (poor bulbs should be discarded). But such is not necessary in naturalized plantings. Naturalized bulbs should receive a balanced fertilizer each year as soon as the leaves appear above the ground.

Narcissus do well in containers. It is important for them to have a good depth of soil under the bulbs, at least 4 in., and 3 to 5 in. of soil over them. Use a regular potting-soil mix, making sure that the containers have good drainage, as the bulbs hate to sit in wet and dank soil. After potting, set the containers in a cool, shaded area where temperatures will remain more or less constant in the 45°F range. Keep moist but not wet. Move the containers into brighter light and more warmth when the shoots are 3 to 4 in. above the level of the soil. Giving them time to root well is essential.

Narcissus are classified by the American Daffodil Society into several divisions, according to their form, size and color. A guide to this system of classification—explaining the defining characteristics most commonly used—and a listing of suggested cultivars follows. The cultivars are recommended because of their proven record in the garden. (New introductions are often more expensive because they are the result of many patient years of hybridizing.)

Trumpet Daffodils.

Trumpets are defined as having one flower per stem, and a trumpet or corona as long as or longer than the perianth segments.

'Dutch Master', large flowers of good texture,

soft yellow; good cut flowers and great in containers; considered by many to be a classic.

'Golden Harvest', very large, clean yellow flowers, often 6 in. in diameter.

'Mount Hood', a strong grower with long-lasting, pure white flowers.

Narcissus 'Mount Hood'
TRUMPET DAFFODIL

Large-cupped Narcissus.

Like the trumpets, large-cupped narcissus have one flower per stem, but their cup or corona is smaller—it must be more than one-third but less than equal the length of the perianth segments.

'Carlton', broad perianth, corona frilled, soft yellow; excellent garden plant.

'Duke of Windsor', pure white with soft orange cup.

'Flower Record', pure white perianth, deep red corona.

'Ice Follies', circular white perianth, large flat corona opens yellow and then turns white.

Small-cupped Narcissus.

Smaller than both the trumpet and large-cupped, the flower of the small-cupped narcissus has a cup or corona that is not more than one-third the length of the perianth segments.

'Barret Browning', pure white perianth with orange cup, one of the earliest to flower.

'Polar Ice', pure white perianth, cup white with just a hint of green.

Double Narcissus.

These selections are defined by their double flowers.

'Irene Copeland', snow-white flowers with yellow segments.

'Sir Winston Churchill', creamy-white with touches of yellow and orange.

'Texas', yellow with brilliant fiery-orange segments, very large flowers.

Poetaz or Tazetta Narcissus.

The characteristics of any of the *N. tazetta* group are clearly evident in these popular garden hybrids.

'Cheerfulness', double white flowers.

'Geranium', pure white with orange-red cup, long in flower.

'Yellow Cheerfulness', soft yellow, double flowers.

Poeticus Narcissus.

These flowers feature the characteristics of the *N. poeticus* group without admixture.

'Actaea', large flowers, snow-white perianth, yellow cup tinged with red.

Butterfly or Orchid-flowered Narcissus.

Corona of these flowers is split for at least a third of its length.

'Marie Jose', creamy-white perianth, with an orange-yellow star in the butterfly-shaped collar.

'Mistral', golden-yellow cup, split into six segments in front of a pure white perianth.

Pink Daffodils.

These large-cupped flowers feature a distinct pink color.

For best color, these should be grown in partial shade. If used as cut flowers, cut only when fully open (if cut in bud, the color will be disappointing).

Narcissus 'Flower Record'
LARGE-CUPPED NARCISSUS

Narcissus 'Carlton'
LARGE-CUPPED NARCISSUS

Narcissus

Narcissus tazetta 'Paper White Grandiflora'

Narcissus 'Actaea'
POETICUS NARCISSUS

'Mrs. R.O. Backhouse', white perianth with a long trumpet of shell-pink.

'Sentinel', corona apricot suffused with pink, with a background of a pure white perianth.

Triandrus Hybrids.

One of the parents of these hybrids is *N. triandrus*.

'Hawera', 8 in. in height, four to six waxy flowers of clear lemon-yellow per stem.

'Liberty Bells', soft clear yellow, three to four flowers per stem.

'Thalia', 24 in. in height, two to three snow-white flowers per stem, great garden plant.

Narcissus 'Geranium'
POETAZ NARCISSUS

Cyclamineus Hybrids.

One of the parents of these flowers must be *N. cyclamineus*, often with a Trumpet cultivar but showing typical *cyclamineus* characteristics.

'February Gold', lovely yellow, long in flower, often in flower in Feb.

'Tête-à-Tête', 6 to 8 in. tall, lemon-yellow with orange cup.

In addition to being listed here a number of hybrids are mentioned in the *N. cyclamineus* entry.

Polyanthus Narcissus.

'Grand Monarque', white perianth with yellow corona.

'Grand Soleil d'Or', yellow with small orange cup, very free flowering.

Jonquilla Narcissus.

'Sundial', pale lemon-yellow with orange cup, 6 in. in height.

'Trevithian', good yellow, fragrant, two to three flowers per stem, excellent cut flower.

N. asturiensis (as-too-ree-*en*-sis).

A species growing on the upper slopes of mountains in Portugal and Spain. The small bulb produces two to three erect leaves, 6 in. in length. The flowers are perfect miniatures, only 4 in. high, and are golden-yellow. March-flowering. The little flowers need protection from heavy rains, which can flatten them. The selection 'Giant' is nursery-grown, a practice that protects those bulbs still in their native habitat, which for years were harvested. Zones 3 to 9.

N. bulbocodium (bul-boh-*coh*-dee-um).
HOOP-PETTICOAT NARCISSUS.
The "petticoats" vary from globular, with a narrow hoop, to a wide-opening flaring skirt. Flowers are pale to deep orange-yellow, solitary, 4 to 6 in. in height, and appear in March–April. Foliage is grasslike, 8 to 12 in. in length. A delightful little species that grows well in poor soil and will naturalize. Ideal for the rock garden. Zones 3 to 9.

N. cyclamineus (sik-la-*min*-ee-us).
A charming little species 4 to 8 in. in height. The flowers are solitary, bright golden-yellow, with the corona ¾ in. long, the same length as the perianth segments that flare back and are aptly described by E.A. Bowles as "like the ears laid back of a kicking horse." Flowers in Feb.–March. A number of selections have been made, all of them great garden plants and superb in containers. These include 'February Gold', a good yellow with deeper yellow trumpet; 'Jenny', which opens as a bicolor of yellow and

Narcissus bulbocodium
HOOP-PETTICOAT NARCISSUS

Narcissus cyclamineus 'February Gold'
CYCLAMINEUS HYBRID

DAFFODILS

Many bulbs have been featured in verse, but few if any surpass the recognition given to daffodils when the English poet William Wordsworth (1770–1850) wrote:

I wandered lonely as a cloud
that floats on high o'er vales and hills,
When all at once I saw a crowd,
A host, of golden daffodils;
Beside the lake, beneath the trees,
Fluttering and dancing in the breeze.

Wordsworth does more than just describe a scene; he portrays the ideal setting for naturalizing daffodils—under trees, near water and in an informal shape, such as that of a cloud.

The name of the genus is derived from the Greek *narcoun* (to benumb), referring to the plants' narcotic properties. The genus is confined to Eur., N. Afr., and western Asia. There are thousands of named cultivars, but the exact number of species is difficult to determine. Some authorities list more than seventy species, others regard many of the minor variations as being subspecies of others. Narcissus have been in cultivation for hundreds of years, and the potential of cross-hybridization of two species grown close to one another, as undoubtably has taken place, does not make definitive identification easy. Today, scientists are using advanced techniques such as the minute examination of the chromosomes and genetic characters to aid in identification. The complex variations in form and shape of the perianth segments have led some authorities to suggest dividing genus *Narcissus* into other genera. This complexity of flower form found within the genus and the new work being done on chromosomal and genetic structure have resulted in revisions—and undoubtedly will continue to do so. If you visit a daffodil show and see the many hundreds of cultivars on display, no doubt the need for accurate classification will be appreciated. Those cultivars with the same characteristics should compete with each other, not with just any plant that happens to be a narcissus. Classification of species, while sometimes irksome, is necessary.

Narcissus are good cut flowers, but there is a trick to make them last as long as possible. They should be cut prior to the flowers being fully open; in fact, just prior to opening is best, with perhaps a petal or two showing signs of movement. Also be aware that the cut stems of narcissus will secrete a mucus, which, if the narcissus are to be mixed with other flowers in an arrangement, will harm the other flowers. It is best to set the narcissus in water for twenty-four hours, then take them out and wash the stems. Note, however, that when this is done, the stems should not be recut, as this would cause renewed flow of the harmful mucus. Another way to reduce the amount of mucus is to add five to seven drops of concentrated household bleach to a liter of water, or put a teaspoon of activated charcoal in the vase, add a liter of water and stir. The useful cut flower life can be as much as ten to twelve days, depending on the cultivar. Some gardeners swear that arranging flowers of bulbs in copper containers prolongs their life; others add copper coins to the water. This will not do any harm, and you might wish to try such a simple method of prolonging vase life.

In the garden, there will come a time when the flowers are finished and the plants may begin to look a little untidy. There is an advantage to picking off spent flowers—this stops the plant from wasting strength in forming seed. The foliage should be left as long as possible, however. Tying it into a knot will make it look tidier, or bending it over and slipping a rubber band over it will keep it neat. In a wild setting or where the the plants are naturalized, this is not necessary. The foliage should be allowed to remain on the bulbs as long as possible, to allow for maximum food production to see the bulbs through the winter and provide the energy reserves needed for good flower production the following year.

When it comes time to lift the bulbs, use a garden fork to gently loosen them from the soil and carefully lift, with the foliage attached. Place the bulbs in an airy location on a wire mat or on a shelf with good air circulation. Allow the bulbs to dry. After a few weeks you will find that the foliage is easily removed, and the earth around the bulb is dry enough for the bulbs to be easily cleaned. Put the bulbs in a paper sack and store in an airy place until it is time to replant in the fall. Check for any rot from time to time, removing any damaged bulbs.

Bulbs that are naturalized need not be lifted. But it is important to make sure that they have a resting period toward the end of summer. They should be allowed to become dry, not receiving any moisture for a period of at least a month. This will enable the bulbs to ripen.

It is also important to add to plantings that have naturalized to ensure a good mixture of shapes, forms and flowering times. With planning, a long period of interest can be obtained from such plantings. Many nurseries sell a mixture of types and cultivars suitable for naturalizing, and there is generally a price advantage to purchasing such mixtures. Add "named" kinds to such mixtures of the types you particularly like.

Bulbs grown in containers will frequently not perform as well the second year, and if space is limited the gardener depending on color from a limited area would be advised to purchase new bulbs each year. Bulbs that have been "forced"—that is, brought into flower ahead of the normal time—should also be discarded, as these bulbs are often exhausted after such treatment and will not give many, if any, flowers the following season.

Gardeners who have grown numerous cultivars may well be thrilled by some of the species listed in catalogs. The size of the bulbs of some species can be much smaller than those of the popular hybrids, which might surprise some gardeners, but even the smallest species, with bulbs only ½ in. in diameter, will produce lovely flowers. Bulbs should be firm, not soft, and have a good tunic, not be devoid of tunic and scarred. The base should be undamaged, since it is from this that the roots will be produced.

Narcissus

NARCISSUS
FLOWER FORMS

Trumpet

Triandrus

Tazetta

Large-cupped

Cyclamineus

Small-cupped

Jonquil

Split-cupped

Double

Poeticus

Narcissus bulbocodium (with *N. cyclamineus*)
Hoop-petticoat Narcissus

Narcissus cyclamineus 'Peeping Tom'
CYCLAMINEUS HYBRID

Narcissus 'Grand Soleil d'Or'
POLIANTHUS HYBRID

Narcissus jonquilla 'Suzy'
JONQUILLA NARCISSUS

white and fades to all white; 'Tête-à-Tête', lemon-yellow with deeper yellow cup; and 'Peeping Tom', a deep yellow, superb plant that naturalizes well. Zones 4 to 9.

N. jonquilla (john-*quill*-uh).
The species has a delightful fragrance and rich golden-yellow flowers, often six to a stem, reaching 12 in. in height. The flowers are 2 in. in diameter. Flowering begins in March–April and lasts for several weeks. Foliage is dark green, 12 in. long and rushlike. A number of cultivars are listed in catalogs, including 'Baby Moon', which is sweetly scented, soft yellow and very free flowering; 'Suzy', with a yellow perianth and orange crown that does not fade, and several flowering stems per bulb; and 'Trevithian', an excellent older cultivar and superb cut flower of pale lemon-yellow. Zones 3 to 9.

N. minimus. See *N. asturiensis.*

N. moschatus. A subspecies of *N. pseudonarcissus.*

N. poeticus (poe-*et*-ih-kus).
Narrow foliage, 8 to 16 in. in length, with fragrant flowers that can vary in color and height. Typically, the flowers have perianth segments of white or pale cream color with a corona of yellow with a red margin. Stems are 10 to 16 in. in height and carry one flower per stem. Because of the color in the center of the flower, it has been given the common name pheasant's-eye, and because of the beauty of the flower, it is also known as poet's narcissus. The cultivar 'Actea' (ak-*tee*-uh) has snow-white perianth segments and a yellow corona edged with red, the flowers 4 in. in diameter. It is an outstanding plant and a good cut flower. Zones 3 to 9.

N. pseudonarcissus (*sue*-doh-nar-siss-us).
TRUMPET NARCISSUS.
A very variable species, at one time comprising

Narcissus

Narcissus triandrus 'Thalia'
TRIANDRUS HYBRID

Narcissus poeticus

Narcissus cyclamineus

twenty-seven subspecies. Native to much of Eur., it has naturalized in many areas. Leaves are ¾ in. wide, 15 in. long. Flowers vary in color from white to deep yellow, and the corona often has a wavy margin or distinct lobes. 10 to 18 in. in height. Flowering in March or April. The subspecies *obvallaris* (ob-val-*lar*-ris) grows wild in Wales and is a vigorous, golden-yellow-flowered plant that naturalizes and grows well in containers. Zones 3 to 9.

N. tazetta (taze-*set*-tuh).
Up to fifteen flowers per stem are found on this species, which grows wild around the Medit. Stems are 18 in. in height and flowers are very fragrant. Flower color varies from pale to deeper yellow, with the corona often having an orange tinge. The popular Paper-whites, grown indoors for winter bloom, belong in the groups under this species.

N. triandrus (try-*ann*-drus).
ANGEL'S-TEARS.

Native to Spain, Portugal and northwestern France. The leaves and flowering stems are 6 to 12 in. in height. Flowers are solitary, but sometimes two to three per stem, and are pale cream to bright yellow in color. One of the latest species, flowering in April–May. Zones 3 to 9.

Nerine (nee-*rye*-nee).

Amaryllis Family (*Amaryllidaceae*).

Tender bulbous plants from S. Afr. The flowers are in clusters at the top of bare stalks and can be white, pink or red in color. The long, narrow leaves appear after the flowers, which blossom in late summer or early fall. Leaves remain on the plants through the winter and spring and die down in summer. As soon as the flower spike appears, give moisture and keep moist through the growing season until leaves begin to die back. Then keep dry until the cycle begins again. Feed after the flowers have finished with regular applications of liquid fertilizer. Plant the bulbs 3 in. deep and 12 in. apart. In containers use a regular potting mix, and leave the bulbs in the same container for several years. Propagate by lifting the bulbs when the foliage has died down and removing the freely produced offsets. Plants are easily raised from seed, which should be sown as soon as ripe. Use a sandy, free-draining soil mix and never let the seedlings dry out. In areas where frost occurs, protect by mulching heavily or bring the containers indoors.

N. bowdenii (bow-*den*-ee-eye).
Reaches 24 in. in height, with ten to fifteen flowers per stalk. Each is 6 to 8 in. in diameter, carmine-pink in color, and trumpet-shaped. Leaves are present when the plant is in flower but elongate after the flowers are finished, remaining green well into the spring. Zone 8.

N. curvifolia. See *N. sarniensis*.

N. filifolia (fil-i-*foh*-lee-uh).
Pretty pink flowers with wavy petals are small, and there are only five to ten flowers per 10- to 15-in. stalk. Flowers in late summer. The grasslike leaves are nearly evergreen, the bulb resting for only a short period in midsummer. Zones 8 to 10.

N. sarniensis (czar-nee-*en*-sis).
GUERNSEY LILY.

Received its common name when a ship was wrecked on the way from Cape Town, S. Afr., to the Netherlands and the bulbs were washed ashore on the English Channel island of Guernsey, where it naturalized. 18 in. in height. Up to ten flowers per stalk, varying in color from white to deep carmine, with prominent stamens that give the impression the flowers are dusted with gold. Late summer flowering. Several selections

Nerine bowdenii

Nerine

have been made, and the colors range from white to carmine. The cultivar 'Fothergillii Major' (foth-er-*jill*-ee-eye *may*-jor) is a dazzling vermilion-scarlet and makes an excellent container plant. Zones 9 to 10.

Notholirion (no-tho-*leer*-ree-on).
Lily Family (*Liliaceae*).
One species, which appears below, is often listed in catalogues.

N. thomsonianum (tom-soh-nee-*ay*-num).
ROSE-COLORED LILY.
Native to Afghanistan. Up to twenty-five flowers of soft pink are carried on a stem that reaches 36 in. in height. It flowers in April–May, and from early spring until it has finished it must be given moisture. The leaves are long and narrow and produced in late fall and winter. Being tender, it can be grown outdoors only in Zones 9 to 11, but it makes an ideal cool-greenhouse plant in all areas. It appreciates a dry ripening period after the foliage dies. Plant 3 in. deep and 18 in. apart in regular potting soil. Propagate by removing the young bulblets when the bulb begins to go dormant in early summer.

Ornithogalum (or-ni-*thog*-uh-lum).
Lily Family (*Liliaceae*).
Bulbs from S. Afr. and the Medit. region, their hardiness depending on their origin. The foliage is grasslike, and the flowers, which are produced in the spring, are often fragrant, carried in loose clusters at the top of bare stems or scattered along the stems. They are good plants for the garden and for containers. The flowers are waxy and long-lasting. Plants are easy to grow, some species growing so well that they become invasive, producing so many bulb offsets that propagation is not a problem. Plant 2 to 3 in. deep in bold clumps, in full sun. Soil should be well drained

but retentive of moisture in winter and spring and dry in late summer. Space the bulbs 10 in. apart, closer if you are going to cut some of the flowers. When growing plants in containers in colder areas, keep them dry after the foliage has died down, protect them by putting them in a frost-free location in winter and start them into growth in early spring.

Ornithogalum nutans
SILVER-BELLS

O. balansae (ba-*lan*-say-ee).
A dwarf species, 3 to 6 in. in height, from Turkey and Asia Minor. Glossy green leaves are just a little lower than the flowers. Up to five white flowers with a green stripe to the back of the petals are produced in March–May. Easy to grow. Zone 5.

O. nutans (*new*-tans).
SILVER-BELLS.
From southern Eur. Flower spikes are 12 to 18 in.

tall. Flowers are white with a green stripe and are produced in late spring. Leaves are narrow and 24 in. in length. Great for naturalizing in woodland areas and among shrubs. Zone 5.

O. thyrsoides (ther-*soi*-deez).
CHINCHERINCHEE.

Flowers vary from pure white to pale yellow and are cup-shaped, arranged on spikes reaching 24 in. in height. Very long lasting. The common name is an attempt at an onomatopoetic expression of the sound made when the stems are rubbed together. In warmer climates the bulbs can be left in the ground; in colder areas they should be treated as gladiolus, taken up and stored overwinter and replanted in the spring. One of the longest-lasting cut flowers, often lasting three to four weeks and giving a lovely fragrance all the while. Zone 8.

O. umbellatum (um-bell-*ay*-tum).
STAR-OF-BETHLEHEM.

Up to twenty star-shaped white flowers, striped with green on the reverse, on racemes reaching 8 to 10 in. in height, are produced in April–May. The flowers are unusual in that they open late in the day and close at night. Seeds itself to the point of almost becoming a pest. Leaves are dark green, 6 to 12 in. in length. Great garden plant if it has room to spread. Zone 4.

Oxalis (*ok*-suh-lis).
WOOD SORREL.

Oxalis Family (*Oxalidaceae*).

Low-growing plants with cloverlike foliage, native to S. Afr. and trop. and subtrop. regions of S. Amer. Several species have become so established in the U.S. that they have become weeds. Rootstocks are either bulbs or tubers, and lifting and dividing established plants is the best way to propagate, as the rootstocks multiply profusely.

Grow in any well-drained soil, preferably sandy, in sun. Plant 1 in. deep and 3 to 5 in. apart. Oxalis will survive drought conditions but prefer a little summer moisture. They make good plants for hanging baskets and in colder areas can be grown in containers in a regular potting soil. Fine plants for spaces between paving stones.

✱ O. adenophylla (ad-en-oh-*fye*-luh).

A tuberous-rooted native of Chile, this dwarf is 2 to 4 in. in height, with leaves held in compact rosettes, bluish and with many leaflets. Flowers are pink with darker veins fading to white and are carried on thin, wiry stalks in May–July. Loves full sun and is a good plant for the rock garden. Zone 7.

O. cernua (*sern*-you-uh).
BERMUDA BUTTERCUP.

A S. Afr. species that is invasive and can become quite a pest if not controlled. As many as thirty heads of yellow flowers, 10 to 12 in. in height, are produced in late winter to early spring. The scaly bulbs are small, but each will produce flowers. Leaves are cloverlike, with a brown spot on the doubly lobed leaflets. Zone 8.

O. deppei (*dep*-ee-eye).
GOOD-LUCK PLANT.
LUCKY CLOVER.
FOUR-LEAVED CLOVER.

From Mex., with foliage that is cloverlike with four red-spotted leaflets. Flowers are rose- or reddish-colored, 12 in. in height. The bulb is black, rounded and edible. Flowers from July–Sept. There is a white cultivar known as 'Alba' and another known as 'Iron Cross' because of the pronounced markings on the leaves. Zone 8.

Oxalis

Oxalis versicolor
Wood Sorrel

Pancratium maritimum
Sea Daffodil

O. hirta (*her*-tuh).
This purple- to pink-flowered species, which has a yellow tube, is from S. Afr. It reaches 12 in. in height but is often a trailing plant, and grows well in hanging baskets. Flowers are produced in the leaf axils, and the plant gives the impression of a fern producing flowers. Flowers in late summer. Not hardy but often grown as an annual. Zone 9.

O. lasiandra (lass-ee-*an*-druh).
Purplish-crimson flowers are 12 in. high above foliage of dark green, each leaf having up to ten leaflets. Summer-flowering. Good indoor plant in colder areas. Zone 9.

O. pes-caprae. See *O. cernua*.

O. regnellii (reg-*nell*-ee-eye).
A S. Amer. species with triangular purple leaflets and many soft-pink flowers. Summer-flowering. An excellent plant for indoors in colder areas. Zones 8 to 11.

O. versicolor (ver-*sik*-oh-lor).
This S. Afr. native makes an ideal houseplant, producing flowers of white or purplish-white with violet margins and yellowish tube, carried above unusual straplike leaves. Height is 2 to 8 in. Winter-flowering. The cultivar 'Candycane' has unusual red buds opening to show candy-cane striations. Zone 8.

Pancratium (pan-*kray*-she-um).
Sea Daffodil.
Sea Lily.
Amaryllis Family (*Amaryllidaceae*).
Native to the Old World. The bulbs of this genus are very large, often more than 6 in. in diameter. Foliage is strap-shaped, evergreen, dark green and shiny. Flowers, carried on stems that reach 24 in. in height, are pure white with a green stripe on the outside of the petals. In the very center of the flowers is a staminal cup that is long and toothed. They have a delightful fragrance. Plant in the

spring, placing 2 in. of soil over the tops of the bulbs and spacing them 12 in. apart. Propagate by lifting the bulb and removing the offsets in the spring. Good container plants in colder climates, where they will thrive in ordinary potting soil with good drainage and should be given moisture throughout the year.

P. maritimum (mahr-it-*tee*-mum).
Native to many parts of the Medit. Flowers are often 6 in. in diameter, appearing in July–Sept. Plants must have warmth and never be exposed to frost. They love very sandy soil that is free draining but moisture retentive. Zones 8 to 10.

Polianthes (pol-ee-*an*-theez).
Agave Family (*Agavaceae*).
There is only one species in cultivation, a tender, bulblike, tuberous plant from Mex. The leaves are gray-green and sword-shaped. The tubelike

Polianthes tuberosa
TUBEROSE

flowers, carried in racemes, are white, very fragrant and long-lasting. The plants like sun and grow in any good garden soil. Plant them 3 in. deep and give them good moisture during the summer months. They come into flower in late summer. Planted in early summer, they will flower that year. In colder areas they should be lifted and stored over winter in a frost-free location, but as they do not seem to flower every year, often missing a year, many gardeners prefer to plant new stock each season. In warm climates they can be left in the ground. In colder climates they can be grown in a cool greenhouse and if given additional heat in the spring can be forced into flower in May–June. To ensure flowering, it is advisable to start the plants into growth indoors, planting out when all danger of frost has passed. Propagate by dividing the rootstock.

P. tuberosa (too-burr-*oh*-suh).
TUBEROSE.
Slender iris-like foliage, 30 in. long and ½ in. wide, sheaths the flower spike which reaches to 24 in. in height and carries up to thirty fragrant white flowers in late summer. These are waxy, often 2½ in. in diameter and carried in pairs. Today the plants most often grown are doubles, such as 'Double Excelsior' or 'The Pearl', but there is a single-flowered cultivar, 'Single Mexican Everblooming'. All are superb cut flowers and are frequently found in florists' shops. Each large bulb will produce two to four flowering shoots. Zones 8 to 10.

Puschkinia (push-*kin*-ee-uh).
Lily Family (*Liliaceae*).
Charming plants from Asia Minor, flowering in early spring. The bulbs, which should be planted 2 in. deep and 4 to 6 in. apart, are not fussy with regards to soil as long as it is well drained. Ideal for the rock garden or the front of the border in

Puschkinia

Puschkinia scilloides

Ranunculus asiaticus
PERSIAN BUTTERCUP

full sun, they appreciate a drier resting period after the foliage has died down. Very easy to grow and best left undisturbed, except when an increase in stock is desired, which is easily accomplished by lifting and dividing and then planting the little bulbs that are freely produced.

P. scilloides (sill-*oy*-deez).
(Syn *P. libanotica.*) Shiny green leaves, 10 in. long and 1 in. wide, appear in spring, soon followed by stems carrying up to eight bell-shaped blue flowers, each with a darker blue stripe in the center of the petals. While the color varies a little, the lighter blue form is most commonly grown. Quite a hardy plant. Zone 5.

✶✶ Ranunculus (rah-*nun*-kew-lus).
BUTTERCUP.
CROWFOOT.
Buttercup Family (*Ranunculaceae*).
A large genus of more than 200 species, widely

scattered over Eur., N. Amer., N. Afr. and New Zealand. Most are easy to grow in ordinary garden soil, but *R. lyallii* (lye-*all*-ee-eye), which is wild on the slopes of Mt. Cook in New Zealand, is a difficult species to grow. The majority of the tubers offered in catalogs have *R. asiaticus* as a parent and are listed as mixed colors, such as Tecolote Strain, containing clean colors of many hues. Plant in the fall except in the coldest climates, where spring planting is preferred. Set the tubers 1 in. deep and 8 to 10 in. apart, in full sun, or in very light shade in the warmest areas. Ideal plants for the perennial border or the wild or rock garden. Propagate by seeds or division, but as these tubers are not expensive, purchasing new tubers each year is recommended.

R. asiaticus (ay-she-*at*-i-kus).
PERSIAN BUTTERCUP.
Hybrid strains with a very wide color range are the most commonly grown. The plants are often

treated as annuals in warmer areas of the South and in Calif. and are easily grown under glass in a cool greenhouse. Pot the tubers in Sept. in good potting soil and keep temperatures in the 45°F range at night. The tubers are quite small and should be planted with the "claws" facing downward. In the garden the tubers can be lifted and saved over winter in the coldest areas, left in the ground in warm areas. They make good container plants, but should be grown in shade until the foliage appears to allow for good rooting. They appreciate a feeding of a balanced fertilizer when growth commences. The flowers are carried on stems 12 to 15 in. in height; foliage is basal. Good cut flowers. Double-flowered cultivars and bicolors are often offered in catalogs. Zones 4 to 9.

Rhodohypoxis (row-doe-hye-*pox*-is).
Hypoxis Family (*Hypoxidaceae*).
Small but delightful little plants produced from a cormlike rootstock and native to S. Afr. They are quite hardy if kept on the dry side and are often grown in the nursery as a small pot plant. Leaves, 3 in. long, are produced in early spring, sheathing the rootstock, and are held flat on the ground. Plant 1 in. deep, 3 to 5 in. apart, in peaty soil that is well drained but moisture retentive. The plants like full sun, except in the warmest areas, where light shade is appreciated. Propagation is by lifting and dividing the rootstock, cutting if necessary. Seed can be sown in the spring in a peaty soil mix. Transplant seedlings to individual pots when they are large enough to handle. Plant in bold groups in the front of the border or in the rock garden.

R. baurii (*bow*-ree-eye).
Flowers from spring through early summer. Many individual flowers are produced, each up to 1½ in. in diameter but only 3 to 4 in. in height,

forming a mat. Color varies from white to pink. The cultivar 'Apple Blossom' has light pink flowers, freely produced. A lovely container plant. Zones 7 to 10.

Scadoxus (ska-*dox*-us).
Amaryllis Family (*Amaryllidaceae*).
This genus has bulbs that are large and fleshy. They should be planted with their shoulders at soil level, spaced 12 in. apart in light shade in a soil that is moisture retentive but free draining. Take care when planting or when lifting to divide established plants not to damage the fleshy roots. In warm areas where little or no frost is experienced they flower in late summer. In colder areas they make great container plants. Put one bulb per 10-in. pot, and as soon as growth is seen make sure the plant is kept moist and fed weekly with a weak solution of liquid fertilizer. Plants will die down over winter and should be kept barely moist during dormancy.

S. multiflorus ssp. katherinae (mul-ti-*floor*-us) (cat-*treen*-eye).
Produces seven to ten leaves, each up to 18 in. in length, which continue to grow after the flowers are past. Flowers on 24-in. stems. The petals are insignificant, but the flowers have many scarlet stamens touched with gold (pollen) and are often more than 10 in. in diameter on well-grown plants. An unusual and eye-catching plant. Zones 10 and 11.

Schizostylis (skiz-oh-*sty*-lis).
Iris Family (*Iridaceae*).
Fleshy-rooted plants from S. Afr. Foliage is grasslike, 10 to 12 in. long. The flowers are like miniature gladioli. Great plants for the cool greenhouse in colder areas and for general garden use in warmer climates. They like to grow with their roots in water and in full sun. If grown in con-

tainers, give them plenty of water during the growing season, drier conditions when foliage has died down. Plant 3 in. deep, 6 to 9 in. apart. Leave undisturbed until the clumps are very large, then lift, divide and replant.

S. coccinea (kok-*sin*-ee-uh).
CRIMSON FLAG.
KAFFIR LILY.
RIVER LILY.
The 18- to 20-in. flower spike is produced in late summer, carrying up to ten flowers of satiny-scarlet, narrow tubular flowers that open almost flat. Several cultivars are listed in catalogs, including 'Mrs. Hegarty', with rose-pink flowers, and 'Vicountess Byng', with pale shell-pink flowers. Zones 8 to 10.

Scilla (*sill*-uh).
SQUILL.
Lily Family (*Liliaceae*).
There are many species of this bulbous plant, native to Eur., Asia, S. Afr. and the Medit. region. The plants have narrow leaves, and most flower in the spring. Flowers are usually blue, but white and pink species also exist. The plants are best grown in large bold plantings in light shade in almost any kind of soil as long as it is moist in the spring. Except for *S. peruviana*, the bulbs should be set 3 to 4 in. deep and 6 to 8 in. apart and left undisturbed for years, lifted and divided only when propagation is undertaken.

S. amethystina. See *S. pratensis*.

S. bifolia (by-*foh*-lee-uh).
One of the finest of the spring-flowering bulbs, coming into flower in Feb–March. Up to eight flowers on each 4- to 8-in. stem. Flowers are blue but sometimes paler, almost white. Great woodland plant. Zones 3 to 8.

Schizostylis coccinea 'Mrs. Hegarty'
CRIMSON FLAG

S. campanulata. See *Hyacinthoides hispanica*.

S. hispanica. See *Hyacinthoides hispanica*.

S. non-scripta. See *Hyacinthoides non-scripta*.

S. nutans. See *Hyacinthoides non-scripta*.

S. peruviana (per-roo-vee-*ay*-nuh).
Native to Portugal and Spain. Summer-flowering, not fully hardy, requiring protection where temperatures drop below 24°F in winter. Foliage is green, 1½ in. wide, 12 in. in length. Flowers are a deep blue, and up to 100 form each densely packed spike, which reach 12 in. in height. An excellent container plant, in colder areas it should be taken indoors just before the first frost and brought outdoors after the last frost in the spring. Plant the bulb so that the neck is at soil level. Zones 8 to 10.

Scilla peruviana

Scilla siberica
SIBERIAN SQUILL

S. pratensis (pray-*ten*-sis).
Grows 6 to 12 in. in height. Bluish-lilac flowers appear in late spring or early summer, on very sturdy stems. Likes full sun and well-drained soil. Zones 4 to 9.

S. siberica (sigh-*beer*-i-cuh).
SIBERIAN SQUILL.
One of the most popular of the spring-flowering bulbs, especially the cultivar 'Spring Beauty'. Bulbs will often produce more than one 8-in. flowering stem, with up to six brilliant blue flowers on each. Leaves are bright green, 8 in. in length. Ideal for planting among shrubs and for naturalizing. A white form is often listed under 'Alba' in catalogs. Zones 3 to 8.

S. tubergeniana (too-ber-jen-ee-*an*-uh).
Flowers are light blue with a darker stripe down the center of each petal. Each bulb will produce

Scilla tubergeniana

Scilla

several spikes 4 in. in height in late Jan. or early Feb., a disadvantage in colder climates but making it an ideal plant for a cool greenhouse. When the flowers are fully open they are almost flat and very showy. Zones 4 to 9.

Sparaxis (spuh-*rak*-sis).
WANDFLOWER.
Iris Family (*Iridaceae*).
S. Afr. cormous plants with sword-shaped leaves forming a basal fan. Funnel-shaped flowers with a flat-spreading edge are carried aloft on wiry stems to a height of 12 to 18 in. In warm climates plant in the fall, setting the corms 2 in. deep and 3 to 4 in. apart in bold clumps. In areas where frost occurs, plant in the spring. Plant in a sunny location where the soil is free draining, but provide moisture when the plants are in growth. After flowering allow the corms to become dry. Leave in the ground in warm areas; bring container-grown plants indoors in colder areas. To propagate, lift after foliage has died down and separate the little corms from the parents. Great cut flowers and should be more widely grown.

S. tricolor (*try*-cul-or).
Called the harlequin flower in its native land due to the great diversity of color of the flowers, which range from white to yellow, crimson to orange with deep yellow centers outlined with black. Flowers often have contrasting colors, especially in certain cultivars listed in catalogs. Flowering is in April–May. The starlike flowers may reach 2 in. in diameter and are long-lasting. Zones 9 to 10.

Sprekelia (spreh-*kee*-lee-uh).
Amaryllis Family (*Amaryllidaceae*).
A native of Mex. having a large bulb and a flower that is often confused with hippeastrum. They make excellent greenhouse plants even though

Sprekelia formosissima
AZTEC LILY

the flowers are solitary, as they remain in flower for a long period of time. Leaves are straplike. Should be planted with the top of the bulb at soil level in well-drained soil in full sun. Propagate by lifting the bulbs in Aug. after the foliage has died down and separate the little bulbs from the parent, then grow them on to flowering size.

S. formosissima (for-moh-*sis*-i-muh).
AZTEC LILY.
JACOBEAN LILY.
ST. JAMES'S LILY.
Very large flowers of deep crimson produced before the straplike leaves in early summer. While solitary, they are of great beauty and long-lasting, and older bulbs will produce more than one spike. The uppermost petal is wide, the two side petals are strap-shaped, and other petals curl and form a tube, making the flower of outstanding interest. Flowers are on 12- to 18-in.-tall stems. Zones 9 to 10.

Sternbergia (stern-*burge*-ee-uh).

Amaryllis Family (*Amaryllidaceae*).

Native to Eur. and the Middle East. One of the finest autumn-flowering bulbs, with narrow straplike leaves and crocus-like flowers. There are no finer golden-yellow flowers, and they are tough, withstanding the frosts and rains, and long-lasting. The bulbs like to have a hot, dry summer resting period and well-drained soil during the winter and spring, when moisture is required. Plant the bulbs 6 in. deep, 6 to 9 in. apart, in the fall or late summer. In areas where temperatures fall below 0°F, protection will be needed. Leave undisturbed for years, lifting to divide when propagation is undertaken, as seed is not generally produced. Inclined to flower in alternate years.

S. lutea (*lew*-tee-uh).

LILY-OF-THE-FIELD.

A native of the Medit. region. Leaves are almost ½ in. wide, 6 to 10 in. long. Flowers are egg-shaped, carried above the foliage to a height of 8 in. Leaves will continue to grow after the flowers are finished. The bulb looks much like a *Narcissus* bulb. Zones 6 to 10.

Tigridia (tye-*grid*-ee-uh).

TIGER FLOWER.

Iris Family (*Iridaceae*).

Native to Mex. and S. Amer., these cormous plants produce sparse swordlike foliage over which the flower stems seem to hover. They are exceedingly colorful, and while individual flowers last only a day, there are many produced and the flowering period lasts many weeks. The three larger petals form a cup in the center of the flowers, with three smaller petals between the larger ones. Flower color can vary from shades of purple and rose to white, yellow and orange. Bulbs should be planted in the spring in all cli-

Sternbergia lutea
LILY-OF-THE-FIELD

mates, set 3-4 in. deep and 6 to 10 in. apart, in well-drained soil in a sunny location. In colder areas lift the bulbs and overwinter in a frost-free area; in warmer climates leave them in the ground. Propagate by lifting and dividing after the foliage has died back, or by sowing seed in a sandy soil mix, keeping them moist and out of the sun, at a temperature of about 60°F at night. When the tiny bulb develops, set the plants outdoors and allow them to grow on. In the following year these little plants should flower.

T. pavonia (pah-*voh*-nee-uh).

TIGER FLOWER.

SHELL FLOWER.

MEXICAN SHELL FLOWER.

This is the best-known and most commonly grown species. Height is 18 to 20 in. Flowers vary in color from yellow to white, and reds to orange, mostly with purple blotches in the cup. Plants are usually sold as "mixed colors". While the flower-

Tigridia pavonia
TIGER FLOWER

ing time is July–Sept., this will depend on the time they are planted. Foliage is sword-shaped, held in a fan; leaves are 10 to 12 in long. Zone 8.

Trillium (*trill*-ee-um).

WAKE ROBIN.

BIRTH-ROOT.

LAMB'S QUARTERS.

Lily Family (*Liliaceae*).

Found from the Himalayas to Japan, but those grown in our gardens are from N. Amer. Aptly named, as the leaves and flowers are tripartite. The rootstock is either a rhizome or a tuber, and the leaves are in a whorl at the top of sturdy stems and are held horizontally. The flowers arise from the leaf whorl, sometimes sessile or on short pedicels, sometimes becoming pendant as the flowers mature, but generally upright. There is only one set of leaves and one flower per stem, but a plant can produce many stems. Trilliums are ideal woodland plants, preferring light shade and soil

that is slightly acid. Plant 4 in. deep, 8 to 12 in. apart. They require moisture throughout the year. Fully hardy, they do not appreciate the warmest climates but will grow there if copious amounts of moisture are given, along with a mulch of leaves to keep the soil cool. Propagation is by lifting and dividing, which should be done in early fall. Seed can be sown as soon as ripe. Use a peaty soil mix and keep cool and in moderate light, with good moisture. The young plants will reach flowering size in two to three seasons.

T. cernuum (*sern*-you-um).
NODDING WOOD LILY.
Reaches up to 24 in. in height, often less. Leaves are nearly sessile. There are two or three stems per plant. Small white (rarely pink) flowers appear on drooping, short stems in April–May. Zones 3 to 8.

T. erectum (ee-*rek*-tum).
Native to eastern N. Amer. and often found in woodland areas. Up to 12 in. in height. Flowers are more than 1 in. in length, mostly in reddish hues, but white, yellow and green forms are known, often listed under the cultivar names 'Album' (*all*-bum), white, and 'Luteum' (*lew*-tee-um), yellow. Zones 3 to 8.

★**T. grandiflorum** (gran-di-*flohr*-um).
From the same areas as *T. erectum*, this is possibly the finest of all trilliums. 12 to 18 in. in height. The flowers are white, up to 3 in. in diameter and almost side-facing. Flowers in April–June. The variety *roseum* (row-*zee*-um) has rose-colored flowers, and the variety *rubrum* (*roo*-brum) has flowers that become deep pink as they age. Zones 3 to 8.

T. sessile (*sess*-i-lee).
Grows to 10 to 12 in. in height. The leaves are

Trillium grandiflorum

Trillium grandiflorum var. *rubrum*

large and mottled light and dark green. Dark crimson flowers are sessile, and they come into flower in April–June. There is a yellow form sometimes listed in catalogs. This species needs to be planted in bold groups. Zones 3 to 8.

Triteleia (treye-*tell*-ee-uh).
Lily Family (*Liliaceae*).
Cormous plants, mostly from the western U.S. They have grasslike leaves that disappear in the summer and, according to the species, will produce white, purple, red or yellow flowers in clusters on slender stalks. They are good plants for naturalizing, especially in warmer climates, and enjoy the dry conditions in summer found in well-drained gritty soils of a rock garden. Where temperatures fall into the 20°F range, protect the plants with a mulch of leaves or lift in late summer and store over winter, planting them again in the spring.

T. laxa (*lax*-uh).
Ithuriel's Spear.
(Syn. *Brodiaea laxa*.) Native to Ore. and Calif., this species has the largest umbels in the genus, often 6 in. in diameter with each flower 1 in. across. Flowers are deep blue on stems 24 in. in height and make good cut flowers. The cultivar 'Queen Fabiola' is a little taller, has stronger stems and is just a little later in flower, blooming in June or July. Zone 8.

Triteleia laxa
Ithuriel's Spear

Tritonia (try-*toh*-nee-uh).
Blazing Star.
Montbretia.
Iris Family (*Iridaceae*).
This S. Afr. genus is growing in popularity. From quite small corms, swordlike rigid leaves are produced, arranged in equal ranks on the side of the flowering stem. The flowers are arranged alternately on each side of the stem, giving a zigzag look to the flower spike. They are held

Tritonia

erect, are bowl-shaped, and are generally in the orange to red shades. Set the corms 2 in. deep and 4 to 6 in. apart in a sunny border. In colder climates they should be lifted in early fall, stored over winter in a frost-free area and planted again about two weeks before the last frost is expected. Propagation is best achieved by lifting the corms and removing the smaller ones, which are freely produced. Seed can be sown as soon as ripe. Sow the seeds in a peaty soil and keep the temperatures at night in the 55°F range. While the corms should have moisture during their growing season, they must never be in wet soil and prefer a dry period in late summer after flowering.

T. crocata (crow-*cay*-tuh).
Reaching up to 15 in. in height. The bowl-shaped flowers are mostly in the yellow to orange range, but white, cream and pink flowers can be obtained if the mix of colors is good. Flowers in May–June. Foliage is stiff, pointed and sword-shaped. Plant in the fall in Zones 7 to 11, and in the spring in other climates, lifting in the fall for wintering. These plants are easy to grow and thrive in good garden soils. They like fertilizer in poorer soils, which will increase the number and size of the flowers, up to 1½ in. in diameter.

Tulbaghia (tool-*badge*-ee-uh).
SOCIETY GARLIC.
SWEET GARLIC.
PINK AGAPANTHUS.
Amaryllis Family (*Amarlyllidaceae*).
Native to S. Afr. The common names are easy to understand, as the foliage has an onion smell when crushed and the flowers are in umbels, like an agapanthus, but pink in color. The rootstocks are tuberous or cormous, sometimes fat and rhizomatous. Of the several species, only *T. violacea* is commonly listed in catalogs, and it is the prettiest. It makes a good bedding plant in warmer

climates, where it will flower most of the summer in full sun or light shade. Plant 1 to 2 in. deep, 6 to 12 in. apart, in good soil with moisture-retentive qualities. In colder zones lift after the foliage has died down and store over winter in a frost-free area. In areas where bulbs are left in the ground, feed occasionally in early spring. Propagate by lifting and dividing the rootstock while dormant. Seed should be sown in the spring in a sandy soil mix, with temperatures in the 50°F range at night. They make good container plants, but grow them in large containers so they can remain undisturbed and multiply.

T. cepacea. See *T. violacea*.

T. violacea (vye-oh-*lay*-see-uh).
Plants are easy to grow and have a long flowering season from late spring through midsummer. Umbels of up to twenty pink flowers on 12- to

Tulbaghia violacea
SOCIETY GARLIC

18-in. stems above attractive green leaves that are up to 12 in. in length. It will form colonies if allowed to remain in the soil, making it an ideal plant among shrubs, as it adds interest to the border when the shrubs are not in flower. Zone 8 with winter mulch, Zone 9 without protection.

✦✦ Tulipa (*too*-li-puh).

TULIP.

Lily Family (*Liliaceae*).

Native to southern Eur. and the Near East, some to Siberia and Asia. Tulips are hardy spring-blooming bulbs that rival the narcissus in popularity. Most of the commercially grown tulips sold in the U.S. come from Holland, site of the world's largest bulb fields. Holland's Keukenhoff Gardens have probably the most extensive and extravagantly beautiful displays of tulips to be found anywhere. Dutch interest in tulips goes back several hundred years, and it was so intense in the seventeenth century that it amounted to hysteria. "Tulipmania" is the term applied to this period in Holland's history, when speculation in tulip values caused a crisis in banking and wiped out many individual speculators. At that time a single bulb could be worth between $10,000 and $50,000. The Dutch government finally put a stop to the speculation, but Holland remains the tulip center of the world. Some bulbs are raised commercially in the U.S., whose tulip centers are around Holland, Mich., Pella, Iowa, and Seattle, Wash.

Tulip varieties range in height from short to very tall (Darwin) and bloom generally from mid-spring (species and early tulips) to early summer (gardeners' tulips), although in a sunny, protected spot some of the species bloom as early as Feb. Their range of colors extends to all shades except blue, and there are also blotched and striped varieties ("broken" tulips). Tulips are beautiful planted in clumps of at least ten of one variety in spring borders and among foundation plantings, but they are most often massed in formal beds. Tulip fanciers treat the bulbs as annuals; they dig and discard the current season's bulbs and replant newly purchased stock in fall to guarantee top-quality blooms the following year. During the summer they plant the tulip beds with annuals. Gardeners with no helpers and with low maintenance in mind plant tulips more deeply, where the bulbs seem to deteriorate less over the years, and treat them as perennials. Bedding tulips that would otherwise be discarded may be replanted in naturalized settings where the view will not be affected by the likelihood that the tulips may become less spectacular as the years go by.

The bulbs are planted in mid- to late fall and will bloom from spring to early summer, depending on the species and variety. Set the bulbs broad side (meaning flat or root side) down in their planting beds or holes. Rich soil, well amended with compost and containing enough sand for really good drainage, is required. Since tulip roots go down, it is important that good soil, well worked and fertilized, be available below the bulb, particularly if the bulbs are not to be discarded after the first season. In preparing beds for tulips, avoid fresh or only partly decomposed manure; thoroughly decayed manure is a good fertilizer, as is rotted compost. Bone meal, scattered at the rate of one cup per square yard, is another good source of nutrients for tulips. Bulbs to be left in the ground benefit from an early application of a complete garden fertilizer when shoots are 1 to 2 in. high in spring.

Tulips are bulbs that require special treatment if they are to bloom south of Zone 8. Where winters are almost frost-free, tulip bulbs must be stored in a refrigerator for from four to six weeks before planting time, which is about or shortly after the third week in Nov. They must not be

Tulipa

TULIPS

Greek mythology has given names to many of our beautiful flowering bulbs: crocus, hyacinth, narcissus. It is the mythology of Persia, however, that brings us the story of the tulip. Ferhad loved the young maiden Shirin, but unfortunately, his love was spurned. When he went into the desert to die, each tear he shed turned into a flower called lale in Persian, the flowering bulb we call the tulip. This name is actually derived from the Turkish *tulbend* (turban), so called because of its resemblance to the traditional Turkish headdress. Eventually, the word evolved to *tulipam*.

In Islamic culture, the tulip was well regarded. Omar Khayyám mentioned it in his writing prior to the thirteenth century. Species were collected by Mohammed Babur, the first Mogul ruler in India, in the early part of the sixteenth century. Pierre Belon, the French naturalist, travelling in Turkey in that same century, described the gardens as having many "red lilies"—in all probability a reference to tulips. While the tulip was known in much of Eur. in the early part of the sixteenth century, it was not until the Ottoman sultan Suleiman the Magnificent was besieging Vienna, in 1529, that the events that propelled the tulip into prominence took place.

The emperor of Austria, Ferdinand I, wished to talk peace with Suleiman. As his emissary, he sent Augier Ghislain de Busbecq. A fortunate choice, as while passing through the countryside de Busbecq noticed and admired the tulips, and those growing in the gardens of Constantinople.

He bought a number of them and had them shipped back to the gardens of Ferdinand in Vienna, where the bulbs came under the care of Carolus Clusius. A short time later, Clusius left Vienna to take up an appointment as professor of botany at the University of Leiden in the Netherlands, and he took his bulbs with him. For many years bulb-growing in the Netherlands was centered in and around Leiden.

By the beginning of the seventeenth century, there was such a demand for tulip bulbs that many people gambled fortunes to obtain these wonderful bulbs that multiplied by themselves.

Today the exportation of tulip bulbs still plays a major role in the economy of the Netherlands.

In early times, the value of a tulip bulb that produced flowers streaked with other colors was highly valued. It was thought that such bulbs had "magical" qualities, and they were much sought after. If such a bulb happened to rot, it was rubbed against a healthy bulb in the hope that these "magical" qualities would be transferred. What was transferred instead was the virus that caused the streaking. Viral diseases were unrecognized in those days.

Today a new cultivar of exceptional merit will still command an extremely high price. What must be appreciated is that it may take as long as seven years to produce just one exceptional cultivar, and this may be the end result of a grower raising thousands of seedlings. It is not unusual to find that from more than 250,000 seedlings raised, only two or three are worthy of being introduced onto the market.

Selecting tulips for cut flowers is not difficult. Darwin hybrids can be harvested when half the bud is colored and half is green. Other cultivars should be cut when the whole bud is colored. Commercial growers harvest flowers several times a day, which makes the tulips more uniform within the bunches, resulting in more even keeping quality. Tulip stems will grow quite rapidly in water and the stems will bend. Storing the flowers in a vertical position and tightly wrapped will avoid stem bending. Cut stems will last a few days in storage before they should be sold, while tulips pulled from the soil with the bulbs may be stored for two to three weeks.

Gardeners are often concerned about planting winter- and spring-flowering annuals over the top of tulips, thinking that the shoots will be harmed if they run up against the roots of the annuals and not be able to work their way through to flower. There is no need for such concern, as the tulips, in fact all bulbs, will work their way through without any problem and without any damage to themselves or the annuals.

Certain tulips will flower again a second year, but the size of the flowers will be reduced. In the home garden a good practice is to plant the bulbs close together for their second flowering season and then either enjoy them "en masse" or cut them for indoor decoration.

Tulips that have been lifted should be stored in a paper bag and examined regularly. About 6 to 8 weeks prior to normal planting time for your area, the bulbs should be placed in the vegetable section of the refrigerator to allow them to ripen completely and to stimulate the formation of the flower bud inside the bulb. The ideal temperature is 40°F.

It is estimated that there are some 100 species of tulip. This is only an estimate, since hybridizing took place many years ago, prior to the introduction of the tulip into cultivation. Some plants regarded as species were found to have been in fact hybrids, albeit very close to species. Today it is thought that the bloodlines of all species and cultivars are known, but this is still not 100% certain.

As to the number of cultivars, there are thousands. By 1948 there were more than 4,000 names registered. Registration of names is very important, because there are several centers of production in the world. Tulips are raised not only in the Netherlands, but also in the U.S. and in Japan. If you purchase a named cultivar from any vendor, and for example it is called 'Gudoshnik' you are assured that you will have exactly that, and the color of the flowers will be the same no matter where the bulb was produced. There might be some variation in height and in exact time of flowering, but this will be due to climatic variances during growth.

Tulipa

frozen. Southern gardeners may buy precooled bulbs from local garden-supply centers. The tulips will grow well after cool winters in the South, but the gardener must expect to treat them as annuals.

In cool areas north of Zone 8, bulbs need not be refrigerated and are planted in Oct. for the early tulips, and late Oct. or early Nov. for varieties that bloom in May. Bulbs of the species tulips do well planted at 4 to 5 in.; taller tulip varieties may be planted at 8 in. but are less apt to be eaten by rodents if planted at closer to 12 in. (Cages made of hardware cloth keep rodents from the bulbs, and rodent repellents help, too.) A distance of about 6 in. between bulbs is recommended.

The plants may simply be dug up and the bulbs discarded. But if the bulbs are to be saved, remove the fading flower heads when the season of bloom is over and allow the foliage to ripen until it yellows and dies down. Then dig the bulbs and set in an airy, roofed-over place outdoors to dry for a few days. Clean off the soil, dust with sulfur, and store in shallow layers on screens or hang in nylon bags from rafters in a cool, dry, well-ventilated room until it is time to plant again in fall. Bulbs may be moved before the foliage has died if you need the beds for other plantings. Dig the plants carefully, taking as large a clump of soil as possible, and replant or heel-in in 4-in. trenches in a sunny location. Water well after planting. When the foliage has died down, lift, dry, clean and store the bulbs as described above.

Tulips are divided by many authorities into varied classifications. A basic division is between the species tulips, which might be called the wild tulips, and gardeners' tulips, which have been bred and improved, and which stem primarily from two of the species, *T. gesneriana* and *T. suaveolens*. The species tulips are generally propa-gated by seed, and the gardeners' tulips (most varieties planted today) by bulb offsets. Species tulips are less spectacular and generally smaller; most bloom early, may have up to three blooms to a stem, and are used often in rock gardens, where they can be left for many years. Gardeners' tulips are the ones for formal displays, and most carry a single bloom on each stem.

The basic classification for *Tulipa* is a simple division according to the time of flowering— Early Flowering, Midseason Flowering and Late Flowering—with a fourth division, Species, into which all species are placed. Within this classification are 15 classes.

Early Flowering Tulips

SINGLE EARLY TULIPS.
These are the first to bloom, starting in mid-April. Especially early is the strain Duc van Tol, with an average height of about 6 to 8 in. and very bright colors.

DOUBLE EARLY TULIPS.
These flower a little later than the Single types and are a little taller. 'Carlton', a good deep red, is one cultivar often listed in catalogs.

Midseason Flowering

MENDEL TULIPS.
These are not quite as popular as they were, but 'Apricot Beauty', a salmon pink, and 'Athlete', a pure white, are still found in catalogs. These are generally 18 to 24 in. in height and will grow well in light shade. Mendels are used in greenhouses, as they force well.

TRIUMPH TULIPS.
These have good texture, making them ideal for outdoor planting. There is a wide color range and

Tulipa acuminata

Tulipa 'Marjolein'
LILY-FLOWERED TULIP

Tulipa 'Queen Wilhelmina'
DARWIN TULIP

Tulipa 'Flaming Parrot'
PARROT TULIP

Tulipa

unique combinations, the edges often margined with another color. The cultivar 'Merry Widow' is a deep red edged with silver. There are also pure colors, such as 'Hibernia', a pure white.

DARWIN HYBRID TULIPS.
Possibly the best types for warmer climates. The flower stems are tall, often more than 30 in. in height, with the individual flowers often as much as 6 in. in diameter when fully open. While the color range is not as great as in other classes, mostly falling in the red and orange ranges, there are some "sport" flowers that arise from another bulb and have flecks of other colors. Such a cultivar is 'Gudoshnik', a sulfur-yellow flecked with red, with every flower a little different. The form of the flowers varies a little, from almost triangular to rounded. 'Apeldoorn' is scarlet with a black base; 'Yellow Apeldoorn', a yellow with a black base.

Late Flowering

DARWIN TULIPS.
Possibly the best-known type, generally reaching more than 30 in. in height and having a flat bottom and top, making them almost rectangular. Flowers in late April or early May. There is an almost satiny quality to the petals. In this class can be found cultivars that have been grown for many years; for example, 'Clara Butt', a salmon-pink that was introduced in 1920 and is still grown today. 'Sunkist', a pure lemon-yellow, and 'Aristocrat', a soft violet-rose, are but some of the cultivars available.

LILY-FLOWERED TULIPS.
These have very pointed petals, but despite their exotic looks they are quite tough and are excellent cut flowers. Flower in late April–May. Among the cultivars are 'West Point', a good clear yellow;

'Queen of Sheba', a red edged with golden-yellow; and 'China Pink', a clear light pink.

COTTAGE TULIPS.
These have oval flowers and were once called Single Late Tulips. The flowers are large, and in this class can be found cultivars that will carry as many as six flowers per stem, making them ideal for containers as well as for bedding. Many pastel colors are found in this class, some with a distinct green rib in the center of the petals. Among the cultivars are 'Mrs. John T. Scheepers', a golden yellow; 'Greenland', pink with a light green rib edged with yellow; and 'Red Bouquet', a clear scarlet with several flowers per stem.

REMBRANDT TULIPS.
These are the "broken" tulips, so called because the colors are striped or blotchy, and are the tulips often featured in the paintings of the Old Masters. Types previously known as Bizarre and Bijbloemen are now classed under Rembrandt. They flower in early May, and cultivars include 'Victor Hugo', a light rosy-pink on a white ground, and 'Pierrette', a pale violet streaked with darker hues.

PARROT TULIPS.
These have fringed flowers, 20 to 24 in. in height, and flower in May. The flowers are often very large and are best planted where they have some protection from the wind. The finely shredded, scalloped or undulating edges to the petals make the plants most attractive. 'Black Parrot' is very dark maroon-brown; 'Texas Gold', a deep yellow with a hint of red to the cut edges of the petals; and 'Fantasy', deep rose streaked with green.

DOUBLE LATE TULIPS.
The flowers are large and are also known as Peony-flowered. They come into bloom in late

Tulipa 'Estella Rijnveld'
PARROT TULIP

Tulipa 'Angelique'
DOUBLE LATE TULIP

Tulipa 'Lilac Perfection'
DOUBLE LATE TULIP

Tulipa clusiana
LADY TULIP

Tulipa

May and are 16 to 24 in. in height. The heads are very large and require some protection in order for them to reach maturity and not be ravaged by the wind. 'Bonanza' is a deep red with petals edged with gold; 'Mount Tacoma' is a large pure white.

Species
Cultivars in these different classes strongly reflect their parentage.

KAUFMANNIANA CULTIVARS AND HYBRIDS (kauf-man-ee-*ay*-nuh).
Very early flowering, often in March. Height is generally less than 12 in. The leaves are mottled. The tulips in this class are ideal for colder climates and one of the few types that will naturalize. Often having two-toned flowers, the cultivars include 'Daylight', scarlet and yellow; 'Shake-speare', salmon-red and yellow; and 'Stresa', the interior of the flowers yellow, the outside red with a yellow border.

FOSTERIANA HYBRIDS (foss-ter-ee-*ay*-nuh).
These have large flowers on strong stems and flower in April. Many of the cultivars have striped or mottled foliage. Flower colors are clean and bright. Generally about 15 to 18 in. in height. Included in this class is the famed 'Red Emperor', a brilliant vermilion-red with a yellow base to the petal, and 'Candela', a soft golden-yellow.

GREIGII HYBRIDS (*greg*-ee-eye).
These plants have striped or mottled foliage and flower in April, reaching a height of 8 to 16 in. The colors are bright, and the outside of the petals is a different color than the inside. 'Cape Cod' has a bronzy interior, and the exterior petals have a broad red stripe surrounded by apricot-yellow.

OTHER SPECIES AND VARIANTS.
Descriptions of species often offered in catalogs are given below.

T. acuminata (ah-kew-mi-*nay*-tuh).
Native to Turkey. It has long twisted petals 3 to 4 in. in length, 18 in. in height, flowering in April or early May. The color is yellowish and red, superb for mixed bouquets with other spring flowers. Zones 4 to 8.

T. aucheriana (aush-eer-ee-*ay*-nuh).
Native to Iran and Syria. It is seldom more than 5 in. in height yet produces one to three flowers of a lovely pink with brownish blotches at the base of the petals, and greenish or brown veins on the exterior. Flowers open flat. Leaves are strap-shaped with wavy margins. Great in the rock garden, where it flowers in April. Zones 4 to 8.

T. australis. See *T. sylvestris.*

T. bakeri (*back*-er-eye).
A dwarf species from Crete, 4 to 6 in. in height, with large purple flowers with a yellow base. The cultivar 'Lilac Wonder' has circular flowers, with a deep lemon base to the petals of light purple and pastel mauve. A great plant for the rock garden, flowering in March. Zones 4 to 8.

T. batalinii (bat-al-*en*-ee-eye).
Native to Bokhara. Plants are only 4 to 6 in. tall, buff yellow with a yellow-gray blotch. The leaves are in a rosette. 'Bright Gem' has sulfur-yellow flowers; 'Bronze Charm' is a bronzy hue. Zones 4 to 8.

T. biflora (bye-*flohr*-uh).
Native to the Caucasus. Plants are only 4 in. in height but will produce one to five small, flat-opening flowers, which are white with a yellow

Tulipa fosteriana 'Princeps'

Tulip kaufmanniana 'Hearts Delight'
KAUFMANNIANA HYBRID

Tulipa greigii 'Plaisir'

Tulipa praestans 'Fusilier'

Tulipa

center, the outer segments stained green and crimson on the back. Flowers in early March. Zones 4 to 8.

T. celsiana (sell-see-*ay*-nuh).
Native to Morocco and Spain. Plants are 6 in. in height, and produce one to three flowers which are fragrant, star-shaped when open, and yellow with red tinting. May flowering. Zones 4 to 8.

T. chrysantha (kris-*an*-thuh).
This species has not been found in the wild. It grows 6 to 8 in. in height and produces a small yellow flower with exterior of petals red. 'Tubergen's Gem' has larger flowers. Zones 4 to 8.

T. clusiana (cloo-see-*ay*-nuh).
Lady Tulip.
Candy Tulip.
Native to Iran, Iraq and Afghanistan. Flowers are solitary, 12 in. in height, and flat and starry when fully open. The interior is white, the exterior red with a dark blue base. The cultivar 'Stellata' has a yellow blotch on the inside of the petals. This species will naturalize. Zones 4 to 8.

T. cornuta. See *T. acuminata*.

T. dasystemon. See *T. tarda*.

T. fosteriana (foss-ter-ee-*ay*-nuh).
Native to eastern Uzbek. It is 8 in. in height, very sturdy and well suited for colder areas, and produces bright red flowers with a black base, edged with yellow. Crossed with the Darwin tulip it gave the famed Darwin Hybrids. The cultivar 'Red Emperor' is a taller plant with the same colors as the species. Flowers in March or April. Cultivars include 'Purissima' (purr-*iss*-i-muh), a creamy-white, and 'Princeps' (pran-*seps*), which flowers a little later. Zones 4 to 8.

T. greigii (*greg*-ee-eye).
Native to Turkestan. It has cup-shaped flowers, and the inner petals remain upright while the outer curl back. Scarlet with a dark blotch on the yellow base. 6 to 8 in. in height. Leaves are distinctive as they have purple-brown stripes and are 3 in. wide. Flowers in April. Cultivars include 'Red Riding Hood', with a good deep color, and 'Plaisir' (play-*zere*), which is creamy-white with red stripes. Zones 4 to 8.

T. hageri (*hay*-jer-eye).
Native to Greece. It sometimes produces up to four flowers per stem, which are copper to near scarlet, with inner segments sometimes margined yellow. 5 to 6 in. in height. Flowers in April. The variety *splendens* is 8 in. in height, produces three to five flowers per stem and is coppery-bronze. Zones 4 to 8.

T. humilis (*hew*-mill-liss).
(Syn. *T. pulchella*.) Native to Asia Minor, Iran and the Caucasus. A variable species, the flowers are solitary and small, with color varying from rose-pink to quite a dark purple with blotches of yellow, black or purple at the base of the petals. 4 in. in height. Early flowering. Zones 3 to 8.

T. kaufmanniana (kauf-man-ee-*ay*-nuh).
Native to Turkestan. Solitary flowers open to a star shape. 6 to 8 in. in height. Flowers in March. There are numerous cultivars, including 'Ancilla', with the exteriors of the flowers flushed pink, inside white with yellow; 'Shakespeare', a salmon-red and yellow; and 'Josef Kafka', a buttercup-yellow overlaid with vermilion on the reverse to the petals. Zones 4 to 8.

T. kolpakowskiana (kol-pak-oh-skee-*ay*-nuh).
Native to Turkestan. It produces one to two

flowers per stem, bright yellow without a blotch, the reverse to the petals olive with a red flush. Flowers in April. Zones 4 to 8.

T. linifolia (lynn-i-*foh*-lee-uh).
Native to Bokhara. The undulating foliage has red margins. Flowers are scarlet-red. 4 to 6 in. in height. May-flowering. Zones 4 to 8.

T. marjoletti (mar-joh-*let*-tee).
Reaches 20 in. in height. The flowers are soft primrose-yellow when first open, turning rosy-red with age. Early May-flowering. Zones 4 to 8.

T. orphanidea (or-fan-eye-*dee*-uh).
Native to Greece and Turkey, often called the Spartan tulip. Flowers are bronzy-orange with a green center. 8 to 10 in. in height. April-flowering. The variety *flava* (flay-vuh) has yellow flowers tinged with orange and green and lasts a long time in flower. Zones 4 to 8.

T. praestans (*press*-stans).
Native to central Asia. Reaches 16 in. in height. Up to four cup-shaped flowers are produced per stem, dark red, flowering in late April. The cultivar 'Fusilier' (few-*sill*-ee-ay) is shorter, with up to five flowers per stem; 'Unicum' is orange-scarlet, with leaves having off-white margins; 'Tubergen's Variety' is earlier in flower and is darker red. Zones 4 to 8.

T. pulchella. See *T. humilis*.

T. sylvestris (sill-*vess*-triss).
FLORENTINE TULIP.
(Syn. *T. australis*.) Native to Eur., Iran and N. Afr. It produces one to two fragrant, clear yellow flowers with red and green backs, 10 to 12 in. in height. April–May flowering. Zones 4 to 8.

T. tarda (*tar*-duh).
(Syn. *T. dasystemon*.) Native to Turkestan. It produces as many as six flowers per stem, 4 to 6 in. in height. Color is yellow at the base, white with red and green markings on the exterior. May flowering. Zones 4 to 8.

T. turkestanica (turk-kah-stan-*nee*-kuh).
Native to Turkestan and China. One to seven flowers per stem, pointed petals, 3 to 10 in. in height, white with orange centers. Flowers early in February. Zones 3 to 8.

Vallota (val-*loh*-tuh).
GEORGE LILY.
KNYSNA LILY.
SCARBOROUGH LILY.
Amaryllis Family (*Amaryllidaceae*).
The only species is a S. Afr. bulb with straplike evergreen leaves, 18 in. long and more than 1 in.

Vallota speciosa
SCARBOROUGH LILY

wide. It is a good garden plant for warmer areas and an excellent greenhouse or windowsill plant in colder areas. Plant in containers using a regular potting mix, placing one bulb per 6-in. pot, barely covering the top of the bulb with soil. Keep moist and give full sun, except during the hottest days in summer, when a little shade will be appreciated. Outdoors plant the bulbs 6 to 8 in. apart. After planting leave undisturbed both in pots and in the garden; lift only to repot after several years. Propagate by seed sown in spring, using a sandy soil mix and potting the seedlings into individual small pots when they are large enough to handle easily. Older plants will produce a few offsets that can be grown on. Feed occasionally in the spring but not heavily.

V. speciosa (spee-see-*oh*-suh).
Flowers in late summer, each leafless stem reaching a height of 18 to 24 in. and carrying up to eight trumpet-shaped flowers, 4 to 5 in. long and with an equal diameter. The color is mostly in the pink shades, but white and orange-reds are known. A delightful garden plant for warm areas. Zones 9, with some protection, to 10.

Veltheimia (vel-*thyme*-ee-uh).
RED-HOT-POKER.
Lily Family (*Liliaceae*).
A small genus of S. Afr. bulbs that make superb plants for the cool greenhouse or indoors and are excellent in the garden in frost-free areas. Their common name describes the form of the flower spike, with flowers held in a dense raceme. They are waxy in appearance, tubular and long-lasting. The foliage is attractive, the margins crisped or wavy. Plant with the tops of the bulbs at soil level, 6 to 10 in. apart, and leave undisturbed, lifting only to separate the little bulbils, which provide the best means of propagation. The plants prefer light shade, good drainage and moisture

throughout the year, but not as much in late summer, when they appreciate a resting period.

V. bracteata (brak-tee-*ay*-tuh).
A large bulb up to 6 in. in diameter, with the leaves forming a rosette, often flecked with a lighter green. The flower stalk is also mottled with purple, with the flowers drooping a little, often more than fifty being densely packed together. Flowers in Dec. to March, reaching up to 20 in. in height. A lovely container and garden plant. Zones 9 to 10.

Watsonia (wat-*soh*-nee-uh).
Iris Family (*Iridaceae*).
This genus from S. Afr. is not unlike a gladiolus in appearance, with swordlike leaves and flowering early in the summer. It is very popular in warmer climates. Plant 3 in. deep and 6 in. apart in a sunny, well-drained border. In colder areas the corms can be lifted, stored over winter and planted again in the spring. In cold climates treat as gladiolus (zones 4–7). Propagation is by separating the many little corms that are produced and growing them on; this should be done after the foliage has died down.

W. iridifolia. See *W. obrienii.*

W. longifolia. (long-ji-*foh*-lee-uh).
Often more than 48 in. in height, it produces many spikes of upward-facing flowers of white, pink tones or salmon. Stems are often branched. The long leaves are 30 in. long and 1 in. wide. Zones 4 to 10.

★**W. obrienii** (oh-bry-*en*-ee-eye).
The flowering stems are often branched, reaching a height of 48 in. Flowers are 2 in. in diameter, in shades of white, with a hint of pink, in early summer. Today mostly cultivars are grown,

which include 'Malvern', with large pink flowers; 'Mrs. Bullard's White'; and 'Rubra', a fuchsia-red. Zones 4 to 10.

Zantedeschia (zan-tee-*des*-ee-uh).
CALLA LILY.
Arum Family (*Araceae*).
A very popular florists' flower, native to S. Afr. The plants have a thick rhizome and produce arrowhead-shaped leaves, which are themselves quite attractive. The flowers are crowded on a spadix, around which is wrapped the spathe, the attractive part of the flower head, and which can be white, yellow or pink, depending on the species grown. A popular greenhouse plant and easily grown in a regular potting mix. Set the rhizomes 4 in. deep and 12 in. apart in the garden and in pots. The plants are not hardy outdoors below 20° to 30°F, but they can, in colder areas, be started into growth in the spring and planted out when danger of frost has passed. Lift in the fall and overwinter in a frost-free area. Calla lilies enjoy moisture and prefer some light shade. Much grown in Calif. for the cut flowers, they are of easy culture and well worth growing in gardens. Propagate by division of the roots, cutting if necessary.

Z. aethiopica (eeth-ee-*oh*-pik-uh).
COMMON CALLA.
Creamy-white flaring spathe often 10 in. long. Leaves are bright green, 10 in. across and 15 in. long. Plants can reach 6 ft. in height but are generally much less, around 36 in. Flowers in April–July. These callas are evergreen in warmer areas, losing their leaves in colder climates. Zones 9 to 10.

Z. albomaculata (all-bow-mack-you-*lay*-tuh).
SPOTTED CALLA.
Up to 24 to 30 in. in height. Leaves are spotted with white. The spathe is 5 in. long, greenish white, spotted crimson at the base. Zones 9 to 10.

Z. elliottiana (ell-ee-ot-ee-*ay*-nuh).
Produces a bright yellow spathe, 6 in. in length. Leaves are bright green with silver blotches. 36 in. in height. Summer flowering. An unusual plant; flowers are attractive and quite freely produced. Zones 9 to 10.

Z. pentlandii. (pent-*land*-dee-eye).
A lovely golden-yellow, 24 in. in height, flowering in June–July. Zones 9 to 10.

Z. rehmannii (ray-*man*-ee-eye).
Perhaps the loveliest of the species. The spathe varies in color from white through shades of pink to deep maroon, 4 to 5 in. long, 24 in. in height. Cultivars include 'Flame', a yellow-flushed red;

Zantedeschia aethiopica
COMMON CALLA

'Gem', a lavender-rose; and 'Sunrise Mix', containing a mixture of colors. Zones 7 to 10.

Zantedeschia rehmannii

Zephyranthes (zeff-er-*ran*-theez).
ZEPHYR LILY.
Amaryllis Family (*Amaryllidaceae*).
Native to C. and S. Amer. and the southwestern U.S. The bulbs grow in wet areas, producing grasslike foliage. The funnel-shaped flowers are solitary, mostly white, sometimes flushed with pink or green; there are also yellow species. The plants need bright light, abundant moisture and rich soil. Where winter temperatures do not fall below 20°F they can be left in the ground. Plant 1 to 2 in. deep, 3 to 4 in. apart. Propagate by division of the bulbs, or by seed sown in the spring and kept at a night temperature of 55°F. Good plants for the cool greenhouse. Flowers are produced at intervals through the summer months.

Z. candida (*kan*-did-uh).
From S. Amer. The stiff, narrow leaves, 12 in. long, are evergreen. Flowers are crocus-like in appearance on stems 4 to 8 in. in height, white with a hint of pink on the outside, appearing in Sept.–Oct. Zones 8 to 10.

Z. robusta (row-*bust*-ta).
From S. Amer., it is now correctly called *Habranthus robustus*. In catalogs cultivars listed include 'Alamo', with rose-pink flowers flushed with yellow; 'Apricot Queen', a yellow with a pink flush; 'Prairie Sunset', with light yellow flowers and a pink flush; and 'Ruth Page', a rich pink. All of these are good garden plants, giving sporadic color through the summer months, and are good pot plants in areas where frosts are experienced, but they have to be moved indoors for winter protection. Zones 8 to 10.

Zephyranthes candida
ZEPHYR LILY

UNDERSTANDING THE ZONE MAP

Gardening is an inexact science, but one unshakable truth is that plants grow, mature, bloom and produce seeds. The key to their success is location—the right plant in the right place will succeed. A plant provided with the right sunlight exposure in a setting where the native climate, moisture and soil conditions meet its needs will largely take care of itself.

Climate comes first. The encyclopedias in the *Hearst Garden Guides* are zone-keyed to the United States Department of Agriculture Hardiness Zone Map, reproduced below. The lower the number, the colder the winter minimum temperatures are in that zone. The zones identified in the encyclopedia describe the recommended zone range in which the plant usually will thrive. Thus, *Hyacinthus orientalis* (common hyacinth), which is listed as Zones 4 to 8, grows well in Zones 4, 5, 6, 7 and 8. North of Zone 4 (Zone 3 and lower), the winter low temperatures are too cold for it to survive. South of Zone 8 (Zones 9, 10 and 11), the summers are too warm and the winters are not cold enough for it to succeed.

The dictates of the zone map are an oversimplification, however; they are a generalization that ignores microclimates. For example, an L-shaped wall with southern exposure, or a windbreak to the north, can create pocket climates in which plants prove hardy north of their normal range. Conversely, an exposed or north-facing slope will jeopardize a plant that is marginally hardy in the region.

Plants have individual soil requirements as well as climate preferences. In fact, if the soil is ideal, the plant may stand up to adverse weather conditions. Most evergreens require well-drained, slightly acid soil. You can grow evergreens in a region where soils are alkaline if you take the trouble to create and maintain suitable soil conditions. But that plant will not really be "in the right place," and it will demand higher maintenance and find the going tougher. You can grow tender cacti and other succulents in the North in the heated indoors in winter, and bog plants in the desert if you create a bog. But the low-maintenance way to success is to select plants that like to live where you garden.

The most accurate indicators of which plants will thrive in a given location, with its specific microclimate and soil conditions, are the plants that are thriving in the neighboring gardens. The plants that do well there will probably also thrive in your own garden. Local nurseries can provide gardeners with valuable regional information about the soil, annual rainfall and fluctuations in temperature.

HARDINESS

Hardiness, commonly accepted as the ability of a plant to withstand low temperatures, should rather be considered a plant's ability to grow well in the presence of a complex variety of physical conditions, including low and high temperatures, drought and humidity (rainfall), altitude, soil characteristics, orientation and exposure (sun, shade, prevailing winds), day length (latitude), air circulation and ground drainage.

PLANT HARDINESS

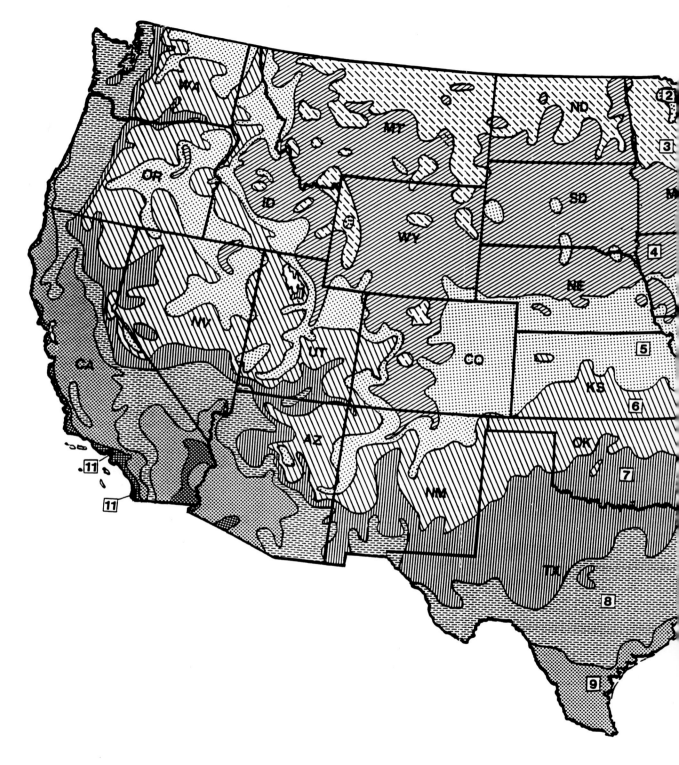

Z O N E   M A P

RANGE OF AVERAGE ANNUAL MINIMUM TEMPERATURES FOR EACH ZONE

ZONE 1	BELOW −50° F	
ZONE 2	−50° TO −40°	
ZONE 3	−40° TO −30°	
ZONE 4	−30° TO −20°	
ZONE 5	−20° TO −10°	
ZONE 6	−10° TO 0°	
ZONE 7	0° TO 10°	
ZONE 8	10° TO 20°	
ZONE 9	20° TO 30°	
ZONE 10	30° TO 40°	
ZONE 11	ABOVE 40°	

Narcissus, tulips and checkered lilies add vibrant color to the garden.

COMMON NAME INDEX

GLORY LILY. See *Gloriosa*.

GLORY-OF-THE-SNOW. See *Chionodoxa*.

GOLD BAND LILY. See *Lilium auratum*.

GOLDEN GARLIC. See *Allium moly*.

GOLDEN RAYED LILY. See *Lilium auratum*.

GOLDEN SPIDER LILY. See *Lycoris aurea*.

GOOD-LUCK PLANT. See *Oxalis deppei*.

GRAPE HYACINTH. See *Muscari*.

GREEK ANEMONE. See *Anemone blanda*.

GUERNSEY LILY. See *Nerine sarniensis*.

GUINEA-HEN FLOWER. See *Fritillaria meleagris*.

HARLEQUIN FLOWER. See *Sparaxis tricolor*.

HARRIET'S FLOWER. See *Agapanthus*.

HOOP-PETTICOAT NARCISSUS. See *Narcissus bulbocodium*.

HOT-WATER PLANT. See *Achimenes*.

HYACINTH. See *Hyacinthus*.

INDIAN SHOT. See *Canna*.

ITALIAN ARUM. See *Arum italicum*.

ITHURIEL'S SPEAR. See *Triteleia laxa*.

IVY-LEAVED CYCLAMEN. See *Cyclamen neapolitanum*.

JACOBEAN LILY. See *Sprekelia formosissima*.

JAPANESE IRIS. See *Iris kaempferi*.

JAPANESE PANSY. See *Achimenes*.

JONQUIL. See *Narcissus jonquilla*.

KAFFIR LILY. See *Schizostylis coccinea*.

KNYSNA LILY. See *Vallota*.

KIMONO PLANT. See *Achimenes*.

LADY TULIP. See *Tulipa clusiana*.

LAMB'S QUARTERS. See *Trillium*.

LILY. See *Lilium*.

LILY LEEK. See *Allium moly*.

LILY-OF-THE-FIELD. See *Sternbergia lutea*.

LILY-OF-THE-NILE. See *Agapanthus*.

LUCKY CLOVER. See *Oxalis deppei*.

MADONNA LILY. See *Lilium candidum*.

MARIPOSA LILY. See *Calochortus*.

MEADOW SAFFRON. See *Colchicum*.

MEXICAN SHELL FLOWER. See *Tigridia pavonia*.

MONTBRETIA. See *Tritonia* or *Crocosmia*.

NAKED LADY LILY. See *Amaryllis*.

NAPLES ONION. See *Allium neapolitanum*.

NEOPOLITAN CYCLAMEN. See *Cyclamen neapolitanum*.

NODDING WOOD LILY. See *Trillium cernuum*.

ONION. See *Allium*.

PAPER-WHITE NARCISSUS. See *Narcissus tazetta*.

PERSIAN BUTTERCUP. See *Ranunculus asiaticus*.

PERUVIAN LILY. See *Alstroemeria*.

PHEASANT'S-EYE. See *Narcissus poeticus*.

PINK AGAPANTHUS. See *Tulbaghia*.

POET'S NARCISSUS. See
Narcissus poeticus.

POPPY-FLOWERED ANEMONE.
See *Anemone coronaria.*

PURPLE SENSATION. See
Allium aflatunense

RED-HOT POKER. See
Veltheimia.

RETICULATED IRIS. See *Iris
reticulata.*

RIVER LILY. See *Schizostylis
coccinea.*

ROSE-COLORED LILY. See
Notholirion thomsonianum.

RUBRUM LILY. See *Lilium
speciosum.*

SAFFRON CROCUS. See
Crocus sativus.

ST. JAMES'S LILY. See
Sprekelia formosissima.

SCARBOROUGH LILY. See
Vallota.

SEA DAFFODIL. See
Pancratium.

SEA LILY. See *Pancratium.*

SHELL FLOWER. See *Tigridia
pavonia.*

SIBERIAN IRIS. See *Iris sibirica.*

SIBERIAN SQUILL. See *Scilla
siberica.*

SILVER BELLS. See
Ornithogalum nutans.

SHELL FLOWER. See *Tigridia
pavonia.*

SNOWDROP. See *Galanthus.*

SNOWFLAKE. See *Leucojum.*

SOCIETY GARLIC. See
Tulbaghia violacea.

SPANISH BLUEBELL. See
Hyacinthoides hispanica.

SPANISH SQUILL. See
Hyacinthoides hispanica.

SPARTAN TULIP. See *Tulipa
orphanidea.*

SPIDER LILIES. See *Lycoris.*

SPIDER LILY. See
Hymenocallis.

SPOTTED CALLA. See
Zantedeschia albomaculata.

SPRING MEADOW SAFFRON.
See *Bulbocodium vernum.*

SPRING SNOWFLAKE. See
Leucojum vernum.

SPRING STARFLOWER. See
Ipheion uniflorum.

SQUILL. See *Scilla.*

STAR-OF-BETHLEHEM. See
Ornithogalum umbellatum.

STAR OF PERSIA. See *Allium
christophii.*

SUMMER SNOWFLAKE. See
Leucojum aestivum.

SUMMER HYACINTH. See
Galtonia.

SWEET GARLIC. See
Tulbaghia.

TIGER FLOWER. See *Tigridia
pavonia.*

TIGER LILY. See *Lilium
lancifolium.*

TROUT LILY. See *Erythronium.*

TRUMPET NARCISSUS. See
Narcissus pseudonarcissus.

TUBEROSE. See *Polianthes
tuberosa.*

TUBEROUS BEGONIA. See
Begonia tuberhybrida.

TULIP. See *Tulipa.*

TURKESTAN ONION. See
Allium karataviense.

WAKE ROBIN. See *Trillium.*

WAND FLOWER. See *Sparaxis.*

WHITE MARIPOSA LILY. See
Calochortus venustus.

WHITE MARIPOSA TULIP. See
Calochortus venustus.

WILD HYACINTH. See *Camassia
scilloides.*

WINDFLOWER. See *Anemone.*

WINTER ACONITE. See
Eranthis.

WOOD ANEMONE. See
Anemone nemerosa.

WOOD SORREL. See *Oxalis.*

ZEPHYR LILY. See
Zephyranthes.

Narcissus cyclamineus

GLOSSARY

alternate. Referring to the way twigs, branches or, especially, leaves have their point of attachment or emergence at different levels, not opposite one another, on stem or trunk. Technically, one leaf at each node (joint) of a stem. Compare opposite and whorl.

angiosperm. A plant that produces seeds inside a closed ovary, which may take the form, for example, of a pod, berry or fleshy fruit. Contrast gymnosperm.

annual. A plant that completes its life cycle, from germination to seed formation, in one year. Contrast biennial, perennial.

anther. The part of a stamen in which pollen is produced by a seed plant. The anther opens when the pollen is ripe.

aril. An outer covering or appendage on some seeds. It is often colored, as in *Celastrus* (bittersweet).

awn. A bristly appendage on some anthers and on the fruits of some plants, notably on grains such as wheat and oats.

axil. The angle formed where a leaf, stalk or branch diverges from the main stem.

beard. The fringelike, often bristly, growth on a petal, as on many irises.

biennial. A plant that requires two years to complete its life cycle. In the first year, it makes only vegetative growth (although some biennials will flower if started early in the year). In the second year, it flowers and produces seed, then dies. Contrast annual, perennial.

bigeneric. Involving two genera. Commonly referring to a hybrid produced by crossing plants of different genera.

bipinnate. Twice pinnate; with leaves arranged in double-feather fashion.

bisexual. Term commonly applied to a flower having both stamens and pistils.

blade. Strictly, the more or less flat, expanded part of any leaf (not to be confused with the leafstalk or petiole). Loosely, blade is a common term for any long, narrow, pointed leaf, as in grass.

bolt. To set seed suddenly, rapidly and prematurely.

bract. One of the small, scalelike leaves that emerge from a flower stalk and enclose a flower bud. Although usually green, bracts may be beautifully colored. The "flowers" of dogwood and poinsettia, for example, are really bracts.

bulb. Loosely, any globular or markedly swollen underground stem that produces top growth and basal roots. Strictly, a true bulb is a modified plant bud enclosed in thick, fleshy scales held together by a fibrous base that sends forth roots. Examples: daffodil, hyacinth, lily, onion, tulip. Crocus, dahlia, gladiolus, iris are produced from related rootstocks classed as corms, rhizomes or tubers.

bur. The spiny, prickly covering of a fruit such as the chestnut. Also, any plant that bears burs.

calyx. The small, petal-like or leaflike sepals that surround the true petals of a flower. The calyx is commonly green, but in some flowers, such as the lily and the anemone, it assumes the flower's color.

chlorosis. The state of a plant abnormally characterized by the loss of green coloring matter in leaves and stems.

clone. Also clon. A group of identical plants, all descended by vegetative or asexual reproduction by cuttings, division, layering, from a single plant produced from seed. Examples: 'Baldwin' apple, 'Concord' grape and named varieties of many common garden plants.

column. The structure formed by the union of stamens and pistil, used especially in reference to the orchid.

compound. Composite; composed of two or more similar parts in one organ, usually in a flower or leaf. A compound leaf, for example, has two or more leaflets.

corm. A swollen but flattish underground stem that resembles a bulb but is more solid and lacks the typical thick scale leaves of a bulb. Gladiolus and crocus are cormous plants.

cormel. A small corm produced at the base of a corm.

corolla. Usually, the showy parts of a flower, consisting of petals.

corona. The circular crown—which may be cup-shaped or tube-shaped—immediately surrounding the stamen of a flower. For example, the cup of a daffodil.

corymb. A flower cluster that is flat on top because of the elongation of the side stems to match the height of the central vegetative stem. The flowers bloom from the edges in. Contrast cyme.

cotyledon. The first seed leaf (or one of the first pairs or whorl) to develop within a seed.

crested. Having an elevated, sometimes toothed ridge. The fasciated inflorescence of cockscomb is described as crested. Some irises show a raised ridge, called a crest, on the surface of the petals (where the beard is in common garden irises).

crown. The upper part of the rootstock from which shoots grow, as in lupine, peony, delphinium and Shasta daisy. Also, the entire foliage of a tree and the corona or corolla of a flower, which is usually the part between petals and stamens.

cultivar. Abbreviation: cv. A new plant developed in cultivation through a breeding program. By contrast, a variety occurs spontaneously, either in the wild or in cultivation, and is simply selected, propagated and named by the plantsman.

cutting. A rootless piece of plant used to produce a new plant.

cyme. A large, broad, sometimes flat flower cluster that blooms from the center outward—always with a flower at the end of the main or central stalk. Example: phlox. Contrast corymb.

dicotyledon. Sometimes shortened to dicot. A plant with two seed leaves (two leaflike structures on the embryo plant within a seed). Contrast monocotyledon.

dioecious. With staminate and pistillate flowers on separate plants. Contrast monoecious.

disbud. To remove certain buds in order to produce better flowers from remaining buds or to induce stronger growth or a more symmetrical shape.

disk. The central portion of the flower head of plants of the Daisy Family. Also, the part of the inflorescence producing the tubular central flowers.

divide. To cut, pull apart or otherwise separate the roots or crowns of a plant or clump in order to produce additional plants. See division, propagation.

division. A method of propagating multi-crowned plants (usually herbaceous ones) by separating the roots into smaller portions capable of independent growth.

dorsal. The back or underside of a plant part. In a leaf, the dorsal side is the surface turned away from the main stem, hence the underside.

embryo. The microscopic plant inside a seed. When the seed is ripe, the embryo comprises root, stem and leaf cells—all arranged in a way characteristic of the mature plant into which it will develop.

endemic. Referring to a plant native to, and found wild only in, a particular region.

endosperm. The tissue inside a seed that contains nourishment for the embryo.

entire. Referring to a leaf with smooth, continuous edges. For example, a rhododendron leaf. An elm or beech leaf is not entire, because its edges are toothed.

epicotyl. The stem tip (above the cotyledons or seed leaves) of an embryo plant. From it develop the true leaves, stems, flowers and fruits of the full-grown plant. See hypocotyl.

epidermis. The "skin" of a leaf.

equitant. Overlapping; said of leaves whose bases overlap the leaves within or above them, as in many irises.

escape. Colloquially, a cultivated plant that has gone wild and perpetuates itself without further care. Also, the naturalization of such a plant. Lily-of-the-valley and daylily frequently escape from the strictly cultivated state.

everlasting. A plant that retains its form and color when dried.

exotic. A plant that is not native to a particular country or region.

exserted. By derivation, extended or protruding. In application, relating especially to staminate or pistillate flower parts that project beyond the corolla. Contrast included.

eye. The growth bud on a tuber (potato, dahlia, peony) or on the stem of a plant. Also, the distinctive center of a flower, as in some members of the Composite (daisy) Family.

fall. In iris, one of the flower's three outer, reflexed segments. The three inner parts are called standards.

female. Referring to pistillate flowers or flower parts. Also, colloquially, a plant having pistillate flowers.

fertile. Referring to a plant able to produce fruit (seeds); to a flower possessing the organs of reproduction; to a soil abundantly supplied with the ingredients necessary to plant growth and in a condition appropriate to the support of that growth.

fibrous-rooted. Plants with finely divided, fiberlike roots, as opposed, for example, to fleshy, tuberous or bulbous roots.

filament. The slender stalk that supports the anther and, with it, constitutes the stamen of a flower.

floret. One of the flowers in a composite cluster; loosely, any single flower, usually small, in any multiple inflorescence.

flower. The popular term for the combination of structures having to do with complex plants. The concept usually includes color and a definite organization. If plants did not have flowers, they could not produce seed with which to reproduce their kind.

funnelform. The shape of certain flowers, in which the tube gradually widens upward and outward like a trumpet.

gamopetalous. A flower whose petals are completely or almost completely fused. For example, the bellflower, morning-glory, snapdragon.

genus. Plural, genera. A quite closely related and definable group of plants that includes one or more species. The genus name is the first half of the horticultural name of a species.

glabrous. Smooth; lacking hairs. Contrast pubescent.

glaucous. Covered with a thin layer of whitish powder that can be rubbed off, as on the needles of blue spruce, the "bloom" of many fruits.

glomerate. Clustered, often referring to dense, globular flower heads.

gymnosperm. Literally, naked seed. Hence, a plant that produces unenclosed seeds, as in a cone. All conifers are gymnosperms. Contrast angiosperm.

gynandrous. Having both male and female organs, united in a column called agynandrium, as with orchids.

haft. A narrow claw (stemlike part) at the base of the petals of iris and some other plants.

half-hardy. A half-hardy perennial is one used outdoors in summer and returned to the hotbed, greenhouse or window garden over the winter. Half-hardy annuals cannot stand frost, so are bedded out or seeded when danger of frost is past.

head. A dense flower or leaf cluster that more or less resembles a head. Commonly, anything from a composite flowerhead (daisies) to a head of lettuce.

heart-shaped. Usually applied to leaves that are ovate (egg-shaped) and bear two rounded basal lobes; cordate.

herb. By definition, a seed plant having soft, fleshy tissue rather than the persistently woody tissue associated with trees and shrubs. Such plants are generally termed herbaceous. Commonly, "herb" refers to plants used for medicinal or culinary purposes.

herbaceous. Plants that have soft, fleshy tissues. Also (but rarely), sepals and bracts that have the color, texture and appearance of leaves.

homozygous. Referring to a plant (homozygote) that has two dominant genes or two recessive genes for the same character—size, growth habit, flower color, for example. Contrast heterozygous.

hybrid. The progeny resulting from the cross-fertilization of one genus, species or variety of plant with another, different plant. Hybrids occur naturally in the wild; they are also the preoccupation of many plant breeders.

hypocotyl. In a newly germinated seedling, the stem below the cotyledons and above the root. (The stem above the cotyledons is part of the epicotyl.)

imperfect. A flower that produces male or female reproductive organs (stamens or pistils) but not both. Contrast perfect.

included. Referring to stamens or pistils that do not protrude beyond a flower's corolla. Contrast exserted.

incurved. Referring to flowers having parts curved toward the center; also to the parts themselves, such as an incurved ray petal.

indeterminate. Plants in which the vegetative growth does not terminate in flower or fruit clusters. Such plants continue to extend shoot growth indefinitely, at the same time producing flowers and fruit until frost.

inferior. A plant ovary that develops beneath a flower calyx. The rose has an inferior ovary, familiarly known as the rose hip. Contrast superior.

inflorescence. The general and total flowering arrangement of a plant; also, the way individual florets are arranged in a cluster.

inserted. Attached by natural growth (as with certain flower parts).

internode. The part of a plant stem between nodes.

involucre. A whorl of bracts or small, often scalelike leaves around the base of a flower or fruit (conspicuously on *Centaurea*, zinnia and many other members of the Composite Family).

irregular. An unsymmetrical flower, in which various parts differ in size or shape from the other parts in the same flower group. For example, all orchid flowers are irregular.

jointed. With nodes (joints)—places at which a leaf or bud is attached to the stem. Separation is natural at these nodes. Bamboo stems are jointed.

keel. A ridge on the back of a leaf or petal, somewhat resembling a boat keel and V-shaped in section.

lateral. A branch, shoot or bud borne at the side of a plant. Contrast terminal.

leader. The topmost growing point of the trunk of a woody plant; the apical or terminal shoot.

leaf. Basically, a leaf consists of a more or less flat, wide part, known as the blade, and a stalk, known as the petiole. Some leaves also have two small bracts, called stipules, at the base of the petiole, where it joins the stem. Though variously shaped, most leaves have a one-piece blade and are therefore called simple leaves. But in some leaves, such as in the rose, the blade is divided into several leaflets. Such leaves are called compound.

leaflet. One part of a compound leaf's whole blade.

linear. Long and uniformly narrow, as are many leaves.

lip. The protruding, sometimes pendulous, liplike part of an irregular corolla, as in the orchid, snapdragon and violet.

lyrate. Deeply cut, with a large terminal lobe.

male. Referring loosely to a plant bearing only staminate (pollen-producing) flowers.

midrib. The principal, usually central, vein or rib of a leaf. The exposed midrib of a pinnately compound leaf is a rachis.

monocarp. A plant that flowers and sets seeds once, then dies. All annuals and biennials are monocarps.

monocotyledon. Sometimes called monocot. A flowering plant with only one seedleaf (a single leaflike structure on the embryo). Its flowers have three (or a multiple of three) petals, sepals and stamens; its leaves are parallel-veined. Among the monocotyledons are amaryllis, irises, lilies, orchids and the grasses. Contrast dicotyledon.

monoecious. A plant with separate male and female flowers, but with both kinds on the same plant. For example, cucumber, oak and walnut. Contrast dioecious.

monotypic. Referring to a genus having only one species.

multifid. Divided into many parts, referring especially to leaves.

mutant. A sport resulting from a mutation, due to genetic changes in a particular plant or part of a plant.

mutation. A natural, spontaneous change in a plant gene that results in the development of a new variety. Also, the result of such a change.

native. A plant indigenous to a particular region. Contrast exotic.

neck. The stemlike extension at the top of many bulbs.

nectar. A dilute sugar solution formed by many flowers. By attracting insects and birds, it aids in pollination.

nectary. A flower part, usually a gland near the base of petal or stamen, that exudes nectar.

node. The joint at which a leaf, bud or branch meets the stem; hence, often, a joint, sometimes quite conspicuous. The space between two nodes is an internode.

obovate. Egg-shaped, with the wide part upward; commonly referring to the shape of a leaf. Contrast ovate.

offset. A short shoot that runs laterally from the base of a plant, producing leaves and usually roots at the end, thus forming a new plant. For example, a strawberry runner. Also, a small bulb that forms at the base of a mature bulb.

opposite. Referring to two leaves or branches attached to a stem directly across from each other, so they seem like pairs. Whether a plant has opposite or alternate leaves is one of the chief and obvious determinants of plant identification. Contrast alternate and whorl.

ovate. Egg-shaped, with the wide end downward; commonly referring to the shape of a leaf. Contrast obovate.

ovule. One of the globular bodies within an ovary that develop into seeds after fertilization.

own-root. Referring to a grafted plant developed on a rootstock from another plant of the same species.

palmate. A leaf with lobes or veins that radiate from a common point at the base, finger-fashion. Typical palmate leaves with palmate veining are those of English ivy, maple.

panicle. A loose flower cluster with the earliest-blooming florets at the bottom. The flower stem does not have a terminal floret bloom. Yucca produces a typical panicle, as do the tall garden phlox and many grasses.

parted. Leaves, or sometimes petals, divided almost to the base.

pedicel. The stalk of any floret in a flower cluster; a division of a peduncle.

peduncle. The stalk of a single or solitary flower when branched. The branches are pedicels.

peltate. A leaf with its stem attached at or near the center, not at the margin. Examples: nasturtium, lotus.

perennial. A plant that lives from year to year. All trees, shrubs and many flowering bulbs are perennial; but the word is applied most commonly to herbaceous plants, especially the better-known border flowers. Contrast annual, biennial.

perfect. A bloom that contains both male and female reproductive organs (stamens and pistils). Contrast imperfect.

perianth. Technically, all the floral leaves of a blossom. The word is used especially where the calyx is almost indistinguishable from the corolla. Among gardeners, perianth most commonly designates the petals from which the cup or crown of a narcissus rises.

petal. Strictly, the leaf of a corolla. Colloquially, the leaf or segment blossom.

petaloid. Sepals or stamens that have the form, appearance or texture of a petal.

petiole. The stalk of a leaf.

petiolule. Strictly, the petiole of the leaflet in a compound leaf.

pinnate. A compound leaf of which the leaflets or leaf parts are similarly arranged on either side of a principal stem, feather-fashion. Also, a single leaf of which the principal veins branch off at a number of points along a midrib.

pinnatifid. A leaf having a pinnately divided margin, deeply cut but with clefts that do not reach the midrib. Example: some oak leaves.

pinnule. The smallest and ultimate division of a compound leaf.

pip. Commonly, the individual root-stock (a single stem bud with roots) of the lily-of-the-valley (occasionally also anemone and some others). Colloquially, a seed of an apple, orange or pear.

pistil. The female reproductive organ of a flower. It consists of three parts: The swollen, bulbous base, the ovary, contains the ovules that develop into seeds. Leading from it is a fleshy, tubelike stalk called the style (not always definable). The enlarged tip of the style is the stigma, with a sticky surface on which pollen adheres and is conveyed through the style to the ovary.

pistillate. Having only a pistil (no stamens); female.

pod. Strictly, a dry, dehiscent fruit, such as a peapod. Loosely, any dry fruit or podlike organ that contains seeds.

pollen. The microscopic grains, usually resembling yellow dust, produced on the anther of a stamen. When ripe, dry pollen becomes wind-borne; sticky pollen is picked up by insects and birds. After pollen is deposited on the stigma of a pistil, it will produce the sperm cells that may fertilize ovules.

polycotyledon. A plant with more than two cotyledons or seed leaves, as the pine and other conifers.

polygamous. A plant with both perfect and imperfect flowers.

polyploid. A plant with more than two sets of chromosomes.

prickle. Technically, a weak or tender, but sharp protrusion from just beneath the epidermis of a stem.

pseudobulb. False bulb. Commonly referring to the enlarged, often bulbous internode of many orchids.

pubescent. Covered with soft, fine hairs. Contrast glabrous.

raceme. A long flower cluster with only one main stem, from which the stems of individual florets branch. The cluster blooms from the bottom upward. There is no flower at the end of the main stem. (A compound raceme is produced when the main stem is branched.) Examples: honey locust, lily-of-the-valley.

rachis. The main stalk of a flower cluster; the main leaf stem (petiole) of a compound leaf.

radical. Pertaining to or proceeding from the root.

radicle. The root portion of an embryo. Also, the first root developed by a germinating seed.

ray. Strictly, a flattened corolla radiating from the central disk of a composite flower head (aster, sunflower). Loosely, any flat, straplike petal in the outer part of a flower.

receptacle. The torus or receptacle is the part of the stem on which the flowers are borne. A rose hip is an enlarged receptacle. So is the strawberry.

regular. A flower that is basically symmetrical in the arrrangement of petals, sepals, etc.; daisy, for example. Most flowers are regular.

remontant. A plant that blooms twice in the same season; rose, for example.

revolute. Leaves or petals with margins or tips rolled backward or downward.

rhizome. The fleshy, somewhat elongated rootstock (underground stem) of some her-

baceous perennials. It has stem buds on the upper side and small roots on the lower side.

root cutting. A piece of root or rootstock
used for propagation.

root hair. One of the countless delicate hairs
somewhat above the tips of the smallest roots.
The hairs are the actual food- and water-
gatherers.

root-hardy. Referring to perennial plants of
which the roots survive even though above-
ground parts may die because of climatic ex-
tremes.

rootstock. A fleshy, underground stem with
eyes and roots, as herbaceous peony or rhu-
barb. It differs from the actual root in that it
stores food but does not gather it. Also, colloquially, the root or rooted understock upon
which a scion or bud is grafted.

salver-form. A flower with a slender tube
topped by an expanded, flat circle of petals; a
phlox blossom, for example.

scale. One of the scalelike leaves protecting a
bud before it opens. Also, a small, thin, often
dry bract. Also, short for scale insect.

scape. A single leafless, branchless stem ris-
ing from the ground and topped by a flower or
an inflorescence, as in amaryllis, bloodroot,
daylily, narcissus.

seed. The fertilized and ripened ovule of a
flowering plant that contains an embryo plant
capable of germination and growth.

seed pod. Commonly, any pod or capsule
containing a seed. Technically, a dry fruit that
splits open. Example: the pea.

segment. A division of a leaf or petals. Leaflets are often called segments.

self-sow. Referring to plants that seed themselves and produce new plants without human
assistance.

self-sterile. A plant that cannot be fertilized
by itself or by another plant of the same variety
is self-sterile. This is true of many apples, avo-
cados, carnations, cherries, gladiolus, pears,
plums, poppies.

sepal. One of the outermost, usually green,
scales of a flower bud. First leaflike, later often
petal-like, the sepals make up the calyx.

sessile. Lacking a stalk.

set. A part of a plant used for propagation, as
an onion set. Also refers to the potential con-
version of flowers into fruit. Example: The
tomato plant sets many fruits.

sheath. The plant part that encases the lower
end of a stalk in many plants, notably the
grasses. Also refers to the envelope that protects
buds of cattleya orchids until they are ready to
open.

shoot. A young branch that may produce
flowers or leaves or both.

simple. A single flower or a leaf with a single
whole blade. Also, but rarely, a medicinal herb.

sinus. The cleft or open space between the lobes, or points, of a leaf—notably, in many oaks.

spadix. The thick flower spike (with fleshy, cylindrical center) characteristic of plants in the Arum Family and some others. The spadix is usually enclosed in a spathe, which is often the showy part of the flower. The most familiar example is the Jack-in-the-pulpit (*Arisaema triphyllum*), in which the club-shaped spadix (Jack) is surrounded by the arching green-and-purple spathe (pulpit).

spathe. The leaflike bract or pair of bracts sheathing an inflorescence (often a spadix), as in calla lily and Jack-in-the-pulpit.

species. A group of plants within a genus. Species of the same genus are all different but contain one or more common characteristics. Species may reproduce themselves from seeds and may often be interbred, sometimes in nature.

spike. An elongated flower cluster in which each individual blossom is connected without a stalk to the main stem. Example, mignonette.

spikelet. A small spike, as the inflorescence of grasses.

sprig. A young shoot. Also, the act of planting stolons of some turf species, such as the bents, to make a lawn.

sprout. Referring to the development of new growth.

spur. A long, hollow appendage of the corolla or calyx of plants such as columbine and larkspur. Also, a short flower- or fruit-bearing shoot on a tree (called a fruit spur) and a comparable shoot producing foliage (leaf spur).

stalk. The stem or main axis of a plant. The word also has such specialized meanings as leafstalk (petiole), flower stalk (peduncle), a slender stalk (pedicel), a short stalk or fern stalk (stipe), the stalk of an anther (filament).

stamen. The male reproductive organ of a flower. It comprises a slender stalk (the filament) and a swollen tip (the anther). The latter produces pollen.

staminate. Having stamens; male.

staminode. A stamenlike organ that does not produce pollen.

standard. A tree or shrub with a single straight stem topped by a compact head of foliage. Examples: weeping mulberry, tree rose, catalpa. Also, the erect, upper-petal of a pea flower. Also, one of the three erect petals of an iris bloom (as contrasted with the drooping petals or "falls").

stele. The central part of the stem or root of most vascular plants. It consists of the vascular bundles that carry water and sugars and the pith that forms the structural material. In monocotyledons, however, there is no clear definition between stele and cortex, as the vascular bundles are scattered throughout the stem.

stem. A confusing term with several meanings: Most commonly, it refers to the main axis of a plant, as the trunk of a tree or the stalk of a zinnia. A rootstock or rhizome is an underground stem. Broadly, any leaf- or flower-bearing stalk is also a stem.

sterility. A plant's inability to reproduce. Some plants are absolutely sterile; others are sterile only under certain circumstances.

stigma. In pistillate flowers, that part of the style, usually the expanded tip, that receives the pollen from the anthers of staminate flowers. A stigma is said to be receptive when its surface becomes sticky, so that it holds the pollen for the initiation of the fertilization process.

stipule. One of the small, leaflike appendages at the base of many petioles.

stock. The rooted plant to which a scion is grafted.

stoma. Plural, stomata. An infinitesimal pore in the epidermis of a leaf that opens during the day to admit essential carbon dioxide and permits water vapor to escape, closes at night when carbon dioxide cannot be used.

strain. A group of plants of the same variety that have a distinct common characteristic, such as greater vigor, longer stems, better flowers than the type.

style. The stalklike or tubelike growth that connects the ovary to the terminal stigma of a pistil.

sucker. A shoot, often undesirable (azaleas, roses) or a nuisance (lilacs) arising from the roots, trunk or branches of a plant. Technically, branch suckers are called water sprouts and occur especially on fruit trees.

superior. Usually a plant ovary borne above, rather than below, the calyx, as in lilies. Contrast, inferior.

systemic. A pesticide applied to the roots of a plant and absorbed through the plant's system.

taproot. The large, central root of many plants. It usually goes straight down to considerable depth.

tender. Plants that cannot survive the winter in the region concerned.

terete. Cylindrical (with a circular cross-section); said of plant stems or leaves, as of some orchids.

terminal. Buds or flowers at the tip of a stem. Contrast lateral.

tetraploid. A plant in which the chromosomes are produced in fours. Tetraploids may occur naturally or be artificially produced.

throat. The opening of the tubular part of many flowers.

trichome. A hair or hair-like bristle.

triploid. A plant that has three sets of chromosomes instead of the normal one set. Triploids rarely can be reproduced by seeds, but are propagated vegetatively.

truss. Colloquially, any flower cluster at the end of a stalk, such as lilac.

tube. The cylindrical or funnel-shaped basal portion of a united calyx or corolla.

tuber. A fleshy, swollen stem, usually underground, having lateral as well as terminal growth buds or "eyes" and producing roots along its length or at the distal end.

umbel. A flat-topped or dome-shaped flower cluster, as in the Carrot Family and the alliums. All the flower stems rise from a common point on the main stalk.

unisexual. Flowers having stamens or pistils but not both. Also, loosely, plants having such flowers on separate plants.

variety. The lowest, or final, natural classification of plants. Not all species have natural varieties, but most species have several. Each variety retains the species' basic character, but has one or more distinctive characteristics of its own.

vascular. Referring to vessels or tubes that convey fluid. In plants, such vessels are contained in the xylem and phloem and are grouped into vascular bundles that carry water and minerals from the roots to the leaves and sugar from the leaves to the roots. For example, the strings of celery are vascular bundles, as are the veins in leaves.

venation. The arrangement of veins in a leaf.

ventral. The inner surface of a plant part, as the surface of a petal facing toward the center of the flower.

vernalization. Exposing seeds or plants to low temperature to induce flowering. Literally, the approximation of the effects of spring.

vernation. The arrangement of leaves within a bud.

viviparous. Plants that produce organs of reproduction or living sprouts while attached to the parent plant. Examples: the sprouting leaf edges of kalachoes; bulbils of the multiplier onion.

whorl. A circle of three or more petals, leaves, twigs or flowers, all from the same point on a stalk.

xerophyte. A plant adapted by nature to withstand drought, by storing water or by resisting waterless conditions for long periods.

zygomorphic. An irregular flower that can be divided into two similar parts on one plane. Snapdragons and all orchids are examples.

ACKNOWLEDGMENTS

The text for *The Hearst Garden Guides* is based on *The Good Housekeeping Illustrated Encyclopedia of Gardening*, a sixteen-volume set originally compiled under the auspices of the Editors of *Good Housekeeping* and published in 1972. The project began as the work of Ralph Sargent Bailey, garden editor for more than a quarter of a century at *House Beautiful* and *House and Garden* (now *HG*); unfinished at the time of Mr. Bailey's death, the work was completed by then Garden Editor at *House Beautiful*, Elvin McDonald.

Mr. McDonald assembled some of the finest garden writers of the day to work on different sections of the encyclopedia. In addition to Messrs. Bailey and McDonald, we would like in particular to acknowledge Elizabeth Lawrence, author of the gardening classic, *The Little Bulbs*, C. Jacques Hahn and Jean Lawson for their essays on bulbs, which were the basis for the essays herein.

For this edition, Sue Baldwin-Way and her husband Robert G. Way did a great deal of work on organizing the manuscript. We would also like to thank Ruth Lively for her tireless efforts in editing the series and Nancy J. Stabile for thoroughly copyediting the text.

Andrew Lawson shot all of the glorious specimen and general garden photographs for the book, except *Gladiolus tristis* (page 97), from Harry Smith Horticultural Photographic Collection and *Gladiolus* cultivar (page 98, top left), reprinted courtesy of the Netherlands Flower-Bulb Information Center. The following photographs are copyright © by Andrew Lawson: the photo on the center of the jacket front and the ones that appear on pages 50, 52, 55 (left), 59, 63 (left), 67, 70, 71 (left), 73 (right), 76, 78 (top left), 88 (top left & bottom left), 93 (left), 94 (right), 96 (right), 100 (left), 103, 105 (left & right), 107 (top left), 113 (left), 114 (top & bottom), 115 (top), 117 (bottom), 118 (top & bottom), 124, 125 (top), 126 (right), 127 (bottom), 130, 131 (top & bottom), 132 (right), 137, 140 (bottom), 142, 144, 145, 146 (left), 148, 150, 152, 153 (top), 163 (bottom left & top right), 165, 168 (left) and 176. Laura B. Goodwin and Lisa Zador created illustrations that lend beauty as well as crisp visual references for the book.